MACMILLAN/McGRAW-HILL

Math

Assessment Guide

Grade 2

 **Macmillan McGraw-Hill**

GRADE 2
CONTENTS

© Macmillan/McGraw-Hill

How to Use the Assessment Guide

Macmillan/McGraw-Hill Math includes opportunities to assess students' knowledge on both a formal and an informal basis. This Assessment Guide is intended to assist you in developing, organizing, and managing multiple assessment strategies.

It is the philosophy of this series that the primary purpose of assessment is to improve students' learning, not just to grade their work. Assessment should provide an occasion for students to learn and to evaluate their own work. It should be an integral part of instruction, not simply an end point. Therefore, strategies for monitoring progress as well as summative measures, such as chapter tests, are all included in this guide.

The following is a brief description of the six assessment strategies provided in this program.

Teacher Interview

The Teacher Interview is an informal assessment strategy designed to help you measure your students' understanding of math concepts. This guide includes a **Teacher Interview Questionnaire** (see page 15) that you can use to document your interviews with students. It also provides information on questioning strategies and help with interviewing techniques.

Journal Writing

Journal Writing is another informal assessment strategy. Here students are given the opportunity to write down how they think about math concepts in their journals. The program provides numerous opportunities for journal writing.

Paper-and-Pencil Tests

Inventory, chapter, unit and final tests in this Assessment Guide provide a snapshot of the content that the student has mastered. These tests are available in multiple-choice and free-response formats. They are easy to grade, and they measure student understanding, skill level, and problem-solving ability.

How to Use the Assessment Guide *(continued)*

Performance Assessment

Each unit test contains a Performance Assessment. Here, students are asked to perform math procedures and make problem-solving decisions that require an understanding of math concepts. The emphasis is on problems set in realistic situations outside of school.

Portfolio Assessment

Portfolios give you a means of evaluating students' understanding of concepts and abilities to reason and communicate mathematically. Blackline Masters are provided for both student and teacher to help with selecting and documenting student portfolios.

Self-Assessment

Self-assessment gives the students opportunity to look at their work and assess how well they are doing. This guide provides a checklist for students to use as they review their work.

Teacher Interview

The **Teacher Interview** is an informal technique designed to be part of the process of monitoring student progress. Interviews can help you assess your students' knowledge of math concepts. The purpose of the interview is to try to discern a student's thinking well enough to determine what to do next. By using questioning strategies, you can learn how each of your students is understanding the concepts you are teaching.

Where to Begin

A generic **Teacher Interview Questionnaire** (see page 13) is included in this Assessment Guide. You may customize this questionnaire to suit your needs. In addition, later in this guide you will find a Teacher Interview section for each chapter. These interview questions focus on the major ideas of each chapter. Another possibility is the **Write about it!** question in each Pupil Edition lesson as a starting point for the interview.

Classroom Management

Select a time when groups of students are engaged in different activities. As students work, you can either interview small groups or individuals at your desk, or move around the room to talk to students. Conduct the interviews in whatever manner best suits your own teaching style. Target a few students each day. Over the course of two weeks, you should be able to interview all the students in your class.

Recordkeeping. One of the most important things to remember is to date the notes you take. In this way a student's progress can be monitored. If you are using the **Teacher Interview Questionnaire** (see page 13), you can write student responses on this form. Another technique would be to keep a class roster with enough space under each student's name for you to take notes about the student's answers to questions.

Teacher Interview *(continued)*

Some Hints for Questioning Strategies

- Try to ask open-ended questions.

- The question could be a follow-up to work the student has done or to a response the student has made.

- Clarifying Questions: "What do you mean by...?" or "How did you do that?"

- Probing Questions: "Do you think that will always be the case?" or "How can you prove that your answer is right?"

- Challenging Questions: "What if the problem was changed in the following way?"

- Try not to pose questions that lead the students to the correct answer.

Interviewing Techniques

- Try to keep a relaxed atmosphere. Get students off to a positive start with a question you are sure that they can handle.

- Tell the students what you are doing. Explain that you are questioning them so that you can learn how they think when they solve math questions. Emphasize the thinking process as opposed to getting a correct answer.

- Rephrase your question if the student doesn't understand it.

- The interview session is not a time for you to teach or correct a student's errors. Concentrate on learning more about the student's thought processes. You may want to take notes on problems you need to help the student with at another time.

- Observe your student's behavior during the interview. You can often gain insight into a student's thinking through his or her actions.

- After you've asked a question, give the student some time to answer. Your focus should be on observing. Allowing the students to do most of the talking will supply you with a wealth of information on the way they think about math.

*See page 13 in this Assessment Guide for the **Teacher Interview Questionnaire.***

© Macmillan/McGraw-Hill

Journal Writing

Journal Writing is the second component of monitoring student progress. Journals provide an opportunity for students to use writing and drawing to show their understanding of math concepts. Math journals can provide you with valuable information about how and what your students are thinking about math.

The Value of Journal Writing

Writing helps students develop thinking skills. Expressing understanding of a concept in writing is also a means of discovering that understanding. Journal writing gives the student the opportunity to clarify, reflect on, and summarize math lessons. Students can pose a question, explore a train of thought, support an argument, or come to a conclusion. Writing can itself be a form of problem solving.

Journal Writing can:

- Help students become comfortable with reflecting on their own learning
- Promote self-assessment of the student's math thinking
- Give students the opportunity to restate information they just learned
- Provide you with information on how a student is thinking about concepts taught.

Where to Begin

Macmillan/McGraw-Hill Math provides several opportunities for students to write in their journals. You will find a feature on journal writing for each chapter of this guide. In addition, journal prompts can be found in the **Performance Assessment** section of the Pupil Edition. All prompts are specific to the material covered in the unit.

Journal Writing *(continued)*

Talking to Your Students About Journal Writing

Emphasize clarity and focus, rather than fluency, in math journals. Tell your students that the idea is to explain a math idea, using illustrations when appropriate, in a way that is to the point.

Discuss the prompts and notify the students if any of their journal entries will be seen by their peers.

Classroom Management

Students can use folders, spiral notebooks, or sections of binders in which to keep their journals. Just be sure that they keep their writing together so that you can easily keep up a dialog with the student.

Assessment and Feedback

It would be best to read and respond to the journals at least once each unit. You may want to write directly in the journal. Encourage students to respond to your entries. Try to provide constructive feedback that will help students further their understanding of a particular topic.

Paper-and-Pencil Tests

Macmillan/McGraw-Hill Math includes four levels of paper-and-pencil tests. The **inventory test** is given at the beginning of the school year. **Chapter tests** and **unit tests** are available to measure student progress throughout the school year. The **final test** is designed to assess student understanding of the content of the entire year. *All* tests provide a multiple-choice format (Form A) and a free-response format (Form B) that contain different item content. Both forms test the same objectives and have the same number of items.

By using both the multiple-choice and the free-response formats, you may help ensure that students get practice taking standardized tests and also have an opportunity to demonstrate higher level thinking skills.

Inventory Test

The inventory test is given at the beginning of the school year. Its intent is to provide a measure of individual and class level of performance at the beginning of the program, establishing a baseline. The inventory test for each grade is the equivalent of the final test of the grade previous to it. There are 10 questions in each form. The inventory test is designed to be scored by the previous grade's objectives and by total test.

Chapter Tests

The chapter tests in this Assessment Guide are aligned with the 28 chapters in the **Macmillan/McGraw-Hill Math** Pupil Edition. The chapter tests measure progress on individual chapter objectives as the students progress through the program. There are about 10 questions in each form of every chapter test. Each test is designed to be scored by objective and by total test.

Unit Tests

The unit tests in this Assessment Guide are aligned with the 7 units in the **Macmillan/McGraw-Hill Math** PE, occurring after every 4 chapters. The unit tests measure progress on individual chapter objectives within that particular unit. There are about 20 questions in each form of every unit test. Each test is designed to be scored by objective and by total test.

Final Test

The final test is given at the end of the school year and measures student progress on skills covered throughout the school year. There are 20 questions in each form. The final test is designed to be scored by the year's objectives and by total test.

Paper-and-Pencil Tests *(continued)*

Administering the Tests

The tests are not timed. In most cases they may be administered in one sitting. For the multiple-choice tests, students may mark their answers on the generic **Student Answer Sheet** (see page 14) or on the test page. Responses to the free-response Form B tests should be marked directly on the test.

It is very important that your students understand exactly what they are supposed to do. Review the directions and the test items before giving the test. During the test, monitor the students to make sure that they are following directions, working on the appropriate task, and indicating their responses correctly.

Try to make the environment as comfortable as possible. Make an effort to minimize distracting noises or activities that might draw the students' attention away from the test.

Evaluating Test Scores

Each test provides an indication of each student's general math achievement at different periods. Achievement on all tests is reported by objective AND by total test. Scores on these tests may indicate if a student has mastered one or more of the math areas tested. The test scores, therefore, can be used to plan further activities, either for reteaching or enrichment.

> *See page 14 in this Assessment Guide for the **Student Answer Sheet.***

> *See pages 15–16 in this Assessment Guide for the **Monitoring Student Progress** form.*

> *See page 17 in this Assessment Guide for the **Monitoring Class Progress** form.*

Performance Assessment

In math, performance assessment emphasizes what the student *does* and *thinks* with problems that involve realistic situations outside of school. Students are asked to perform math procedures and make problem-solving decisions that require an understanding of math concepts.

The Goals of Performance Assessment

The **Performance Assessment** tasks at the end of each unit:

- Assess the "big ideas" in the unit
- Balance concept and process, knowing and doing
- Elicit reasoning
- Provide opportunities for varied learning styles and intelligences
- Set a "real-world" context as often as possible
- May involve teamwork

Where to Begin

At the end of each unit of the Pupil Edition, there is a Performance Assessment task. This task is designed to allow students to apply their knowledge of the unit in a practical situation. The problem-solving, activity-based assignments in each unit also offer important assessment opportunities with more extended time frames and greater potential for students to explore math in engaging situations.

Evaluating Student Performance

Responses in this type of assessment are not simply right or wrong, but rather show a continuum of the degree of understanding. To evaluate students in a fair and consistent way, **Macmillan/McGraw-Hill Math** provides you with scoring rubrics. At the end of each unit in the Teacher Edition you will find a scoring rubric specifically designed for that unit's **Performance Assessment** task. These rubrics are 3-point scales that provide you with specific criteria on which to evaluate students' work. You might want to distribute these rubrics to your students so that they understand how they will be assessed. Students should receive feedback about their performance with respect to the criteria. In this way, assessment will serve to improve student performance, not just monitor it.

Portfolio Assessment

A portfolio is a collection of students' work that can be used as an important assessment tool. Portfolio assessment:

- Focuses attention on performance criteria
- Documents the improvement of students' work over time
- Fosters students' self-assessment and reflection
- Develops students' ownership in learning
- Communicates with students, parents, and other teachers
- Evaluates the instructional program

What Goes in a Portfolio?

The portfolio is a place for student work that highlights their understanding of concepts, problem solving, reasoning, communication, and connection making. Any task that provides evidence of these abilities is a candidate for inclusion in the portfolio. In particular, **Macmillan/McGraw-Hill Math** provides the following features for use in the portfolio:

- Performance Assessment
- Journal Writing
- Write a Problem
- Linking Math and Science
- Problem Solving Prcatice
- Decision Making
- Unit Project

One important goal of the portfolio is to foster student ownership of his or her work. Therefore, material to go in the portfolio should always be selected with the student. You may prefer to keep a "working" portfolio where all student work is held. Then every three or four weeks, you and the student can determine which pieces will go in the "showcase" portfolio, which is shared with external audiences, such as parents and next year's teacher.

Selecting the Showcase Portfolio

Selecting the showcase portfolio is very important. It is a significant part of a student's self-assessment. Have your students use **My Portfolio** (see page 18) to write about the selections they've made. In addition, each piece may be

Portfolio Assessment *(continued)*

annotated by the student or teacher indicating where it demonstrates specific portfolio criteria, such as using appropriate problem-solving criteria. Since portfolios collect student work over time, be sure to include work that shows improvement. Remember to write the date on all work.

You may also want to consider a multimedia portfolio. Here students who are not strong in writing can demonstrate their math proficiency through photographs, audio or video tapes, and computer software.

Classroom Management

Working portfolios need to be used in ongoing instruction and therefore must be accessible to students. Cardboard boxes or milk crates can be used to house working portfolios. As students complete performance tasks and other appropriate exercises, they will need to store drafts of their work. When students revise their work they will need access to their portfolios again. If possible, allow students to move about the room to access their portfolio material. Learning to take responsibility for one's own work can be a fruitful by-product of using a portfolio.

As selections are made for the showcase portfolio, those materials not selected can be sent home to parents or discarded. Showcase portfolios need not be accessible on a daily basis and may be stored in a file cabinet or closet.

Small-Group Strategies

Teachers who use portfolios often find that by using flexible grouping strategies they are able to work intensively with small groups of students on particular topics while other students work independently. Since students generally finish performance-oriented tasks at different rates, this approach works well with portfolio work. It can also free you up to confer with individuals or groups concerning portfolio work.

Reviewing Portfolios

A good strategy for reviewing portfolios is to look at just a few each day. Even if each portfolio is reviewed every two weeks, this schedule can provide you with enough information to meet with students to discuss their portfolios.

> *See page 18 in this Assessment Guide for the student's **My Portfolio** form.*
> *See page 19 in this Assessment Guide for the teacher's **Portfolio Assessment Form.***

Self-Assessment

Self-assessment empowers the students and gives them the sense that they are in control of an important aspect of their school work. Students should be able to look at their work and assess how well they are doing. Self-assessment is an important aspect of the process of selecting a showcase portfolio as well.

Checklist

Macmillan/McGraw-Hill Math provides a checklist for students to use in the self-assessment process. The **Self-Assessment Checklist** (see page 20) uses simplified language to provide students with a means of comparing their work against established criteria. This list correlates to the teacher's blackline master **Portfolio Assessment Form** (see page 19). It is particularly suitable for extended tasks, such as performance assessment tasks. To promote and guide student self-assessment, you might want to attach checklists to the work in the student's portfolio. Then use this information in conferences to improve your student's understanding of classroom standards.

*See page 20 in this Assessment Guide for the student's **Self-Assessment Checklist**.*

Teacher Interview Questionnaire

Student Name _____ Date _____

Chapter _____ Lesson _____

For Individual Students

Tell how you got your result.

_____

_____

What were some of the things you were thinking when you solved the problem?

_____

_____

Show how to prove that your answer is right.

_____

_____

What would happen if (you changed)…

_____

_____

What have you learned in class that might have helped you solve this problem?

_____

_____

For Students in a Group

How would you solve this problem differently than the other students in your group suggested?

_____

_____

Tell me more about how you would solve this problem.

_____

_____

Student Answer Sheet

Student Name _____ Date _____

Macmillan McGraw-Hill Math
GRADE 2

☐ **Inventory** _____ ☐ **Chapter** _____ ☐ **Unit** _____ ☐ **Final**

Choose One

1. Ⓐ Ⓑ Ⓒ Ⓓ   11. Ⓐ Ⓑ Ⓒ Ⓓ
2. Ⓕ Ⓖ Ⓗ Ⓙ   12. Ⓕ Ⓖ Ⓗ Ⓙ
3. Ⓐ Ⓑ Ⓒ Ⓓ   13. Ⓐ Ⓑ Ⓒ Ⓓ
4. Ⓕ Ⓖ Ⓗ Ⓙ   14. Ⓕ Ⓖ Ⓗ Ⓙ
5. Ⓐ Ⓑ Ⓒ Ⓓ   15. Ⓐ Ⓑ Ⓒ Ⓓ
6. Ⓕ Ⓖ Ⓗ Ⓙ   16. Ⓕ Ⓖ Ⓗ Ⓙ
7. Ⓐ Ⓑ Ⓒ Ⓓ   17. Ⓐ Ⓑ Ⓒ Ⓓ
8. Ⓕ Ⓖ Ⓗ Ⓙ   18. Ⓕ Ⓖ Ⓗ Ⓙ
9. Ⓐ Ⓑ Ⓒ Ⓓ   19. Ⓐ Ⓑ Ⓒ Ⓓ
10. Ⓕ Ⓖ Ⓗ Ⓙ   20. Ⓕ Ⓖ Ⓗ Ⓙ

Monitoring Student Progress

Student Name _____

Inventory Test	Form A		Form B		Comments
	Score	%	Score	%	
	/20		/20		

Chapter	Form A		Form B		Comments
	Score	%	Score	%	
1	/20		/20		
2	/20		/20		
3	/20		/20		
4	/20		/20		
5	/20		/20		
6	/20		/20		
7	/20		/20		
8	/20		/20		
9	/20		/20		
10	/20		/20		
11	/20		/20		
12	/20		/20		
13	/20		/20		
14	/20		/20		
15	/20		/20		
16	/20		/20		
17	/20		/20		
18	/20		/20		
19	/20		/20		
20	/20		/20		
21	/20		/20		
22	/20		/20		
23	/20		/20		
24	/20		/20		
25	/20		/20		
26	/20		/20		
27	/20		/20		
28	/20		/20		

Student Name _____

Chapter	Form A		Form B		Performance Task	Comments
	Score	**%**	**Score**	**%**	**Score**	
1	/20		/20			
2	/20		/20			
3	/20		/20			
4	/20		/20			
5	/20		/20			
6	/20		/20			
7	/20		/20			

Final Test	Form A		Form B		Comments	
	Score	**%**	**Score**	**%**	**Score**	
	/20		/20			

Monitoring Class Progress

This chart is to be used in monitoring your class progress unit by unit. Please photocopy this page and use one page for every unit in the **Macmillan/McGraw-Hill Math** program. Fill in the correct chapter and unit numbers in the chart as you complete the columns.

UNIT _____   PA = Performance Assessment

Student	Chapter _____		Chapter _____		Unit _____		
	Form A	Form B	Form A	Form B	Form A	Form B	PA

A = Form A   B = Form B   PA = Performance Assessment

My Portfolio

Name _____

Name of Work	Why this is in my portfolio.
1. _____	_____ _____
2. _____	_____ _____
3. _____	_____ _____
4. _____	_____ _____
5. _____	_____ _____
6. _____	_____ _____
7. _____	_____ _____
8. _____	_____ _____
9. _____	_____

Portfolio Assessment Form

Student Name _____ Grade _____

Teacher _____ Date _____

This portfolio shows evidence that the student:	Little Evidence	Partial Evidence	Adequate Evidence	Substantial Evidence
Understands concepts				
Selects appropriate strategies to solve problems				
Provides quality explanations				
Expresses concepts, ideas, and thinking in an organized and clear way				
Uses math representations (models, graphs, charts, pictures, diagrams, numerals, symbols, math vocabulary) appropriately and accurately				
Makes connections to real-world situations, other math ideas, or other subject areas				

I would characterize the quality of the work in this portfolio as —

_____

_____

This student shows growth in —

_____

_____

This student would benefit from instruction in —

_____

_____

Self-Assessment Checklist

Name _____

Look over your math work. Check ✔ the things you did.

Understanding

☐ My work shows that I know about the big math "idea."

Problem Solving

☐ I answered the whole question.

☐ I showed how I got my answer.

Reasoning

☐ I explained why I did my work the way I did.

☐ I explained why my answer is a good one.

Communicating

☐ My writing was clear.

☐ I used models, pictures, or charts with my work.

Now complete these sentences.

The math strategy I used to solve this problem was —

_____

From this problem I learned —

_____

Inventory Test – Monitoring Student Progress

☐ **Form A**   ☐ **Form B**

Student Name _____ Date _____

Directions: This test targets selected objectives. For each item that is answered incorrectly, cross out the item number. Then record the number of correct responses in the column labeled **Number of Correct Responses**. Add to find the **Total Number of Correct Responses** and record the total. Use this total to determine the **Total Test Score** and the **Total Percent Correct**.

Strand • Objective(s)	Item Numbers	Number of Correct Responses
Number Sense, Concepts, and Operations • Count, read, write, and represent numbers to 31. • Identify ordinal numbers. • Add, facts to 18. • Subtract, facts to 18. • Identify and extend skip-counting patterns. • Find the value of a set of coins. • Add three numbers. • Identify fractional parts of a whole group. • Add and subtract two-digit numbers.	1, 2, 3, 5, 6, 8, 9, 10, 11, 16, 17, 18, 20	/13
Measurement and Geometry • Tell and write time to the hour and half hour. • Measure length in customary and metric units. • Read temperatures. • Identify 2-dimensional shapes and 3-dimensional figures and their attributes.	7, 13, 14, 15	/4
Statistics, Data, and Probability • Read, make, and use bar graphs.	4, 12	/2
Mathematical Reasoning • Use a calendar to solve problems.	19	/1
Total Number of Correct Responses		
Total Test Score		/20
Total Percent Correct		%

Read each question carefully. Darken the circle for the correct answer.

1. Count how many.

   Ⓐ 4   Ⓒ 6

   Ⓑ 5   Ⓓ 7

---

2. 6 + 5 = ▨

   Ⓕ 9   Ⓗ 11

   Ⓖ 10   Ⓙ 12

---

3. What number comes just before 25?

   Ⓐ 23

   Ⓑ 24

   Ⓒ 26

   Ⓓ 27

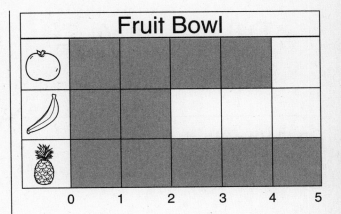

Fruit Bowl

4. How many fewer 🍌 than 🍎?

   Ⓕ 1

   Ⓖ 2

   Ⓗ 3

   Ⓙ 4

---

5. 7 + 7 = ▨

   Ⓐ 12

   Ⓑ 13

   Ⓒ 14

   Ⓓ 15

GO ON ▶

6. $12 - 5 = $ ■

- Ⓕ 8
- Ⓗ 6
- Ⓖ 7
- Ⓙ 5

---

7. What is the time?

- Ⓐ 6:06
- Ⓒ 7:06
- Ⓑ 6:30
- Ⓓ 7:30

---

8. Count the money.

- Ⓕ 50¢
- Ⓗ 48¢
- Ⓖ 49¢
- Ⓙ 47¢

---

9. Choose the fraction for the part shaded.

- Ⓐ $\frac{1}{4}$
- Ⓑ $\frac{1}{5}$
- Ⓒ $\frac{1}{6}$
- Ⓓ $\frac{1}{8}$

---

10. Which shape is third?

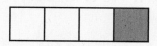

- Ⓕ
- Ⓖ
- Ⓗ
- Ⓙ

GO ON ▶

11. Write the missing number.

10, 20, 30, ▩ , 50, 60

Ⓐ 32   Ⓒ 36

Ⓑ 34   Ⓓ 40

Fruits

apples	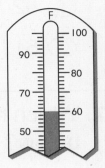
bananas	
peaches	

12. What is the range of the fruit?

Ⓕ 1

Ⓖ 7

Ⓗ 8

Ⓙ 9

13. What is the temperature?

Ⓐ 50°F

Ⓑ 60°F

Ⓒ 70°F

Ⓓ 80°F

14. Measure the line in inches.

Ⓕ 1 inch   Ⓗ 3 inches

Ⓖ 2 inches Ⓙ 4 inches

15. Which solid figure matches the one below?

Ⓐ   Ⓒ

Ⓑ   Ⓓ

GO ON ➡

Name ____________________

INVENTORY TEST
FORM A
PAGE 4

16. 43 + 9 = ▢

Ⓕ 42 Ⓗ 52

Ⓖ 51 Ⓙ 53

17. Which number is shown below?

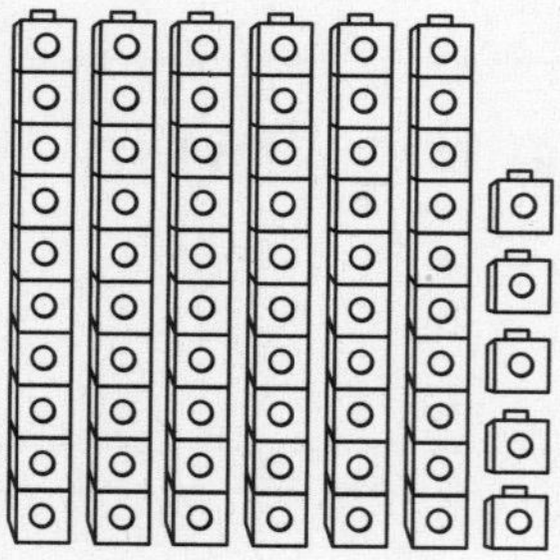

Ⓐ 11

Ⓑ 56

Ⓒ 65

Ⓓ 66

18. 5 + 4 + 5 = ▢

Ⓕ 14

Ⓖ 13

Ⓗ 12

Ⓙ 11

September 2004

Sun	Mon	Tues	Wed	Thurs	Fri	Sat
			1	2	3	4
5	6	7	8	9	10	11
12	13	14	15	16	17	18
19	20	21	22	23	24	25
26	27	28	29	30		

19. Andrea goes on vacation on the fourth Wednesday in September. What day is her vacation?

Ⓐ September 1

Ⓑ September 8

Ⓒ September 15

Ⓓ September 22

20. 51 − 7 = ▢

Ⓕ 58

Ⓖ 54

Ⓗ 45

Ⓙ 44

STOP

Read each question carefully. Write or circle your answer in the space provided.

1. Write how many.

_____

2. $8 + 4 =$ _____

3. What number comes just after 26?

_____

Fruit Bowl

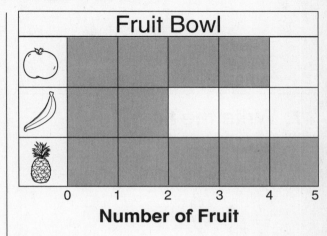

Number of Fruit

4. How many fewer 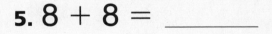 than 🍍 ?

_____

5. $8 + 8 =$ _____

GO ON ▶

6. $11 - 6 =$ _____

7. Write the time?

_____ : _____

8. Count the money.

_____ ¢

9. Choose the fraction for the part.

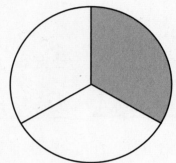

_____

10. Circle the shape that is first.

GO ON ➡

© Macmillan/McGraw-Hill

11. Write the missing number.

5, 10, 15, _____, 25, 30

The Zoo						
monkeys						
birds						
elephants						
	0	1	2	3	4	5	6

12. What is the range of the animals?

_____

13. What is the temperature?

_____ °F

14. Measure the line in inches.

|———————————|

_____ **inches**

15. Circle the 3-dimensional figure that matches the figure below?

GO ON ⯈

16. $37 + 8 =$ _____

17. Write the number in a different way.

_____ tens _____ ones

18. $7 + 4 + 6 =$ ___

June 2004						
Sun	Mon	Tues	Wed	Thurs	Fri	Sat
		1	2	3	4	5
6	7	8	9	10	11	12
13	14	15	16	17	18	19
20	21	22	23	24	25	26
27	28	29	30			

19. Timmy goes on vacation on the third Wednesday in June. What day is his vacation?

June _____

20. $72 - 8 =$ _____

Chapter 1 – Teacher Interview

Core Concept: *Exploring Number Relationships*

Student Activity: The student demonstrates an understanding of the use of numbers, skip-counting, and addition and subtraction facts to 12. Have 12 small objects such as coins, buttons, or markers available for the student. Ask the student such questions, as "If you have 6 pairs of shoes, how many socks do you have?"

Teacher Question 1:

• What are three ways we use numbers?

Understanding Student Response	Practice and Improvement
Student cannot name three ways.	Review lesson 1 to help the student understand that numbers can be used in different ways.
Student does not name counting.	Review lesson 1 to help the student learn to use numbers to count.

Teacher Question 2:

• How many toes are there on 5 feet?

Understanding Student Response	Practice and Improvement
Student does not skip-count to answer.	Review lesson 2 to help the student learn to skip-count by fives.
Student gives a close, but incorrect response.	Review lesson 2 to help the student learn to skip-count.

Teacher Question 3:

• There are 9 kittens in a store. 3 find homes. How many kittens are left?

Understanding Student Response	Practice and Improvement
Student adds instead of subtracts.	Review lesson 3 to help the student understand addition and subtraction.
Student subtracts but gets an incorrect difference.	Review lesson 3 to help the student review how to subtract.

Chapter 1 – Journal Writing

Encourage students to generate their own journal entries related to math ideas in general or to concepts in this chapter. Present the following journal prompt and have students share their drawing/writing with a partner:

- Write down 5 + 2 = 7, and then write the turnaround fact. Draw a picture showing why the sum does not change when you turn the addends around.

  (Responses should show two sets of seven objects, one indicating 5 added to 2, the other indicating 2 added to 5. Students should be able to explain why the sum does not change.)

FOLLOW-UP

To follow up, review the concept of turnaround facts. Ask students to think of any times that day when you or they had occasion to add two quantities (for example, adding points during a game at recess.) Use counters to show the turnaround facts for the sum.

Have students find all the turnaround facts for 3 consecutive sums (such as for 4, 5, and 6 or for 10, 11, and 12 depending on ability). Have the students draw conclusions about the number of facts for each sum and also write about how they found all the facts. Have students share their conclusions with a math partner.

Chapter 1 – Monitoring Student Progress

☐ **Form A**   ☐ **Form B**

Student Name _____ Date _____

Directions: For each item that is answered incorrectly, cross out the item number. Then record the number of correct responses in the appropriate Student Score column. If the student has not met the Criterion Score for an objective, circle the student's score. Recommended assignments are listed in the Prescription Table on the next page.

Objective	Item Numbers	Criterion Score	Student Score
A. Count, read, write, and represent numbers.	1, 9	1/2	/2
B. Identify number patterns.	2, 8, 10	2/3	/3
C. Demonstrate the meaning of addition and subtraction.	3, 4, 5	2/3	/3
D. Use strategies and skills to solve problems.	6, 7	1/2	/2
Total Test Score		6/10	/10
Total Percent Correct			%

Chapter 1 – Prescription Table

The following chart correlates the tested objectives for this chapter to supplementary materials that meet the individual needs of the students. The Reteach and Practice pages are designed for students who need further instruction in the math concepts taught in this chapter. The Enrich pages are designed for students who need advanced challenges.

Objective	Reteach	Practice	Enrich
A. Count, read, write, and represent numbers.	1	2	3
B. Identify number patterns.	4	5	6
C. Demonstrate the meaning of addition and subtraction.	7	8	9
D. Use strategies and skills to solve problems.	10	11	12

Read each question carefully. Darken the circle for the correct answer.

1. How many marbles?

(A) 4

(B) 6

(C) 14

(D) 24

2. What number is missing?

20, 25, 30, 35, ____, 45

(F) 36

(G) 38

(H) 40

(J) 42

3. 10 − 0 = □

(A) 10

(B) 8

(C) 5

(D) 0

4. 9 − 2 = □

(F) 11

(G) 9

(H) 7

(J) 6

5. 5 + 4 = □

(A) 9

(B) 8

(C) 2

(D) 1

GO ON

6. 7 turtles were sitting on a log. A duck landed and scared 5 of them into the water. Which number sentence shows the number of turtles left on the log?

(F) 7 + 5 = 12

(G) 5 + 7 = 12

(H) 12 − 7 = 5

(J) 7 − 5 = 2

7. 4 people are walking their dogs in the park. 3 more people join them. Which number sentence shows how many people are walking their dogs in the park?

(A) 4 + 3 = 7

(B) 7 − 4 = 3

(C) 4 − 3 = 1

(D) 4 + 3 = 8

8. What number is missing?

40, 50, 60, _____, 80, 90

(F) 62   (H) 70

(G) 65   (J) 75

9. How many marbles?

(A) 7   (C) 17

(B) 10   (D) 37

10. How is the student counting?

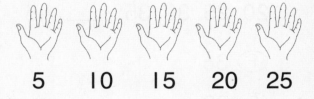

5   10   15   20   25

(F) by ones

(G) by twos

(H) by fives

(J) by tens

STOP

Read each question carefully. Write your answer on the line.

1. How many marbles?

_____

2. What number is missing?

30, 35, 40, 45, _____

3. 7 − 1 = _____

_____

4. 4 + 8 = _____

_____

5. 10 − 9 = _____

GO ON

6. 10 turtles were laying in the sun. A rabbit ran by and scared 10 of them into the water. Write a number sentence that shows the number of turtles left.

_____

7. 8 children are ready to ride the carousel. 3 more children get on. Write a number sentence that shows how many children are ready to ride the carousel.

_____

8. What number is missing?

40, 50, 60, 70, 80, _____

9. How many marbles?

_____

10. How is the student counting?

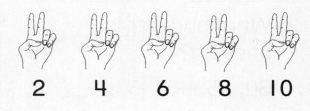

2   4   6   8   10

_____

_____

STOP

Chapter 2 – Teacher Interview

Core Concept: *Addition Strategies and Facts to 20*

Student Activity: The student demonstrates an understanding of adding facts to 20. Have 20 small objects, such as coins, buttons, or markers, and a number line available for the student. Ask the student such questions as, "If you add 3 buttons to 5 buttons, how many will you have?"

Teacher Question 1:

• Here are 5 buttons. If you add 3 buttons to the group, how many will there be?

Understanding Student Response	Practice and Improvement
Student gives an incorrect response, such as '7' or '9'.	Review lesson 2 to help the student count on from 5 to 8 on a number line. Practice with similar questions.
Student gives a response that indicates they have subtracted instead of added.	Review lesson 3 from Chapter 1 to remind the student that adding means increasing the total, not decreasing it. Ask the student to use the number line to practice adding and have them make up other examples.

Teacher Question 2:

• What happens to the sum if you turn around the addends?

Understanding Student Response	Practice and Improvement
Student says that the sum increases or decreases.	Review lesson 1 to show that the sum will not change. Have the student use the number line to add, starting with one addend the first time and then the other addend the next time. Compare the results.
Student says that addition must always start with the larger addend.	Review "turnaround facts" in lesson 1 and have the student do examples like those in the **Practice** section in lesson 1.

Teacher Question 3:

• If you have 11 cookies and add 4 more, how many do you have?

Understanding Student Response	Practice and Improvement
Student subtracts instead of adds.	Review lesson 3 from Chapter 1 and discuss key words that indicate addition is necessary in a problem.
Student gives a reasonable, but incorrect, response.	Review lesson 2 and then have the student count forward 4 from 11 on the number line. Assign examples like those at the end of lesson 2.

Chapter 2 – Journal Writing

Encourage students to generate their own journal entries related to math ideas in general or to concepts in this chapter. Present the following journal prompt and have students share their drawing/writing with a partner:

- John, Ben, and Susan have just started to collect baseball cards. John has 8 cards, Ben has 4, and Susan has 7. How many do they have together? Write a number sentence that will tell the sum and illustrate it with a picture.

  (Responses should show one set of 4 cards, one set of 8, and another set of 7, along with the number sentence 4 + 8 + 7 = 19.)

FOLLOW-UP

Later in the day, review the idea of adding facts to 20. Present students with a set of 20 like items, such as counters or pennies. Have students use the items to create and solve addition problems. Encourage students to write number sentences from their problems.

Have students write at least 5 number sentences with an explanation of what they added. Ask the students to make a picture story with one of their number sentences in their journals. Have students share their picture stories and sentences with a math partner.

Chapter 2 – Monitoring Student Progress

☐ **Form A**   ☐ **Form B**

Student Name _____ Date _____

Directions: For each item that is answered incorrectly, cross out the item number. Then record the number of correct responses in the appropriate Student Score column. If the student has not met the Criterion Score for an objective, circle the student's score. Recommended assignments are listed in the Prescription Table on the next page.

Objective	Item Numbers	Criterion Score	Student Score
A. Add, facts to 20.	1, 2, 3, 4, 8, 9	5/6	/6
B. Add three 1-digit numbers.	5, 7, 10	2/3	/3
C. Use strategies and skills to solve problems.	6	1/1	/1
Total Test Score		8/10	/10
Total Percent Correct			%

Chapter 2 – Prescription Table

The following chart correlates the tested objectives for this chapter to supplementary materials that meet the individual needs of the students. The Reteach and Practice pages are designed for students who need further instruction in the math concepts taught in this chapter. The Enrich pages are designed for students who need advanced challenges.

Objective	Reteach	Practice	Enrich
A. Add, facts to 20.	13, 16, 19	14, 17, 20	15, 18, 21
B. Add three 1-digit numbers.	22	23	24
C. Use strategies and skills to solve problems.	25	26	27

Read each question carefully. Darken the circle for the correct answer.

1. Which is another way to write this fact?

$5 + 3 = 8$

Ⓐ $4 + 4 = 8$

Ⓑ $7 + 1 = 8$

Ⓒ $3 + 5 = 8$

Ⓓ $6 + 2 = 8$

2. $9 + 0 = \blacksquare$

Ⓕ 0

Ⓖ 9

Ⓗ 10

Ⓙ 11

3. $6 + 3 = \blacksquare$

Ⓐ 2

Ⓑ 3

Ⓒ 6

Ⓓ 9

4. $9 + 2 = \blacksquare$

Ⓕ 11

Ⓖ 9

Ⓗ 7

Ⓙ 6

5. $5 + 4 + 3 = \blacksquare$

Ⓐ 9

Ⓑ 10

Ⓒ 11

Ⓓ 12

GO ON

6. There are 8 lambs in the field. There are 3 fewer lambs in the barn.

Which number sentence tells how many lambs there are in all?

(F) $8 - 3 = 5$

(G) $8 + 3 = 11$

(H) $8 + 4 = 12$

(J) $8 + 5 = 13$

7. $7 + 3 + 2 =$

(A) 11   (C) 13

(B) 12   (D) 14

8. Cara was using her calculator to add 3 to numbers. She added in this order, $2 + 3 = 5$, $3 + 3 = 6$, $4 + 3 = 7$, and then $5 + 3 = 8$. What would the next sum be if she continued this pattern?

(F) 8   (H) 10

(G) 9   (J) 11

9. $9 + 8 =$ ▮

(A) 1   (C) 17

(B) 7   (D) 18

10. $4 + 9 + 7 =$ ▮

(F) 17   (H) 19

(G) 18   (J) 20

STOP

Read each question carefully. Write your answer on the line.

1. Show another way to write this fact.

$7 + 1 = 8$

_____

2. $4 + 0 =$ _____

_____

3. $3 + 6 =$ _____

4. $5 + 2 =$ _____

_____

5. $2 + 7 + 3 =$ _____

GO ON

6. There are 4 chickens in the pen. There are 5 chickens in the hen house.

Write a number sentence that tells how many chickens there are in all.

_____

7. $2 + 5 + 4 =$ _____

8. Taryn was using her calculator to add 5 to numbers. She added in this order, $2 + 5 = 7$, $4 + 5 = 9$, $6 + 5 = 11$, and then $8 + 5 = 13$. What would the next sum be if she continued this pattern?

_____

9. $9 + 9 =$ _____

10. $6 + 7 + 5 =$ _____

STOP

Chapter 3 – Teacher Interview

Core Concept: *Subtraction Strategies and Facts to 20*

Student Activity: The student demonstrates an understanding of subtracting facts to 20. Have 20 counters or small objects, and a number line available for the student. Ask the student such questions as, "If you have 16 pennies and you give your friend 9 pennies, how many do you have left?"

Teacher Question 1:

• How can you use a number line to subtract 10 − 3?

Understanding Student Response	Practice and Improvement
Student does not mention counting back.	Review lesson 1 to help the student learn to use a number line to count back.
Student starts from a number other than 10.	Review lesson 1 to help the student learn to use a number line to count back.

Teacher Question 2:

• If you have 16 pennies and you give away 7, how many do you have left?

Understanding Student Response	Practice and Improvement
Student adds instead of subtracts.	Review lesson 4 to help the student learn to subtract facts to 20.
Student gives a reasonable, but incorrect response.	Review lesson 3 to help the student relate addition facts to subtraction facts.

Teacher Question 3:

• How can you use related facts to subtract?

Understanding Student Response	Practice and Improvement
Student does not mention addition facts in his or her answer.	Review lesson 3 to help the student relate addition to subtraction.
Student does not understand related facts.	Review lesson 3 to help the student relate addition to subtraction.

Chapter 3 – Journal Writing

Encourage students to generate their own journal entries related to math ideas in general or to concepts in this chapter. Present the following journal prompt and have students share their drawing/writing with a partner:

• Min had a total of 17 practice subtraction problems to finish. She has finished 8 so far. How many more does she have to do? Tell your math partner what operation you used and how you checked your answer.

(Responses should show she has 9 problems still to solve, by using 17 − 8 = 9. Students should indicate using the related addition facts 8 + 9 = 17 and 9 + 8 = 17 to check their answer, and possibly the concept of doubles plus one).

FOLLOW-UP

Use real-life situations to demonstrate how students can use subtraction to solve problems. For example, if there are 14 vehicles in line for a student car wash, and 5 of them are SUVs, ask how many of the vehicles are cars. Students can work independently, with a math partner, or as a class to figure out the best way to solve a particular problem.

Have students trade math journals with a math partner and write or draw a problem for their math partner to solve. Afterward, have the partners share their answers.

Chapter 3 – Monitoring Student Progress

☐ **Form A**   ☐ **Form B**

Student Name _____ Date _____

Directions: For each item that is answered incorrectly, cross out the item number. Then record the number of correct responses in the appropriate Student Score column. If the student has not met the Criterion Score for an objective, circle the student's score. Recommended assignments are listed in the Prescription Table on the next page.

Objective	Item Numbers	Criterion Score	Student Score
A. Subtract, facts to 20.	1, 2, 3, 4, 7	4/5	/5
B. Relate addition and subtraction.	5, 6, 8	2/3	/3
C. Use strategies and skills to solve problems.	9, 10	1/2	/2
Total Test Score		7/10	/10
Total Percent Correct			%

Chapter 3 – Prescription Table

The following chart correlates the tested objectives for this chapter to supplementary materials that meet the individual needs of the students. The Reteach and Prcatice pages are designed for students who need further instruction in the math concepts taught in this chapter. The Enrich pages are designed for students who need advanced challenges.

Objective	Reteach	Practice	Enrich
A. Subtract, facts to 20.	28, 31	29, 32	30, 33
B. Relate addition and subtraction.	34, 37, 40	35, 38, 41	36, 39, 42
C. Use stategies and skills to solve problems.	43	44	45

Read each question carefully. Darken the circle for the correct answer.

1. $11 - 8 =$ ▢

    Ⓐ 6

    Ⓑ 5

    Ⓒ 4

    Ⓓ 3

2. $17 - 9 =$ ▢

    Ⓕ 7

    Ⓖ 8

    Ⓗ 9

    Ⓙ 10

3. $7 - 7 =$ ▢

    Ⓐ 0

    Ⓑ 1

    Ⓒ 2

    Ⓓ 3

4. $12 - 0 =$ ▢

    Ⓕ 0

    Ⓖ 1

    Ⓗ 11

    Ⓙ 12

5.

$$\begin{array}{r} 8 \\ + \ ▢ \\ \hline 14 \end{array} \qquad \begin{array}{r} 14 \\ - \ 8 \\ \hline ▢ \end{array}$$

    Ⓐ 4

    Ⓑ 5

    Ⓒ 6

    Ⓓ 7

GO ON

6. Which does NOT name 11?

(F) $5 + 6$

(G) $11 - 0$

(H) $9 + 3$

(J) $7 + 4$

7. $12 - 2 = $ ◻

(A) 10

(B) 9

(C) 8

(D) 7

8.

$$\begin{array}{r} 7 \\ + \ ◻ \\ \hline 16 \end{array} \qquad \begin{array}{r} 16 \\ - \ 7 \\ \hline ◻ \end{array}$$

(F) 10

(G) 9

(H) 8

(J) 7

9. 18 birds are on the sand.

9 birds fly away.

How many birds are on the sand now?

(A) 10 birds

(B) 9 birds

(C) 8 birds

(D) 7 birds

10. Britney saw 12 birds.

Chrissy saw 3 birds.

How many more birds did Britney see than Chrissy?

(F) 7 birds

(G) 8 birds

(H) 9 birds

(J) 10 birds

STOP

Read each question carefully. Write or circle your answer in the space provided.

1. $12 - 9 =$ _____

_____

2. $15 - 8 =$ _____

_____

3. $9 - 9 =$ _____

4. $10 - 0 =$ _____

_____

5.
$$
\begin{array}{r} 6 \\ + \underline{} \\ 14 \end{array}
\qquad
\begin{array}{r} 14 \\ - 6 \\ \hline \end{array}
$$

GO ON

6. Circle the fact that does NOT name 12?

7 + 5

12 − 0

8 + 4

3 + 10

9. 14 gulls are on the sand.

7 gulls fly away.

How many gulls are on the sand now?

_____ gulls

7. 11 − 3 = _____

10. Norah saw 11 birds.

Gwen saw 6 birds.

How many more birds did Norah see than Gwen?

_____ birds

8.
$$5 \quad\quad 13$$
$$+\ \underline{} \quad -\ \underline{5}$$
$$13 \quad\quad \underline{}$$

STOP

Chapter 4 – Teacher Interview

Core Concept: *Relating Addition and Subtraction*

Student Activity: The student demonstrates an understanding of relating addition and subtraction. Have a collection of 20 small objects, such as coins, buttons, or markers, and a number line available for the student. Ask the student to use strategies such as doubles facts and fact families to relate addition and subtraction.

Teacher Question 1:

• What is a doubles fact that will help you find the sum of 9 and 8?

Understanding Student Response	Practice and Improvement
Student does not know what a doubles fact is or how it may help to find the sum.	Review doubles facts as presented in lesson 1. Have the student practice increasing or decreasing various doubles facts by 1.
Student does not know which of the addends to double.	Review lesson 1 to practice doubling the larger addend and subtracting 1 and then doubling the smaller addend and adding 1. Ask the student to create similar examples for extra practice.

Teacher Question 2:

• What is the fact family that relates 15, 11, and 4?

Understanding Student Response	Practice and Improvement
Student gives addition facts correctly, but not subtraction facts.	Review lesson 4 and then use the number line to count down from 15 to 11 and then from 15 to 4. Record the results. Use examples like **Fast Facts** after lesson 9 for further practice.
Student does not understand "fact families."	Review lesson 4. Ask the student to use a number line or counters to help find members of the fact families.

Teacher Question 3:

• Newell painted 14 pictures in two days. He painted 8 on one day. How many did he paint on the second day?

Understanding Student Response	Practice and Improvement
Student tries to add 14 and 8.	Review lesson 8 to point out that this is a "missing addend" problem and then have the student review the fact family relating 8 and 14. Use counters to demonstrate.
Student gives a reasonable, but incorrect, response.	Have the student count back on the number line and ask the student to write (or say) the addition and subtraction fact families relating 14 and 8. Use similar examples to help the student understand the process involved.

Chapter 4 – Journal Writing

Encourage students to generate their own journal entries related to math ideas in general or to concepts in this chapter. For students requiring guidance, present the following journal prompt:

• Dawn knows that 7 + 8 = 15. What other addition and subtraction facts does she know without having to compute?

(Responses should include 8 + 7 = 15, 15 − 8 = 7, and 15 − 7 = 8.)

FOLLOW-UP

Use real-life situations to demonstrate how students can use doubles to help them add or subtract. Have students think of things that come in twos such as shoes, gloves, etc. and use the items to create and solve fact families. Encourage students to write number sentences from their problems.

Have students write at least 4 sets of fact families with doubles and an explanation of what they added and subtracted. Ask the students to make a picture story with one of their doubles fact families in their journals. Have students share their picture stories and fact families with a math partner.

Chapter 4 – Monitoring Student Progress

☐ **Form A**   ☐ **Form B**

Student Name _____ Date _____

Directions: For each item that is answered incorrectly, cross out the item number. Then record the number of correct responses in the appropriate Student Score column. If the student has not met the Criterion Score for an objective, circle the student's score. Recommended assignments are listed in the Prescription Table on the next page.

Objective	Item Numbers	Criterion Score	Student Score
A. Use 10 to add and subtract 7, 8, and 9.	1, 3, 4, 5, 9, 10	5/6	/6
B. Use fact families to add and subtract.	2, 8	1/2	/2
C. Use strategies and skills to solve problems.	6, 7	1/2	/2
Total Test Score		7/10	/10
Total Percent Correct			%

Chapter 4 – Prescription Table

The following chart correlates the tested objectives for this chapter to supplementary materials that meet the individual needs of the students. The Reteach and Practice pages are designed for students who need further instruction in the math concepts taught in this chapter. The Enrich pages are designed for students who need advanced challenges.

Objective	Reteach	Practice	Enrich
A. Use 10 to add and subtract 7, 8, and 9.	49, 52	50, 53	51, 54
B. Use fact families to add and subtract.	55	56	57
C. Use strategies and skills to solve problems.	58, 59	60	

Read each question carefully. Darken the circle for the correct answer.

1. $10 - 5 = $ ▪

    Ⓐ 15

    Ⓑ 10

    Ⓒ 6

    Ⓓ 5

2. What number sentence is missing from this fact family?

$6 + 7 = 13$ $13 - 7 = 6$

$7 + 6 = 13$ _____

    Ⓕ $7 - 6 = 1$

    Ⓖ $6 + 13 = 19$

    Ⓗ $13 - 6 = 7$

    Ⓙ $13 + 7 = 20$

3. $9 + 2$ is the same as:

    Ⓐ $10 + 1$

    Ⓑ $10 + 2$

    Ⓒ $9 + 3$

    Ⓓ $9 + 2$

4. $9 + 7$ is the same as:

    Ⓕ $10 + 2$

    Ⓖ $10 + 4$

    Ⓗ $10 + 6$

    Ⓙ $10 + 7$

5. $8 + 4$ is the same as:

    Ⓐ $10 + 1$

    Ⓑ $10 + 2$

    Ⓒ $10 + 3$

    Ⓓ $10 + 4$

GO ON ▶

6. 7 frogs were sitting on a log. A turtle jumped into the pond and scared 4 of them into the water. Which number sentence shows the number of turtles left on the log?

- Ⓕ 7 + 4 = 11
- Ⓖ 4 + 7 = 11
- Ⓗ 11 − 7 = 4
- Ⓙ 7 − 4 = 3

7. 4 people are riding their bikes. 6 more people join them. Which number sentence shows how many people are riding their bikes?

- Ⓐ 4 + 6 = 10
- Ⓑ 10 − 4 = 6
- Ⓒ 6 − 4 = 2
- Ⓓ 4 + 6 = 9

8. What number sentence is missing from this fact family?

4 + 8 = 12
8 + 4 = 12
12 − 8 = 4

- Ⓕ 8 − 4 = 4
- Ⓖ 4 + 12 = 16
- Ⓗ 12 − 4 = 8
- Ⓙ 12 + 8 = 20

9. 7 + 4 = ▆

- Ⓐ 3　　Ⓒ 11
- Ⓑ 4　　Ⓓ 12

10. 9 + 3 = ▆

- Ⓕ 6　　Ⓗ 12
- Ⓖ 9　　Ⓙ 13

STOP

Read each question carefully. Write your answer on the line.

1. $8 - 5 =$ _____

2. What number sentence is missing from this fact family?

$2 + 6 = 8$

$6 + 2 = 8$

$8 - 6 = 2$

3. $9 + 4$ is the same as:

$10 +$ _____

4. $9 + 8$ is the same as:

$10 +$ _____

5. $7 + 4$ is the same as:

$10 +$ _____

GO ON

6. 2 boys were playing hockey. 8 other children joined them. Write a number sentence that shows how many children are playing hockey.

_____

7. 6 girls are playing soccer. 3 had to go home to have dinner. Write a number sentence to show how many girls are still playing soccer.

_____

8. What number sentence is missing from this fact family?

$4 + 3 = 7$

$3 + 4 = 7$

$7 - 3 = 4$

_____

9. $7 + 6 =$ _____

10. $9 + 8 =$ _____

STOP

Unit 1 Performance Assessment

Pack Your Bags!

- *Target Skill:* Use related facts and fact families to add and subtract.

- *Additional Skills:* Draw pictures to solve addition problems.

Task Description: This task requires students to separate 20 books into two bags and determine how many different ways this can be done.

Preparing: You may wish to have students use the Commutative Property (turnaround facts) and say, for example, that 1 in Tara's bag and 19 in Tim's bag is a different way than 19 in Tara's bag and 1 in Tim's bag.

Materials	Group Size	Time on Task
Pencil Paper Counters	2 to 3 students	1–2 days

Guiding: Remind students that they must put at least one book in each box (20 in one, none in the other is not an option). Suggest to students that they think of all the addends for 20.

Observing/ Monitoring: As you move among the students, pose the following questions:

How do you know you found all the ways to separate 20 books into two bags?

How do addition facts help you to solve this problem?

Unit 1 Performance Assessment Scoring Rubric

Pack Your Bags!

Score	Explanation
3	Students demonstrate an efficient strategy and a thorough approach that enables them to solve the problem completely. A satisfactory answer: • includes all the ways to share 20 books in two boxes (19 including the related addition facts): 1 and 19, 2 and 18, 3 and 17, 4 and 16, 5 and 15, 6 and 14, 7 and 13, 8 and 12, 9 and 11, 10 and 10. Students are able to complete the problem quickly and have all of the above correct solutions.
2	Students demonstrate a strategy that enables them to solve most of the problem correctly. The strategy is somewhat disorganized, making it less efficient. A solution is found but errors are contained. Students may: • find most of the options; • find all of the options, but have no method or organization. Students may have some difficulty determining all solutions correctly but demonstrate an understanding of general concepts.
1	Students demonstrate a confused strategy, which leads to difficulty solving the problem. Most answers are incorrect, but students demonstrate knowledge of at least one concept being assessed. Students may: • find most of the options, but forget to use the turnaround facts.

Unit 1 Performance Assessment
Student Activity

Pack Your Bags!

You will need
- 20 counters
- a piece of paper
- a pencil

Tara and Tim are going on a trip with their family. They bring 20 books to read. All 20 books will not fit into one bag. How many different ways can they sort the books into two bags?

1. Place 20 counters on a table.

2. Draw two large squares on your paper. Label one "Tara's Bag". Label the other "Tim's Bag".

3. See how many different ways you can sort the counters into two bags.

4. Write a number sentence for each way.

_____

_____

_____

_____

Unit I – Monitoring Student Progress

☐ **Form A**   ☐ **Form B**

Student Name _____ Date _____

Directions: This test targets selected objectives. For each item that is answered incorrectly, cross out the item number. Then record the number of correct responses in the column labeled **Number of Correct Responses.** Add to find the **Total Number of Correct Responses** and record the total. Use this total to determine the **Total Test Score** and the **Total Percent Correct.**

Strand • Objective(s)	Item Numbers	Number of Correct Responses
Number Sense, Concepts, and Operations • Count, read, write, and represent numbers. • Identify number patterns. • Demonstrate the meaning of addition and subtraction. • Add, facts to 20. • Add three 1-digit numbers. • Subtract, facts to 20. • Relate addition and subtraction. • Use 10 to add and subtract 7, 8, and 9. • Use fact families to add and subtract. • Use strategies and skills to solve problems.	1, 2, 3, 4, 5, 6, 7, 8 ,9, 10, 11, 12, 13, 14, 15, 16, 17, 18, 19, 20	/20
Total Number of Correct Responses		
Total Test Score		/20
Total Percent Correct		%

Read each question carefully. Darken the circle for the correct answer.

1.
$$5 \\ + \ 1$$

Ⓐ 4   Ⓒ 6
Ⓑ 5   Ⓓ 7

2.
$$10 \\ - \ 3$$

Ⓕ 6   Ⓗ 8
Ⓖ 7   Ⓙ 9

---

3. $7 - 1 =$ ▪

Ⓐ 4   Ⓒ 6
Ⓑ 5   Ⓓ 7

4. Look at this fact family triangle. Which fact belongs in this family?

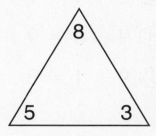

Ⓕ $5 - 3 = 2$
Ⓖ $11 - 3 = 8$
Ⓗ $5 + 3 = 8$
Ⓙ $3 + 8 = 11$

---

5. Which is a related subtraction fact for $6 + 2 = 8$?

Ⓐ $8 - 8 = 0$
Ⓑ $8 - 6 = 2$
Ⓒ $6 - 2 = 4$
Ⓓ $2 + 6 = 8$

GO ON

6. What is the turnaround fact for $5 + 4 = 9$?

(F) $3 + 6 = 9$

(G) $8 + 1 = 9$

(H) $4 + 5 = 9$

(J) $9 - 1 = 8$

7. Which of these is a doubles fact?

(A) $6 + 2$

(B) $3 + 3$

(C) $4 + 1$

(D) $1 + 2$

8. The ▨ of $5 - 4$ is 1.

(F) fact family

(G) difference

(H) addend

(J) sum

9. $8 + 8 = $ ▨

(A) 15

(B) 16

(C) 17

(D) 18

10. $6 + $ ▨ $ = 15$

(F) 7

(G) 8

(H) 9

(J) 10

GO ON

11.   16
     −   8

Ⓐ 6

Ⓑ 7

Ⓒ 8

Ⓓ 9

12. 15 − ▢ = 7

Ⓕ 6

Ⓖ 7

Ⓗ 8

Ⓙ 9

13. Which subtraction fact relates to 5 + 9 = 14?

Ⓐ 14 − 5 = 9

Ⓑ 14 − 14 = 0

Ⓒ 9 − 5 = 4

Ⓓ 14 − 6 = 8

14. Which addition fact relates to 13 − 6 = 7?

Ⓕ 6 + 7 = 13

Ⓖ 6 + 1 = 7

Ⓗ 9 + 4 = 13

Ⓙ 3 + 4 = 7

15. 5 + 5 + 3 = ▢

Ⓐ 10

Ⓑ 11

Ⓒ 12

Ⓓ 13

16.   4
      1
     + 5

Ⓕ 9   Ⓗ 11

Ⓖ 10   Ⓙ 12

GO ON

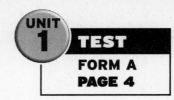

17. There are 6 frogs in the pond. Then 6 more frogs jump in. How many frogs are in the pond now?

Ⓐ 6 frogs

Ⓑ 7 frogs

Ⓒ 11 frogs

Ⓓ 12 frogs

18. Ana has 9 trucks. She gives 4 trucks to Rob. How many trucks does Ana have left?

Ⓕ 4 trucks

Ⓖ 5 trucks

Ⓗ 7 trucks

Ⓙ 8 trucks

19. Kimah has 8 pencils. She buys 7 more. Which number sentence tells how many pencils Kimah has in all?

Ⓐ $8 + 7 = 15$

Ⓑ $9 - 6 = 15$

Ⓒ $15 - 7 = 8$

Ⓓ $15 - 8 = 7$

20. There were 13 cookies on a plate. Erik puts all but 6 of them in his lunchbox. How many cookies did Erik put in his lunchbox?

Ⓕ 5 cookies

Ⓖ 6 cookies

Ⓗ 7 cookies

Ⓙ 8 cookies

STOP

Read each question carefully. Write or circle your answer in the space provided.

1.
$$\begin{array}{r} 4 \\ + \ 5 \\ \hline \end{array}$$

2.
$$\begin{array}{r} 12 \\ - \ 2 \\ \hline \end{array}$$

3.
$$\begin{array}{r} 12 \\ - \ 6 \\ \hline \end{array}$$

4. Look at this fact family triangle. Circle the fact that belongs in this family.

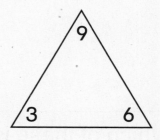

$3 + 3 = 6$

$6 + 3 = 9$

$5 + 4 = 9$

$6 + 6 = 12$

5. Circle the related subtraction fact for $5 + 7 = 12$.

$7 - 5 = 2$

$2 + 5 = 7$

$7 + 5 = 12$

$12 - 7 = 5$

GO ON

6. What is the turnaround fact for $1 + 3 = 4$?

_____

7. Which of these is a doubles fact?
Circle the answer.

$7 + 1$

$8 + 4$

$4 + 4$

$9 + 3$

8. Complete the sentence using one of the following:
fact family, difference, addend, sum.

The _____
of $4 + 1$ is 5.

9. $9 + 6 = $ _____

10. $4 + $ _____ $= 12$

GO ON

11.   14
       −   7

_____

12. 14 − _____ = 8

_____

13. What is the subtraction
fact that relates
to 6 + 7 = 13?

_____

14. What is the addition
fact that relates
to 16 − 7 = 9?

_____

_____

15. 6 + 3 + 4 = _____

_____

16.   3
          5
       + 2

GO ON

17. There are 9 frogs in the pond. Then 2 more frogs hop in. How many frogs are in the pond?

_____ frogs

18. Miguel has 11 fish. He gave 7 fish to his friends. How many fish does Miguel have left?

_____ fish

19. Janell has 6 pencils. She buys 7 more. Which number sentence tells how many pencils Janell has in all?

$$6 + 7 = 13$$

$$9 - 6 = 15$$

$$15 - 7 = 8$$

$$15 - 8 = 7$$

20. There were 11 cookies on a plate. Michael puts all but 6 of them in his lunchbox. How many cookies did Michael put in his lunchbox?

_____ cookies

STOP

Chapter 5 – Teacher Interview

Core Concept: *Understanding Place Value*

Student Activity: The student demonstrates an understanding of reading and writing numbers, and of two-digit place value. Have available a collection of small objects, tens and ones models, a number line, and pencils and paper for the student to use. Ask the student questions such as, "How many tens are in 37?"

Teacher Question 1:

- Think about the number 14. How many tens and ones are in 14?

Understanding Student Response	Practice and Improvement
Student refers only to 14 ones.	Review lesson 2 to reinforce place value. Have student count out 14 objects and then group 10 of the objects together. Show that there is one group of 10 and 4 ones left over. Repeat using other numbers.
Student reverses the places, saying 4 tens and one 1.	Do the counting exercise above. Point out that 4 groups of 10 make 40. Repeat with another number.

Teacher Question 2:

- What is the value of the tens digit in the number 42?

Understanding Student Response	Practice and Improvement
Student says the answer is 0.	Review lesson 2. Point out to student that 42 objects form 4 groups of 10, with 2 ones left over.
Student says the answer is 2.	Point out that 2 tens is equal to 20.

Teacher Question 3:

- Write down the numbers twenty-five, forty-two, and seventeen. Now find them on the number line.

Understanding Student Response	Practice and Improvement
Student cannot write the numbers correctly.	Review lesson 4. Assign practice items from among those given in lesson 4.
Student consistently reverses the order of the digits.	Review lesson 2 and lesson 3 to reinforce place value.

Chapter 5 – Journal Writing

Encourage students to generate their own journal entries related to math ideas in general or to concepts in this chapter. Present the following journal prompt and have students share their drawing/writing with a partner:

- Work with a math partner. Make a list of all the fruits or vegetables you can think of. You can write them down or draw a small picture to show each one. Try to think of at least 20 different kinds. Draw a circle around each group of 10 items in your list. If you have some items left over, do not circle them. How many fruits and vegetables are in your list? Write your answer as a number and in words. What do you notice about the number of circled groups in your list and the number of items left over?

  (Responses should indicate that the number of circled groups equals the number in the tens place of the students' answer, and the number of leftover items equals the number in the ones place. If time allows, repeat the exercise with students making another list, such as a list of all their relatives or all of the students in their class.)

FOLLOW-UP

At the end of the class, review the meaning of place value. Ask the students how the exercise illustrates this concept. Students should have an understanding that 1 ten equals 10 ones.

Now have the students look around the classroom for any items that appear 100 times or more. Ask the students if they can "find 100 of something" in the room. Some examples include legs of chairs, ceiling tiles, and fingers, but try not to give too many examples away. You may want to limit the students' answers to objects they can actually see from their seats, but you should expect some creative responses. Have the students write their ideas down before they share them out loud. Although students are not yet expected to understand 3-digit numbers, this exercise will give them a sense of the size of 100 and may enhance their understanding of place value.

Chapter 5 – Monitoring Student Progress

☐ **Form A**   ☐ **Form B**

Student Name _____ Date _____

Directions: For each item that is answered incorrectly, cross out the item number. Then record the number of correct responses in the appropriate Student Score column. If the student has not met the Criterion Score for an objective, circle the student's score. Recommended assignments are listed in the Prescription Table on the next page.

Objective	Item Numbers	Criterion Score	Student Score
A. Count, read, write, and represent numbers to 100.	4, 5	1/2	/2
B. Identify the place value for each digit for numbers to 100	1, 2, 3, 6	3/4	/4
C. Estimate numbers.	7, 8, 9	2/3	/3
D. Use strategies and skills to solve problems.	10	1/1	/1
Total Test Score		7/10	/10
Total Percent Correct			%

Chapter 5 – Prescription Table

The following chart correlates the tested objectives for this chapter to supplementary materials that meet the individual needs of the students. The Practice and Reteach pages are designed for students who need further instruction in the math concepts taught in this chapter. The Enrich pages are designed for students who need advanced challenges.

Objective	Reteach	Practice	Enrich
A. Count, read, write, and represent numbers to 100.	62, 65 71	63, 66 72	64, 67 73
B. Identify the place value for each digit for numbers to 100.	68	69	70
C. Estimate numbers.	74	75	76
D. Use strategies and skills to solve problems.	77	78	79

Read each question carefully.
Darken the circle for the correct answer.

1. What is another name for 50 ones?

(A) 50 tens   (C) 10 ones

(B) 5 tens   (D) 1 ten

2. What is another name for 7 tens?

(F) 710   (H) 70

(G) 700   (J) 7

3. How many tens and ones are these?

(A) 4 ones 7 tens

(B) 47 tens

(C) 74 ones

(D) 4 tens 7 ones

4. Which number is seventy-three?

(F) 37   (H) 307

(G) 73   (J) 703

5. How do you write 49?

(A) four-nine

(B) nine-four

(C) four and nine

(D) forty-nine

6. What is the value of the number 5 in 85?

(F) 80   (H) 15

(G) 50   (J) 5

GO ON

7. There are 10 beans in the smaller jar.

About how many beans fill the larger jar?

Ⓐ 40　　Ⓑ 30　　Ⓒ 20　　Ⓓ 10

8. This jar holds 20 noodles.

About how many noodles will fill the jar below?

Ⓕ 20　　　Ⓗ 60

Ⓖ 40　　　Ⓙ 80

9. How many marbles are in the picture?

Ⓐ 10　　Ⓒ 30

Ⓑ 20　　Ⓓ 40

10. Marcos mixed flour, eggs, and milk. He poured the batter into the pan, in small circle shapes. He flipped them and when they were done, he put them on a plate. What do you think happened next?

Ⓕ Marcos ate the burgers he made.

Ⓖ Marcos ate the French fries he made.

Ⓗ Marcos ate the cake he just baked.

Ⓙ Marcos ate the pancakes he made.

STOP

Read each question carefully. Write your answer on the line.

1. Write another way to show 7 tens.

_____

_____

2. What is another name for 40 ones?

_____

_____

3. How many tens and ones are these?

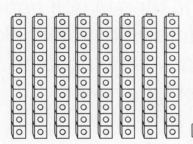

_____ _____

4. Write the number thirty-two.

_____

_____

5. Write the word for 45.

_____

_____

6. What is the value of the number 2 in 72?

_____

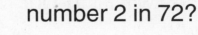

7. There are 15 beans in the smaller jar.

About how many beans fill the larger jar?

_____

8. This small jar holds 25 noodles.

About how many noodles will fill the jar below?

_____

9. How many marbles are in the picture?

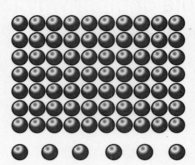

_____

_____

10. Carly took out her paper. Then she got out her pens. She sat and wrote a letter to her grandmother. She folded the letter in half and then in half again. Write what you think Carly is going to do with her letter next.

_____

_____

_____

STOP

Chapter 6 – Teacher Interview

Core Concept: *Comparing and Ordering Numbers*

Student Activity: The student demonstrates an understanding of comparing and ordering numbers to 100. Have available a collection of small objects, such as coins, buttons, or markers; tens and ones models; a number line; and pencils and paper for the student to use. Ask the student questions such as, "Which number is greater: 35 or 53?"

Teacher Question 1:

• Is 73 **greater than** 74, **less than** 74, or **equal to** 74? Show me how to write down the answer.

Understanding Student Response	Practice and Improvement
Student says 73 is greater than 74.	Review lesson 1. Use a number line or tens and ones models to compare the numbers.
Student answers correctly, but writes the answer incorrectly.	Review the >, <, and = symbols in lesson 1. Show the student how the bigger side of the greater than or less than symbol points toward the larger number.

Teacher Question 2:

• What are the numbers just **before** and just **after** the number 37?

Understanding Student Response	Practice and Improvement
Student says the wrong number or just one number.	Review ordering numbers in lesson 2. Have the student make the number 37 using tens and ones models. Take 1 ones model away or add 1 more ones model and name the number.
Student responds with 27 and 47.	Review lesson 2. Count back to 27 from 37 on a number line and then count on to 47 from 37. Show that those numbers are 10 away from 37.

Teacher Question 3:

• Write down the numbers eighteen, sixty-one, and twenty-three. Now put them in the correct order.

Understanding Student Response	Practice and Improvement
Student writes the numbers incorrectly.	Review lesson 4, Chapter 5.
Student writes the numbers correctly, but orders them incorrectly.	Review lesson 2 to remind student that ordering means to write the numbers from smallest to largest. Give student another group of three 2-digit numbers to write and order.

Chapter 6 – Journal Writing

Encourage students to generate their own journal entries related to math ideas in general or to concepts in this chapter. Present the following journal prompt and have students share their drawing/writing with a partner:

- Even numbers are those that end with 0, 2, 4, 6, and 8 in the ones place, and odd numbers are those that end with 1, 3, 5, 7, and 9 in the ones place. If you add 2 even numbers, is the result odd or even? If you add 2 odd numbers, is the result odd or even? What numbers could you add to get an odd result?

  (Responses should indicate that adding two even or two odd numbers together gives an even result, while adding an even number and an odd number gives an odd result.)

FOLLOW-UP

To follow up, review the meaning of odd and even numbers. Have students skip-count by 2 starting at 2, and note that the numbers that they are naming are all even numbers. Then have students skip-count by 2 starting at 1, and note that these numbers are all odd numbers.

Now have the students find and count objects in the room and decide if there is an even or an odd number of that object. Have the students write the name of the object, how many they found, and if they found an even or an odd number. With an object they found, or with counters, have students divide them into two groups of equal size. Ask students to write about even and odd numbers based on this activity. They may draw pictures to illustrate. Have students share their pictures with a math partner.

Chapter 6 – Monitoring Student Progress

☐ **Form A**   ☐ **Form B**

Student Name _____ Date _____

Directions: For each item that is answered incorrectly, cross out the item number. Then record the number of correct responses in the appropriate Student Score column. If the student has not met the Criterion Score for an objective, circle the student's score. Recommended assignments are listed in the Prescription Table on the next page.

Objective	Item Numbers	Criterion Score	Student Score
A. Compare and order numbers to 100.	2, 3, 4, 10	3/4	/4
B. Skip-count to 100.	1, 9	1/2	/2
C. Identify even and odd numbers.	5, 8	1/2	/2
D. Use strategies and skills to solve problems.	6, 7	1/2	/2
Total Test Score		6/10	/10
Total Percent Correct			%

Chapter 6 – Prescription Table

The following chart correlates the tested objectives for this chapter to supplementary materials that meet the individual needs of the students. The Reteach and Practice pages are designed for students who need further instruction in the math concepts taught in this chapter. The Enrich pages are designed for students who need advanced challenges.

Objective	Reteach	Practice	Enrich
A. Compare and order numbers to 100.	81, 84	82, 85	83, 86
B. Skip-count to 100.	87	88	89
C. Identify even and odd numbers.	90, 93	91, 94	92, 95
D. Use strategies and skills to solve problems.	96, 97	98	

Read each question carefully.
Darken the circle for the correct answer.

1. Which set shows skip-counting by 5's?

Ⓐ 5, 10, 12, 20, 25

Ⓑ 5, 9, 15, 20, 23

Ⓒ 5, 10, 15, 20, 25

Ⓓ 5, 10, 15, 20, 24

Use this picture to answer questions 2–3.

2. What is the letter of the runner who finished 5th?

Ⓕ A   Ⓗ C

Ⓖ B   Ⓙ D

3. In which place did runner F finish?

Ⓐ first   Ⓒ third

Ⓑ second Ⓓ fourth

4. Which number is between 48 and 50?

Ⓕ 48   Ⓗ 50

Ⓖ 49   Ⓙ 51

5. Which is an odd number?

Ⓐ fifty-six

Ⓑ fifty-eight

Ⓒ sixty-five

Ⓓ sixty-six

GO ON

6. David sits behind John.
John sits behind Mark.
Isaac sits in front of
Mark.
Who sits in the front?

Ⓕ David

Ⓖ Isaac

Ⓗ John

Ⓙ Mark

7. The square is in front of
the triangle. The circle is
in front of the square.
The rectangle is behind
the triangle. Which
shape is last in the row?

Ⓐ circle

Ⓑ rectangle

Ⓒ square

Ⓓ triangle

8. Which shows a group of
even numbers?

Ⓕ 22, 24, 68, 77

Ⓖ 33, 34, 38, 90

Ⓗ 54, 56, 80, 98

Ⓙ 72, 88, 94, 97

9. What number is
missing?

74, ☐, 78, 80, 82, 84

Ⓐ 75   Ⓒ 77

Ⓑ 76   Ⓓ 79

10. What symbol makes this
sentence true?

42 ◯ 42

Ⓕ >   Ⓗ =

Ⓖ <   Ⓙ +

STOP

Read each question carefully. Fill in the correct answer in the space provided.

1. Finish counting by 3's.

37, 40, 43, 47, 50, _____

Use this picture to answer questions 2–3.

2. Write the position

of .

_____

3. Describe the person standing 6th in line.

_____

_____

_____

4. What number is between 67 and 69?

_____

5. Write an odd number.

_____

_____

GO ON

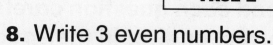
6. Max sits behind Zach.
Zach sits behind
Francis.
Gene sits in front of
Francis.
Who sits in the front?

_____

7. The frog is in front of the
log. The butterfly is in
front of the tulip. The
tulip is behind the log.
What item is in the
front?

_____

8. Write 3 even numbers.

_____

_____

9. Write the missing
number.

39, 42, 45, ____, 51, 54

10. Write <, >, or = to make
a true sentence.

37 ____ 89

STOP

Chapter 7 – Teacher Interview

Core Concept: *Coins and Their Values*

Student Activity: The student demonstrates an understanding of coins and their values. Have a collection of real or realistic play money available for the student. A number line should also be available. Ask the student questions such as, "How can you make 25¢ using different coin combinations?"

Teacher Question 1:

- Chul has two dimes, and Erin has four nickels. Who has more money? Why do you think so?

Understanding Student Response	Practice and Improvement
Student says Chul has more because dimes are worth more than nickels.	Review lesson 1 to help the student write the number of cents each person has. Show that 5¢ + 5¢ = 10¢ = one dime and therefore 2 dimes equal 4 nickels.
Student says Erin has more because she has 4 coins while Chul has only 2 coins.	Review lesson 1 and then use the procedure above. Use pennies, nickels, and dimes to show that size of a coin is not necessarily related to its value.

Teacher Question 2:

- If you buy candy for 25¢, with what different coin combinations can you pay for it?

Understanding Student Response	Practice and Improvement
Student just says a quarter.	Review lesson 2 before asking the student what coins make a quarter. Prompt the student by saying "How many pennies in 25¢?" Then prompt for other coins. If necessary, student may use real or realistic play money.
Student gives one or two correct answers, but cannot produce others.	Review lesson 2 to prompt the student to think of other combinations that will make 25¢. If student does not think of others then ask such questions as, "How many pennies are in 25¢?"

Teacher Question 3:

- At the school bake sale, cupcakes are 35¢ each. If Becky has 3 quarters, how many can she buy?

Understanding Student Response	Practice and Improvement
Student says Becky can buy just one cupcake.	Review lessons 2 and 3. Prompt student to find how many cents Becky has. Then ask how much 2 cupcakes will cost.
Student says Becky can buy 3 or more cupcakes.	Review lesson 3. Then have the student determine the cost of 2 cupcakes and of 3 cupcakes. Point out that 3 cupcakes cost more than $1, and it takes 4 quarters to make $1. Assign practice from lesson 3.

Chapter 7 – Journal Writing

Encourage students to generate their own journal entries related to math ideas in general or to concepts in this chapter. Present the following journal prompt and have students share their drawing/writing with a partner:

- Steven has five coins in his pocket, but he does not know what kinds of coins they are. Draw pictures to show the greatest amount of money Steven could have in his pocket, and the least amount he could have. Could Steven have exactly 1 dollar in his pocket? Explain your answer and draw a picture.

   (Responses should reflect an understanding of the value of coins from the penny to the half dollar, and that different combinations of coins can equal 1 dollar. Students may not be able to calculate the value of 5 half dollars, but they should realize that this combination gives the greatest value.)

FOLLOW-UP

At the end of the class, review the value of each coin and various combinations. Include combinations that total $1.00 in value. Ask students how they knew the answers to the problem. They should understand that since the half dollar has the greatest value, five half dollars would give Steven the most money.

Give the students a variation of the original problem: Steven has five coins in his pocket, and each coin has a different value. How much money does Steven have? Students can make drawings as before, and they should share their reasoning ideas with a partner.

Chapter 7 – Monitoring Student Progress

☐ **Form A**   ☐ **Form B**

Student Name _____ Date _____

Directions: For each item that is answered incorrectly, cross out the item number. Then record the number of correct responses in the appropriate Student Score column. If the student has not met the Criterion Score for an objective, circle the student's score. Recommended assignments are listed in the Prescription Table on the next page.

Objective	Item Numbers	Criterion Score	Student Score
A. Identify coins and their values.	1, 2	1/2	/2
B. Find the value of a set of coins.	3, 4, 5, 7	3/4	/4
C. Make equal amounts.	9, 10	1/2	/2
D. Use strategies and skills to solve problems.	6, 8	1/2	/2
Total Test Score		6/10	/10
Total Percent Correct			%

Chapter 7 – Prescription Table

The following chart correlates the tested objectives for this chapter to supplementary materials that meet the individual needs of the students. The Reteach and Practice pages are designed for students who need further instruction in the math concepts taught in this chapter. The Enrich pages are designed for students who need advanced challenges.

Objective	Reteach	Practice	Enrich
A. Identify coins and their values.	99, 102, 108	100, 103, 109	101, 104, 110
B. Find the value of a set of coins.	105	106	107
C. Make equal amounts.	111	112	113
D. Use strategies and skills to solve problems.	114	115	116

Read each question carefully.
Darken the circle for the correct answer.

1. What is the name of this coin?

- Ⓐ dime
- Ⓑ nickel
- Ⓒ penny
- Ⓓ quarter

2. What is the value of a quarter?

- Ⓕ 1¢
- Ⓖ 5¢
- Ⓗ 10¢
- Ⓙ 25¢

Find the value of the sets of coins.

3.

- Ⓐ 99¢   Ⓒ 49¢
- Ⓑ 81¢   Ⓓ 36¢

4.

- Ⓕ 61¢   Ⓗ 93¢
- Ⓖ 67¢   Ⓙ 97¢

5.

- Ⓐ 68¢   Ⓒ 77¢
- Ⓑ 75¢   Ⓓ 93¢

6. Which of these describes the value of a quarter?

　Ⓕ 5 tens 2 ones

　Ⓖ 2 tens 5 ones

　Ⓗ 7 tens

　Ⓙ 3 ones

7. Which is a way to show 74¢?

Ⓐ

Ⓑ

Ⓒ

Ⓓ

8. Which value shows 4 tens and 9 ones?

　Ⓕ 94¢　　Ⓗ 49¢

　Ⓖ 84¢　　Ⓙ 13¢

9. Dora wants to buy some candy for her friends. How many nickels does she need if the item costs 25¢?

　Ⓐ 4　　Ⓒ 6

　Ⓑ 5　　Ⓓ 7

10. Betty bought a glass of lemonade for 2 quarters. Angel wants to buy a glass for the same price. How many dimes does he need?

　Ⓕ 2　　Ⓗ 6

　Ⓖ 5　　Ⓙ 10

STOP

Read each question carefully. Fill in your answer in the space provided.

1. What is the name of this coin?

_____

2. What is the value of a nickel?

_____

Find the value of the sets of coins.

3.

_____

4.

_____

5.

_____

GO ON

6. Write the value of 5 tens
and 8 ones?

_____ ¢

7. Circle the coins to
show 38¢.

8. What is the place value
of 34¢?

____ tens ____ ones

9. Kai bought an orange
for 4 nickels. Dina wants
to buy an orange for the
same price. How many
dimes does she need?

_____

10. Maurice has 4 dimes
and 10 pennies. He
wants to trade them in
for one coin. Write or
draw the coin he could
trade these in for.

_____

STOP

Chapter 8 – Teacher Interview

Core Concept: *Using Money*

Student Activity: The student demonstrates an understanding of money value in amounts of $1.00 or more, and an ability to compare money amounts and make change. Have a collection of real or realistic play money available for the student. A number line should also be available. Ask the student questions such as, "How much is 1 half dollar, 3 quarters, and 2 dimes?"

Teacher Question 1:

• Jerome has a $1 bill, 2 quarters, and 1nickel in his pocket. How much money does he have in all?

Understanding Student Response	Practice and Improvement
Student does not know the value of a dollar.	Review lesson 1 to remind student that 1 dollar equals 100 cents. Assign practice from lesson 1.
Student does not add money amounts correctly.	Review lesson 2 and practice counting money. Use real or realistic play money to act out the problem.

Teacher Question 2:

• Amy wants to buy a sticker book that costs 1 dollar and 18 cents. She has 1 half dollar, 2 quarters, 1 dime, and 13 pennies. Does she have enough money to buy the sticker book?

Understanding Student Response	Practice and Improvement
Student says she does not have enough because she has only 17 coins.	Review lesson 3 to practice counting and comparing money. Remind student that 1 dime equals 10 pennies.
Student cannot add the half dollar and the quarters correctly.	Review the practice problems in lesson 1. Show student ways to make $1.00 from quarters and half dollars. For more practice review lesson 2, chapter 7.

Teacher Question 3:

• You decide to buy a yo-yo that costs 89¢. You pay for it with a $1 bill. How much change should you get back?

Understanding Student Response	Practice and Improvement
Student tries to use subtraction to solve the problem.	Review lesson 4, reminding student that change can be found by counting up from the price to the amount spent.
Student gets wrong answer, or does not know what to do.	Review lesson 5 and practice acting out change scenarios. Use real or realistic play money to act out the problem.

Chapter 8 – Journal Writing

Encourage students to generate their own journal entries related to math ideas in general or to concepts in this chapter. Present the following journal prompt and have students share their drawing/writing with a partner:

- Georgina buys 2 pieces of candy and a ball. What do you have to know to tell whether she has enough money to pay for it and whether or not she will get any change back?

  (Responses should mention how much one piece of candy costs, how much the ball costs, and how much money she has with her. Responses should suggest that if she has more money with her than the items cost, she will get change back.)

FOLLOW-UP

At an appropriate time, review ways of showing money amounts (Lesson 3) and making change (Lesson 4). Students may practice making change using real or play money, and write or draw a picture about the experience in their journals.

Have students work in pairs. The first student will think of three items to buy. The partner will write down the items and the cost of each item. They will total the cost of the items and the first student will "pay" for the items. If change is needed they will calculate it together and record it in the journal. One student should use addition to check the answer. Students will then reverse roles.

Chapter 8 – Monitoring Student Progress

☐ **Form A**   ☐ **Form B**

Student Name _____ Date _____

Directions: For each item that is answered incorrectly, cross out the item number. Then record the number of correct responses in the appropriate Student Score column. If the student has not met the Criterion Score for an objective, circle the student's score. Recommended assignments are listed in the Prescription Table on the next page.

Objective	Item Numbers	Criterion Score	Student Score
A. Identify a dollar and its value.	2, 4, 5, 8	3/4	/4
B. Compare money amounts.	1, 6, 7	2/3	/3
C. Make change.	3	1/1	/1
D. Use strategies and skills to solve problems.	9, 10	1/2	/2
Total Test Score		7/10	/10
Total Percent Correct			%

Chapter 8 – Prescription Table

The following chart correlates the tested objectives for this chapter to supplementary materials that meet the individual needs of the students. The Reteach and Practice pages are designed for students who need further instruction in the math concepts taught in this chapter. The Enrich pages are designed for students who need advanced challenges.

Objective	Reteach	Practice	Enrich
A. Identify a dollar and its value.	117, 120	118, 121	119, 122
B. Compare money amounts.	123	124	125
C. Make change.	126	127	128
D. Use strategies and skills to solve problems.	129, 130	131	

Read each question carefully.
Darken the circle for the correct answer.

1. Which of these is NOT equal to one dollar?

   Ⓐ 4 quarters

   Ⓑ 10 nickels

   Ⓒ 10 dimes

   Ⓓ 100 pennies

---

2. How much money does Emily have?

   Ⓕ $1.84   Ⓗ $1.64

   Ⓖ $1.74   Ⓙ $1.54

---

3. Miguel buys a flower for 59¢. He gives the clerk 75¢. How much change should he get back?

   Ⓐ 18¢   Ⓒ 16¢

   Ⓑ 17¢   Ⓓ 14¢

---

4. Anne has these coins.

Which coins does Anne need to make a dollar?

   Ⓕ 1 dime, 1 quarter

   Ⓖ 2 nickels, 2 quarters

   Ⓗ 2 quarters, 5 pennies

   Ⓙ 3 nickels, 1 quarter

---

5. How much money is shown?

   Ⓐ $2.92   Ⓒ $2.72

   Ⓑ $2.82   Ⓓ $2.52

GO ON

6. Which is greater than $1.76?

(F)

(G)

(H)

(J)

7. Which is NOT equal to $2.00?

(A) 20 dimes

(B) 4 half dollars

(C) 30 nickels

(D) 200 pennies

8. Jenna has 1 quarter and 2 dimes. She finds 30¢. How much does she have in all?

(F) 33¢   (H) 65¢

(G) 57¢   (J) 75¢

9. Paulo has 3 quarters. He buys a juice box for 60¢. How much change should he get?

(A) 15¢   (C) 57¢

(B) 30¢   (D) 75¢

10. Eli has 8 dimes. He buys a card for 47¢. How much change should he get?

(F) 33¢

(G) 39¢

(H) 43¢

(J) 80¢

STOP

Read each question carefully. Write or circle your answer in the space provided.

1. Draw or write the coins you can use to equal one dollar.

_____

_____

2. How much money does Benito have?

_____

3. Denise buys a flower for 89¢. She gives the clerk $1.00. How much change should she get back?

_____

4. Philippa has these coins.

What coins does Philippa need to make a dollar?

_____

_____

5. How much money is shown?

_____

GO ON

6. Circle the group that is less than $1.52.

7. Draw coins that equal $1.00.

8. Carl had 5 nickels and 8 pennies. He earned 27¢. How much money does he have now?

_____

9. Raylene has 6 dimes and 1 nickel. She buys a hotdog for 37¢. How much does she have left?

_____

10. Leona has 2 dimes and 7 nickels. She buys a book for 19¢. How much does she have left?

_____

STOP

Unit 2 Performance Assessment

How Much Change?

- *Target Skill:*   Make change.
- *Additional Skills:*   Identify dollars and coins and their values; compare money amounts.

Task Description: This task requires students to give the value of a dollar and a set of coins and determine the amount of change to be received back after paying.

Preparing: You may wish to have students make a list of the value of a dollar bill and the following coins: quarter, dime, nickel, and penny.

Materials	Group Size	Time on Task
Pencil Crayons Play money (optional)	1 to 2 students	1–2 days

Guiding: Remind students that they can skip-count for quarters, dimes, and nickels.

Tell students they will have enough money to buy the items and they will be paying more than the cost. This means they will receive change.

Observing/ Monitoring: As you move among the students, pose the following questions:

How do you know if Loretta received the correct change?

How does drawing the coins help you know how much Loretta has?

Unit 2 Performance Assessment Scoring Rubric

How Much Change?

Score	Explanation
3	Students demonstrate an efficient strategy and a thorough approach that enables them to solve the problem completely. A satisfactory answer: • correctly states the change Loretta gets back 46¢, 7¢, and 33¢; • draws the change back correctly; • successfully adds the cost of the change Loretta got back and answers yes to buying the calendar. Students are able to complete the problem quickly and have all of the above correct solutions.
2	Students demonstrate a strategy that enables them to solve most of the problem correctly. The strategy is somewhat disorganized, making it less efficient. A solution is found but errors are contained. Students may: • correctly count the change from each item; • draw the change back, but not add it correctly; • not know why Loretta has enough change to buy the calendar. Students may have some difficulty determining all solutions correctly but demonstrate an understanding of general concepts.
1	Students demonstrate a confused strategy, which leads to difficulty solving the problem. Most answers are incorrect, but students demonstrate knowledge of at least one concept being assessed. Students may: • correctly compute the change for some of the items; • draw some of the change Loretta received correctly.

Name _____

Unit 2 Performance Assessment
Student Activity

How Much Change?

You will need
- a piece of paper
- a pencil

Help Loretta get change for the items above.
Draw coins to help you answer the questions.

1. Loretta buys the picture frame with a dollar. How
much change should she get back?

_____

2. Loretta buys the card with two quarters. How
much change should she get back?

_____

3. Loretta buys the vase with a dollar. How much
change should she get back?

_____

4. Can Loretta buy the calendar with seventy
five cents?

_____

© Macmillan/McGraw-Hill

Unit 2 – Monitoring Student Progress

☐ Form A   ☐ Form B

Student Name _____ Date _____

Directions: This test targets selected objectives. For each item that is answered incorrectly, cross out the item number. Then record the number of correct responses in the column labeled **Number of Correct Responses.** Add to find the **Total Number of Correct Responses** and record the total. Use this total to determine the **Total Test Score** and the **Total Percent Correct.**

Strand • Objective(s)	Item Numbers	Number of Correct Responses
Number Sense, Concepts, and Operations • Count, read, write, and represent numbers to 100. • Identify the place value for each digit for numbers to 100. • Estimate numbers. • Compare and order numbers to 100. • Skip-count to 100. • Identify even and odd numbers. • Use strategies and skills to solve problems.	1, 2, 3, 4, 5, 6, 7, 8, 16, 17	/11
Measurement • Identify dollars and coins and their values. • Find the value of a set of coins. • Make equal amounts. • Compare money amounts. • Make change. • Use strategies and skills to solve problems.	9, 10, 11, 12, 13, 14, 15, 18, 19, 20	/9
Total Number of Correct Responses		
Total Test Score		/20
Total Percent Correct		%

Read each question carefully.
Darken the circle for the correct answer.

1. What number does the picture show?

tens	ones

Ⓐ 9   Ⓒ 63

Ⓑ 54   Ⓓ 64

---

2. How do you write the number sixteen?

Ⓕ 6   Ⓗ 60

Ⓖ 16   Ⓙ 70

---

3. How many tens are in 62?

Ⓐ 2 tens

Ⓑ 6 tens

Ⓒ 20 tens

Ⓓ 60 tens

4. Which is true?

Ⓕ 18 > 34

Ⓖ 72 > 59

Ⓗ 21 > 28

Ⓙ 34 > 43

---

5. What number comes just after 39?

Ⓐ 37

Ⓑ 38

Ⓒ 40

Ⓓ 41

GO ON

6. Skip-count by threes. Which number comes next?

3   6   9

Ⓕ 10   Ⓗ 12

Ⓖ 11   Ⓙ 18

7. Which is an odd number?

Ⓐ 16

Ⓑ 23

Ⓒ 48

Ⓓ 54

8. What are the next three even numbers?

16 18 ▢ ▢ ▢

Ⓕ 19, 20, 21

Ⓖ 20, 21, 22

Ⓗ 19, 21, 23

Ⓙ 20, 22, 24

9. How many cents are in a nickel?

Ⓐ 1¢

Ⓑ 5¢

Ⓒ 10¢

Ⓓ 25¢

10. How many dollars are in $4.23?

Ⓕ 1

Ⓖ 2

Ⓗ 3

Ⓙ 4

11. Which of these coins is a dime?

Ⓐ   Ⓒ

Ⓑ   Ⓓ

GO ON ▶

12. Which set of coins has the greatest value?

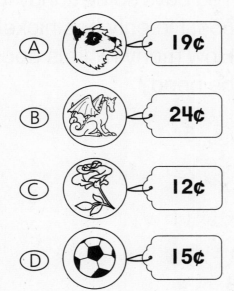

Ⓕ

Ⓖ

Ⓗ

Ⓙ

13. Which toy costs the most?

Ⓐ 19¢

Ⓑ 24¢

Ⓒ 12¢

Ⓓ 15¢

14. Count. How much money?

Ⓕ $1.80   Ⓗ $3.21

Ⓖ $3.15   Ⓙ $3.50

15. Which toy costs the least?

Ⓐ $1.59

Ⓑ $1.25

Ⓒ $1.05

Ⓓ $1.45

GO ON

16. Mr. Ruiz's students are standing in line. How many people are in front of the fifth person in line?

Ⓕ 4 people

Ⓖ 5 people

Ⓗ 11 people

Ⓙ 16 people

17. How many children are on the bus?

The number is between 31 and 46.

There are 4 tens in the number.

The ones digit is greater than the tens digit.

Ⓐ 43 children

Ⓑ 45 children

Ⓒ 47 children

Ⓓ 35 children

18. Kyle has 6 dimes. He buys a drink for 55¢. How much change should he get back?

Ⓕ 1¢   Ⓗ 10¢

Ⓖ 5¢   Ⓙ 50¢

19. Denise has dimes and nickels. How many ways can she buy a cookie for 25¢?

Ⓐ 1 way   Ⓒ 3 ways

Ⓑ 2 ways   Ⓓ 4 ways

20. Ted buys some candy for 65¢. He only has nickels. How many nickels does he need?

Ⓕ 5

Ⓖ 6

Ⓗ 11

Ⓙ 13

STOP

Read each question carefully. Write or circle your answer in the space provided.

1. What number does the picture show?

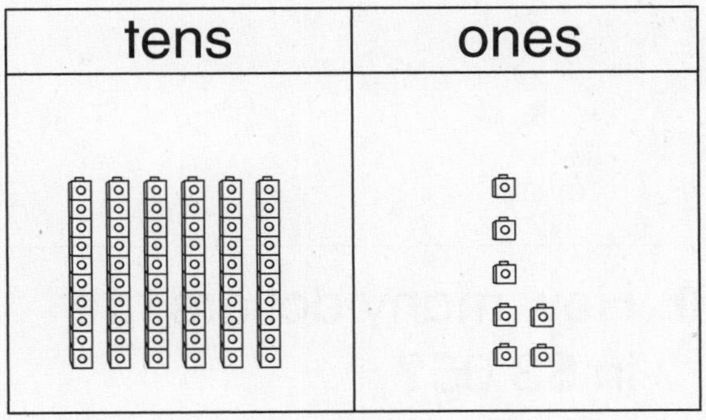

tens	ones

_____

2. How do you write the number eighteen?

_____

3. How many tens are in 79?

_____ tens

4. Circle the comparison that is true.

$50 < 49$

$62 < 85$

$65 < 40$

$95 < 85$

_____

5. What number comes just after 59?

_____

GO ON ▶

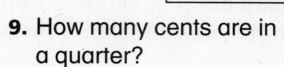

6. Skip-count by threes. Which number comes next?

15   18   21   _____

7. Which is an odd number?

29, 56, 82, or 98

_____

8. Write the next three even numbers.

26   28   __   __   __

9. How many cents are in a quarter?

_____ ¢

10. How many dollars are in $3.05?

_____

11. Circle the penny.

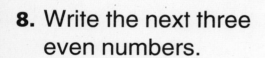

 GO ON

12. Circle the set of coins with the greatest value.

13. Circle the toy that costs the most.

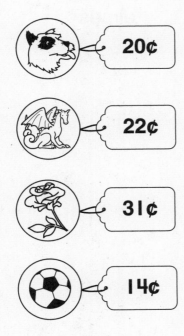

20¢

22¢

31¢

14¢

14. Count. How much money?

$ _____

15. Circle the toy that costs the least.

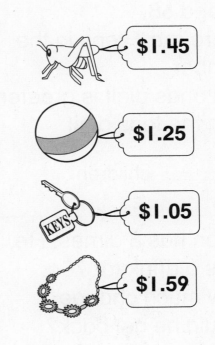

$1.45

$1.25

$1.05

$1.59

GO ON

16. Mrs. Cho's class is standing in line. How many people are in front of the seventh person in line?

_____ people

17. How many children are on the bus?
The number is between 52 and 68.
There are 6 tens in the number.
The ones digit is greater than the tens digit.

_____ children

18. Byron has 8 dimes. He buys a drink for 75¢. How much change should he get back?

_____ ¢

19. Kristen has quarters and nickels. How many ways can she buy a ticket for 35¢?

_____ ways

20. Jan wants to buy a glass of juice for 50¢. How many dimes does she need?

_____ dimes

STOP

Chapter 9 – Teacher Interview

Core Concept: *Telling Time*

Student Activity: The student demonstrates an understanding of reading analog clocks to tell time to 5, 15, and 30 minutes, and the hour. Have worksheets with analog clock faces available for the student. A demonstration clock is desirable. Ask the student questions such as "What is another name for quarter past 6?"

Teacher Question 1:

• What is another name for quarter past 8?

Understanding Student Response	Practice and Improvement
Student says 5:45.	Review lesson 4 to prompt the student for the meaning of "quarter past." Have the student count 15 minutes on an analog clock face and draw hands to illustrate 6:15.
Student is unable to give a response.	Review lesson 4 to help the student learn time before and after the hour.

Teacher Question 2:

• If the hour hand is between the 10 and 11 and the minute hand is on the 6 what time is it?

Understanding Student Response	Practice and Improvement
Student answers 10:06, 10:60, 11:06, or 11:60.	Review lesson 1 to help the student learn that when the minute hand is on the 6 it is 30 minutes past the hour.
Student gives an incorrect response not shown above.	Review lesson 1 to help the student learn to tell time to the hour and half hour.

Teacher Question 3:

• When it is 8:30, why is the hour hand halfway between the 8 and 9?

Understanding Student Response	Practice and Improvement
Student does not know that 30 minutes is half an hour.	Review lesson 1 to help the student learn that there are 60 minutes in an hour and 30 minutes in a half hour.
Student knows that 30 minutes is a half hour but does not understand why the hour hand is halfway between the 8 and 9.	Review lesson 1 to reinforce that the hour hand moves between hours as each hour progresses.

Chapter 9 – Journal Writing

Encourage students to generate their own journal entries related to math ideas in general or to concepts in this chapter. Present the following journal prompt and have students share their drawing/writing with a partner:

- Dolly watches the news from quarter to 6 to half past 7. Write these times. Draw clocks to show these times. What words tell you how to write these times?

  (Responses should show an understanding that some words, such as "past", indicate a time after the hour and other words, such as "to," indicate a time before the hour.)

FOLLOW-UP

At the end of the class, review the concept of time. Model different ways of saying the time. Write these times so students can see and hear them. You may use a model clock to emphasize the motion of clock hands. Show the hand before the hour. Then move the hand and show it after the hour.

Ask students to think of a time when they used a clock today (for example, knowing when it was time for art class). Have them tell the time to a math partner who will write the time down and draw a clock that shows the time.

Chapter 9 – Monitoring Student Progress

☐ **Form A**   ☐ **Form B**

Student Name _____ Date _____

Directions: For each item that is answered incorrectly, cross out the item number. Then record the number of correct responses in the appropriate Student Score column. If the student has not met the Criterion Score for an objective, circle the student's score. Recommended assignments are listed in the Prescription Table on the next page.

Objective	Item Numbers	Criterion Score	Student Score
A. Tell and write time to 5-minute intervals.	1, 2, 3, 4, 5, 6, 7, 8	7/8	/8
B. Use strategies and skills to solve problems.	9, 10	1/2	/2
Total Test Score		8/10	/10
Total Percent Correct			%

Chapter 9 – Prescription Table

The following chart correlates the tested objectives for this chapter to supplementary materials that meet the individual needs of the students. The Reteach and Practice pages are designed for students who need further instruction in the math concepts taught in this chapter. The Enrich pages are designed for students who need advanced challenges.

Objective	Reteach	Practice	Enrich
A. Tell and write time to 5-minute intervals.	133, 136, 139, 142	134, 137, 140, 143	135, 138, 141, 144
B. Use strategies and skills to solve problems.	145	146	147

Read each question carefully.
Darken the circle for the correct answer.

Fill in the correct choice for the time on the clock.

1.

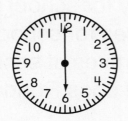

Ⓐ 4:00   Ⓒ 6:00

Ⓑ 5:00   Ⓓ 8:00

2.

Ⓕ 3:30   Ⓗ 4:30

Ⓖ 4:06   Ⓙ 5:30

3.

Ⓐ 10:03   Ⓒ 10:30

Ⓑ 10:15   Ⓓ 10:45

4. Which clock shows 7:25?

Ⓕ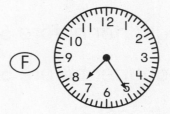

Ⓖ

Ⓗ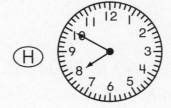

Ⓙ

5. Which is the same as a quarter before 3?

Ⓐ 3:45   Ⓒ 2:45

Ⓑ 3:15   Ⓓ 2:15

6. Which is the same as 5:15?

- F a quarter after 5
- G a quarter before 6
- H a quarter before 5
- J half past 5

7. How many half hours are there in one hour?

A 1 B 2 C 3 D 4

8. Which time is NOT shown?

- F 8:40
- G 20 minutes before 9
- H 40 minutes past 8
- J a quarter before 9

Use the information for exercises 9–10.

Rondell wakes up at 7:00. He gets ready for school at 7:30. He leaves for school at 7:45. He arrives at school at 8:00. What does Rondell do at 7:45?

- A wake up
- B get ready for school
- C leave for school
- D arrive at school

10. Which clock shows when Rondell first does something?

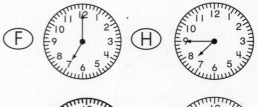

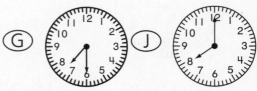

© Macmillan/McGraw-Hill

STOP

Read each question carefully. Write your answer in the space provided.

Write the time.

1.

_____

2.

_____

3.

_____

4. Draw the hands to show 3:35.

5. What time is it when it is quarter past 4?

_____

GO ON

6. What is another way to say 10:45?

_____
_____
_____

7. How many quarter hours are there in 1 hour?

_____

8. Name three ways to say the time on the clock.

_____
_____

Use the information for exercises 9–10.

Judy leaves school at 2:45. She plays softball at 3:00 for an hour. She arrives home at 4:15. She starts her homework at 4:30.

9. How long does Judy play softball?

_____

10. At what time does Judy arrive home?

_____

STOP

Chapter 10 – Teacher Interview

Core Concept: *Time and Calendar*

Student Activity: The student demonstrates an understanding of reading analog clocks and using addition and subtraction to state durations of time. Have worksheets with analog clock faces available for the student, as well as worksheets of current calendar pages. A demonstration clock is desirable. Ask the student questions such as, "What is another name for quarter past 8 in the morning?"

Teacher Question 1:

• What is another name for quarter past 8 in the morning?

Understanding Student Response	Practice and Improvement
Student says "8:15," but does not add "A.M."	Review lesson 1 to point out that since 8:15 occurs twice each day, they must specify A.M. or P.M. to be correct.
Student gives an incorrect response, such as "8:30" or "7:45."	Review lesson 4 from Chapter 9 to prompt the student for the meaning of "quarter past." Have the student count 15 minutes on an analog clock face and draw hands to illustrate 8:15.

Teacher Question 2:

• Here is a calendar showing that today is Wednesday, October 4th (or the current date). One week from today, what will be the date?

Understanding Student Response	Practice and Improvement
Student does not know that one week in the future will be the same day of the week as today.	Review lesson 3 to remind the student that one week contains 7 days. Have the student note that seven days will be the same day of the week as today. Give other examples.
Student knows that it will be Wednesday, but cannot give the date.	Review lesson 3 to point out that since today is the 4th and a week contains 7 days, one week will be Wednesday, the (4 + 7)th or the 11th. Practice items like those following lesson 3.

Teacher Question 3:

• If Khalid can do 10 arithmetic problems in 10 minutes, how many can he do in a half hour?

Understanding Student Response	Practice and Improvement
Student does not know that there are 30 minutes in a half hour.	Review Chapter 9 lessons 1-4 to help the student see that there are 30 minutes in a half hour. Ask how many problems Khalid can do in 30 minutes.
Student knows there are 30 minutes in a half hour, but does not see that Khalid can do one problem each minute, hence 30 problems in 30 minutes.	Review Chapter 9 lessons 1–4 to help the student determine how many problems Khalid can do in 5 minutes, 20 minutes, and other durations leading up to 30 minutes. Create additional items for practice and improvement.

Chapter 10 – Journal Writing

Encourage students to generate their own journal entries related to math ideas in general or to concepts in this chapter. Present the following journal prompt and have students share their drawing/writing with a partner:

- Dorothy practices her music lessons for 20 minutes in the morning and 20 minutes in the afternoon on Monday, Wednesday, and Friday. How many hours does she practice in a week?

  (Responses should state that adding the numbers of minutes is the process required. Students may solve the problem by using a demonstration clock or by drawing on an analog clock face. Students should convert the total minutes to hours, and should be able to explain how they arrived at a solution.)

FOLLOW-UP

At the end of the day, review the concept of time and of elapsed time. Ask students to think of a time when they used a clock today (for example, knowing when it was time for music).

Have the students show what time they have special classes, like art and music, on analog clocks. Have them skip–count by fives to figure out how long each class lasts. Add the times together. Students should show all of their work in their journals and share their entry with a math partner.

Chapter 10 – Monitoring Student Progress

☐ **Form A**   ☐ **Form B**

Student Name _____ Date _____

Directions: For each item that is answered incorrectly, cross out the item number. Then record the number of correct responses in the appropriate Student Score column. If the student has not met the Criterion Score for an objective, circle the student's score. Recommended assignments are listed in the Prescription Table on the next page.

Objective	Item Numbers	Criterion Score	Student Score
A. Find elapsed time of A.M. and P.M.	1, 6, 7, 8, 9, 10	5/6	/6
B. Use a calendar.	3, 4, 5	2/3	/3
C. Use strategies and skills to solve problems.	2	1/1	/1
Total Test Score		8/10	/10
Total Percent Correct			%

Chapter 10 – Prescription Table

The following chart correlates the tested objectives for this chapter to supplementary materials that meet the individual needs of the students. The Reteach and Practice pages are designed for students who need further instruction in the math concepts taught in this chapter. The Enrich pages are designed for students who need advanced challenges.

Objective	Reteach	Practice	Enrich
A. Find elapsed time.	151	152	153
B. Use a calendar.	154	155	156
C. Use strategies and skills to solve problems.	160, 161	162	

Read each question carefully.
Darken the circle for the correct answer.

1. What time do you wake up?

  (A) 7:00 A.M.

  (B) 11:00 A.M.

  (C) 7:00 P.M.

  (D) 11:00 P.M.

---

2. How much time is there until 12:00?

  (F) 3 hours

  (G) 3 hours, 30 minutes

  (H) 4 hours

  (J) 4 hours, 30 minutes

Use the calendar for items 3–5.

March 2004						
Sun	Mon	Tues	Wed	Thurs	Fri	Sat
	1	2	3	4	5	6
7	8	9	10	11	12	13
14	15	16	17	18	19	20
21	22	23	24	25	26	27
28	29	30	31			

3. How many days are in March?

  (A) 28   (C) 30

  (B) 29   (D) 31

---

4. What is the date one week after March 10?

  (F) March 11

  (G) March 15

  (H) March 17

  (J) March 20

---

5. Which date is the fourth Tuesday in March?

  (A) March 18

  (B) March 23

  (C) March 25

  (D) March 30

© Macmillan/McGraw-Hill

6. What time is it 2 hours after 5:30?

Ⓕ 5:32   Ⓗ 7:30

Ⓖ 5:50   Ⓙ 7:52

7. Which clock shows the time 30 minutes after 2:15?

Ⓐ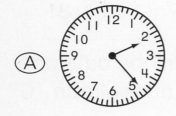

Ⓑ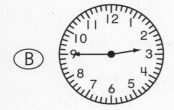

Ⓒ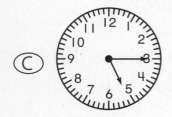

Ⓓ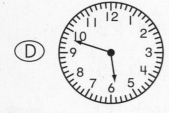

8. How long was Maura at the movies?

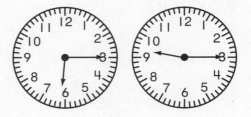

Ⓕ I hour   Ⓗ 3 hours

Ⓖ 2 hours   Ⓙ 4 hours

9. Which unit is best for measuring the length of time it takes to wash your face?

Ⓐ minute   Ⓒ day

Ⓑ hour   Ⓓ week

10. Which unit is best for measuring the length of time it will take for you to enter fourth grade?

Ⓕ day   Ⓗ month

Ⓖ minute   Ⓙ year

STOP

Read each question carefully. Write your answer in the space provided.

1. What time do you go to sleep?

_____

_____

2. How much time is there until 1:00?

_____

Use the calendar for items 3–5.

October 2004						
Sun	Mon	Tues	Wed	Thurs	Fri	Sat
					1	2
3	4	5	6	7	8	9
10	11	12	13	14	15	16
17	18	19	20	21	22	23
24	25	26	27	28	29	30
31						

3. How many days are in October?

_____

4. What is the date one week after October 7?

_____

5. What date is the third Friday in October?

_____

GO ON

6. What time is it 2 hours after 2:30?

_____

7. Show the time 30 minutes after 6:15.

8. How many hours was Manny at the movies?

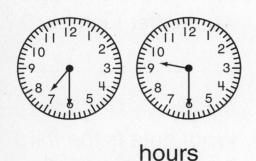

_____ hours

9. What unit is best for measuring the length of time it takes to walk a dog?

_____

10. What unit is best for measuring the length of time it will take for you to become an adult?

_____

STOP

Chapter 11 – Teacher Interview

Core Concept: *Data and Graphs*

Student Activity: The student will demonstrate an understanding of making graphs and interpreting data presented in graphic form. Have graph paper, crayons or markers, pencils, and scratch paper available for the student. Ask the student questions such as, "What is the difference between a pictograph and a bar graph?"

Teacher Question 1:

• Ms. Tollefsen's class made a pictograph in which a small square represents 10 books. If the "animal stories" category showed 3 of these small squares, how many books are represented?

Understanding Student Response	Practice and Improvement
Student does not know what a pictograph is and how it represents data.	Review lesson 4 to explain pictographs and how each square represents 10 books. Have the student skip–count by 10s to find how many books. Ask the student to recalculate based on 1 square = 2 books.
Student understands that one square means 10 books, but cannot interpret 3 squares.	Review lesson 4. Have the student assume each square = 2 books, then skip–count to find 6 books. Go back and skip-count by 10s to get 30.

Teacher Question 2:

• What is the difference between a pictograph and a bar graph?

Understanding Student Response	Practice and Improvement
Student is unable to explain how a pictograph and bar graph differ.	Review lessons 3 and 4 to clarify that in pictographs, each picture represents a certain number of things, while in bar graphs, the length of a bar shows how many.
Student confuses the graph types, or "mixes up" the ways of displaying data.	Review lessons 3, 4, and 6. Point out that the same data can be shown by either method, but that it may be easier to read a bar graph.

Teacher Question 3:

• What is the difference between a bar graph and a line plot?

Understanding Student Response	Practice and Improvement
Student is unable to explain how a bar graph and a line plot differ.	Review lessons 3 and 5 to clarify that in bar graphs, the length of a bar represents a certain number of things, while in line plots, the number of X's show how many.
Student confuses the graph types or "mixes up" the ways of displaying data.	Review lessons 3, 4, and 6. Point out that the same data can be shown by either method, and the advantages of both types.

Chapter 11 – Journal Writing

Encourage students to generate their own journal entries related to math ideas in general or to concepts in this chapter. Present the following journal prompt and have students share their drawing/writing with a partner:

- Imagine that you are going to make a pictograph showing how many books your class has read over a whole year. You want to show how many adventure books, biographies, mysteries, and so on have been read. How will you collect the data? What would be a good picture to use? How many books should each picture stand for?

  (Responses should describe several categories of books. The picture suggested should be appropriate. One way of collecting data would be to survey the class; another would be to put every learner's name on a chart and put a tally mark for every book read. Have students sketch what the pictograph might look like in their journals.)

FOLLOW-UP

At the end of the day, review the concept of representing quantities with pictures. Ask students to think of classroom activities other than reading that might be recorded on a pictograph or bar graph. Have students draw some symbols that would represent those activities, and share them with their math partners.

Have students think of out-of-school events that could be shown graphically, and propose ways to record and interpret the data. Students should share their pictures and stories with a math partner.

Chapter 11 – Monitoring Student Progress

☐ **Form A**   ☐ **Form B**

Student Name _____   Date _____

Directions: For each item that is answered incorrectly, cross out the item number. Then record the number of correct responses in the appropriate Student Score column. If the student has not met the Criterion Score for an objective, circle the student's score. Recommended assignments are listed in the Prescription Table on the next page.

Objective	Item Numbers	Criterion Score	Student Score
A. Read, interpret, and create graphs.	1, 5, 8	2/3	/3
B. Represent the same data set in more than one way.	3, 4, 7, 10	3/4	/4
C. Use strategies and skills to solve problems.	2, 6, 9	2/3	/3
Total Test Score		7/10	/10
Total Percent Correct			%

Chapter 11 – Prescription Table

The following chart correlates the tested objectives for this chapter to supplementary materials that meet the individual needs of the students. The Reteach and Practice pages are designed for students who need further instruction in the math concepts taught in this chapter. The Enrich pages are designed for students who need advanced challenges.

Objective	Reteach	Practice	Enrich
A. Read, interpret, and create graphs.	163, 166, 169,172, 175	164, 167, 170,173, 176	165, 168, 171, 174, 177
B. Represent the same data set in more than one way.	178	179	180
C. Use strategies and skills to solve problems.	181	182	183

Read each question carefully.
Darken the circle for the correct answer.

Use the data for items 1–4.

Favorite Games

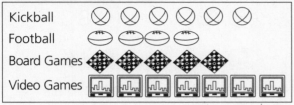

1. Which is the favorite?

    Ⓐ kickball

    Ⓑ football

    Ⓒ board games

    Ⓓ video games

2. How many more children like kickball than football?

    Ⓕ 1   Ⓖ 2   Ⓗ 3   Ⓙ 4

3. Which shows the correct tally marks for kickball?

    Ⓐ |||| Ⓒ ⧸⧸⧸⧸ |

    Ⓑ |||| Ⓓ ⧸⧸⧸⧸ ||

4. Which bar graph shows the data in the picture graph?

Ⓕ
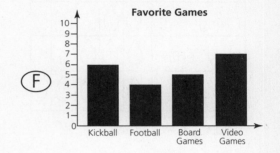

Ⓖ
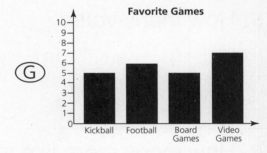

Ⓗ

Ⓙ
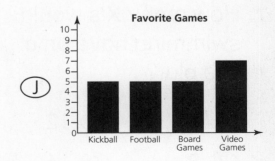

GO ON

Name _____

Use the pictograph for exercises 5–8.

Favorite Water Activities

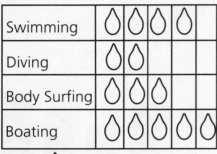

Swimming	
Diving	
Body Surfing	
Boating	

Each ◊ = 2 votes

5. How many voted?

(A) 14   (C) 28

(B) 16   (D) 32

6. How many more like to go boating than diving?

(F) 3   (H) 7

(G) 6   (J) 14

7. How many X's would swimming have on a line plot?

(A) 4   (C) 12

(B) 8   (D) 16

8. How many students like body surfing or boating the best?

(F) 2   (H) 8

(G) 4   (J) 16

9. The class voted for its favorite sport. Jodi said, "I like hitting the ball." Which sport might Jodi have voted for?

(A) high jump

(B) baseball

(C) bowling

(D) cycling

10. 8 girls and 5 boys like tennis. What would a tally mark look like for girls?

(F) |||| (H) ⵜⵜⵜ ||

(G) ⵜⵜⵜ | (J) ⵜⵜⵜ |||

STOP

Read each question carefully. Fill in your answer in the space provided.

Use the data for items 1–4.

Favorite Games

1. Which is the favorite?

_____

2. How many more students like card games than T-ball?

_____ students

3. Write the correct tally marks for soccer.

_____

4. Fill in the bar graph for the data in the picture graph.

GO ON

Use the pictograph for exercises 5–8.

Favorite Water Activities

Beach	☀	☀	☀	☀
Riding Bikes	☀	☀	☀	
Fishing	☀	☀		
Camping	☀			

Each ☀ = 2 votes

5. How many voted?

_____

6. How many more students like to go to the beach than go fishing?

_____

7. How many X's would riding bikes have on a line plot?

_____

8. How many students like going to the beach or fishing the best?

_____

9. The class is voting for their favorite dessert. Brad said, "I usually order a cone."
What dessert might be Brad's favorite?

_____

10. 7 girls like Italian food. 9 boys like Italian food. What would the tally marks look like for each?

_____

_____

STOP

Chapter 12 – Teacher Interview

Core Concept: *Rename Numbers in More Than One Way*

Student Activity: The student will demonstrate an understanding of renaming numbers in order to add them. Have tens blocks and ones blocks available for the students. Ask the student questions such as, "How can you rename 25 in three different ways?"

Teacher Question 1:

• How many tens are there in 36? How many ones?

Understanding Student Response	Practice and Improvement
Student does not know how to group the number into tens and ones.	Review lesson 1 to help the student learn how to regroup numbers.
Student says 36 ones.	Review lesson 1 to help the student learn to regroup 36 as 3 tens and 6 ones.

Teacher Question 2:

• How can you add 18 + 24 using blocks?

Understanding Student Response	Practice and Improvement
Student does not mention regrouping.	Review lesson 3 to help the student add greater numbers through regrouping.
Student adds 3 tens but does not regroup the 12 ones.	Review lesson 3 to help the student add greater numbers through regrouping.

Teacher Question 3:

• How can you rename 25 in three different ways?

Understanding Student Response	Practice and Improvement
Student does not know all three ways.	Review lesson 4 to help the student learn how to regroup two-digit numbers.
Student uses regrouping, but the numbers do not equal 25.	Review lesson 4 to help the student learn how to regroup two-digit numbers.

Chapter 12 – Journal Writing

- Frankie has 8 toys. For her birthday she gets 16 more. How can you use a pattern to find the number of toys Frankie has now?

  (Responses should state that since 8 + 6 = 14, if the addend is increased by 10, the sum will increase by 10, so 8 + 16 = 24. Students may want to make a drawing of 8 toys then 6 toys added on before adding 10 more.)

FOLLOW-UP

At the end of the class, review the concept of regrouping and addition. Ask students to think of times when they have had to add two 2-digit numbers.

Have the students pretend they are in a store to buy two items. They buy a pen for 27¢ and a pencil for 34¢. Have the student use renaming and regrouping to find how much the total cost will be. Ask them how knowing a pattern can help them find the sum. Students can make observations about what happened to the sums as they renamed and regrouped. Have students write these observations and the sum in their math journals.

Chapter 12 – Monitoring Student Progress

☐ **Form A** ☐ **Form B**

Student Name _____ Date _____

Directions: For each item that is answered incorrectly, cross out the item number. Then record the number of correct responses in the appropriate Student Score column. If the student has not met the Criterion Score for an objective, circle the student's score. Recommended assignments are listed in the Prescription Table on the next page.

Objective	Item Numbers	Criterion Score	Student Score
A. Regroup numbers.	1, 2, 4, 7	3/4	/4
B. Rename numbers in more than one way.	3, 5, 6, 8	3/4	/4
C. Use strategies and skills to solve problems.	9, 10	1/2	/2
Total Test Score		7/10	/10
Total Percent Correct			%

Chapter 12 – Prescription Table

The following chart correlates the tested objectives for this chapter to supplementary materials that meet the individual needs of the students. The Reteach and Practice pages are designed for students who need further instruction in the math concepts taught in this chapter. The Enrich pages are designed for students who need advanced challenges.

Objective	Reteach	Practice	Enrich
A. Regroup numbers.	184	185	186
B. Rename numbers in more than one way.	193	194	195
C. Use strategies and skills to solve problems.	196, 197	198	

Read each question carefully.
Darken the circle for the correct answer.

1. 45 = ▢ tens ▢ ones

  Ⓐ 5 tens 4 ones

  Ⓑ 5 tens 5 ones

  Ⓒ 4 tens 4 ones

  Ⓓ 4 tens 5 ones

2. 6 tens 3 ones = ▢

  Ⓕ 9

  Ⓖ 36

  Ⓗ 63

  Ⓙ 99

3. 8 + 7 = ▢

  Ⓐ 13

  Ⓑ 14

  Ⓒ 15

  Ⓓ 16

4. 9 + 9 = ▢ tens ▢ ones

  Ⓕ 1 ten 9 ones

  Ⓖ 1 ten 8 ones

  Ⓗ 1 ten 7 ones

  Ⓙ 1 ten 6 ones

5. 7 + 55 = ▢

  Ⓐ 63

  Ⓑ 62

  Ⓒ 53

  Ⓓ 52

GO ON

6. Which way does NOT name 38?

Ⓕ 3 tens 8 ones

Ⓖ 3 tens 18 ones

Ⓗ 1 ten 28 ones

Ⓙ 0 tens 38 ones

7. How many in all?

tens	ones

tens	ones

Ⓐ 32

Ⓑ 33

Ⓒ 42

Ⓓ 43

8. Which shows 72?

Ⓕ 5 tens 12 ones

Ⓖ 4 tens 22 ones

Ⓗ 3 tens 32 ones

Ⓙ 2 tens 52 ones

9. There are 6 people at a meeting. A bus comes with 48 more people. How many people are there now?

Ⓐ 42   Ⓒ 52

Ⓑ 44   Ⓓ 54

10. There are 7 bagels for the meeting. Someone brings 36 more. How many bagels are there now?

Ⓕ 29   Ⓗ 43

Ⓖ 33   Ⓙ 44

© Macmillan/McGraw-Hill

STOP

Read each question carefully. Write your answer on the line.

1. $67 =$ ___ tens ___ ones

_____

2. 4 tens 6 ones = _____

3. $9 + 7 =$ _____

4. $8 + 6 =$

___ ten ___ ones

_____

5. $9 + 48 =$ _____

GO ON

6. 64 = 4 tens _____ ones

7. How many in all?

tens	ones

tens	ones

_____

8. Show 25 in three different ways.

_____ tens _____ ones

_____ tens _____ ones

_____ tens _____ ones

9. There are 8 adults in the stands and 64 children. How many people are in the stands?

_____

10. There are 8 donuts in a box. Someone brings 39 more donuts. How many donuts are there now?

_____

STOP

Unit 3 Performance Assessment

Picnic Plans

- *Target Skill:* Record data in systematic ways.
- *Additional Skills:* Represent the same data set in more than one way.

Task Description: This task requires students to ask 9 classmates which kind of fruit they would like for a picnic and make a tally chart and a bar graph of this information. Students then need to decide which kind of fruit to bring and why.

Preparing: You may wish to have students list fruits that they know. Talk about how to decide which fruit to bring for a picnic.

Materials	Group Size	Time on Task
Pencil Paper for tally chart	1 to 2 students	1–2 days

Guiding: Suggest that students collect the data first and then create the tally chart once they know which kinds of fruit they will need to record.

Observing/ Monitoring: As you move among the students, pose the following questions:

How did you decide which fruit to bring?

Is there anything else you learned in class that can help you solve this problem?

Unit 3 Performance Assessment Scoring Rubric

Picnic Plans

Score	Explanation
3	Students demonstrate an efficient strategy and a thorough approach that enables them to solve the problem completely. Students may: • include collected data from 9 classmates; • include an organized tally chart and corresponding bar graph; • include a sentence that draws a conclusion from the data. Students are able to complete the problem quickly and have all of the above correct solutions.
2	Students demonstrate a strategy that enables them to solve most of the problem correctly. The strategy is somewhat disorganized, making it less efficient. A solution is found but errors are contained. Students may: • make a tally chart and/or a bar graph that is missing some of the collected data; • make no decisions about the fruit or suggest that you purchase all the fruits. Students may have some difficulty determining all solutions correctly but demonstrate an understanding of general concepts.
1	Students demonstrate a confused strategy, which leads to difficulty solving the problem. Most answers are incorrect, but students demonstrate knowledge of at least one concept being assessed. Students may: • collect some data; • begin a tally chart and bar graph.

Unit 3 Performance Assessment
Student Activity

Picnic Plans

You will need
- a pencil
- paper for a tally chart and bar graph

You are helping to plan a class picnic. Your job is to find out which kind of fruit to bring.

1. Ask 9 classmates which kind of fruit they would like to have at the picnic.

2. Record your results in a tally chart.

3. Record your results in a bar graph.

4. Write a sentence telling which kind of fruit you will bring to the picnic and why?

_____

_____

_____

Unit 3 – Monitoring Student Progress

☐ **Form A**   ☐ **Form B**

Student Name _____ Date _____

Directions: This test targets selected objectives. For each item that is answered incorrectly, cross out the item number. Then record the number of correct responses in the column labeled **Number of Correct Responses.** Add to find the **Total Number of Correct Responses** and record the total. Use this total to determine the **Total Test Score** and the **Total Percent Correct.**

Strand • Objective(s)	Item Numbers	Number of Correct Responses
Number Sense, Concepts, and Operations • Regroup numbers. • Rename numbers in more than one way. • Use strategies and skills to solve problems.	19, 20	/2
Measurement • Tell and write time to 5-minute intervals. • Find elapsed time. • Use a calendar. • Use strategies and skills to solve problems.	1, 2, 3, 4, 5, 6, 7, 8, 17, 18	/10
Data Analysis and Probability • Read, interpret, and create graphs. • Represent the same data set in more than one way. • Use strategies and skills to solve problems.	9, 10, 11, 12, 13, 14, 15, 16	/8
Total Number of Correct Responses		
Total Test Score		/20
Total Percent Correct		%

Read each question carefully. Darken the circle for the correct answer.

1. What time does the clock show?

Ⓐ 12:00   Ⓒ 4:00

Ⓑ 12:20   Ⓓ 4:12

2. How many minutes are in a half hour?

Ⓕ 5 minutes

Ⓖ 15 minutes

Ⓗ 30 minutes

Ⓙ 60 minutes

3. What is the same as 60 seconds?

Ⓐ one minute

Ⓑ a quarter hour

Ⓒ a half hour

Ⓓ one hour

Use the calendar to answer exercises 4–5.

April 2002						
Sun	Mon	Tues	Wed	Thurs	Fri	Sat
				1	2	3
4	5	6	7	8	9	10
11	12	13	14	15	16	17
18	19	20	21	22	23	24
25	26	27	28	29	30	

4. What is the date of the second Tuesday in April?

Ⓕ April 8   Ⓗ April 13

Ⓖ April 12   Ⓙ April 15

5. How many days are there between April 15 and April 26?

Ⓐ 8 days   Ⓒ 10 days

Ⓑ 9 days   Ⓓ 11 days

GO ON ➡

Name _____

6. It is nighttime. What time does the clock show?

- (F) 3:55 A.M.
- (G) 10:15 P.M.
- (H) 11:15 P.M.
- (J) 12:15 A.M.

7. How many hours have passed?

- (A) 2 hours
- (C) 5 hours
- (B) 3 hours
- (D) 7 hours

8. What time does the clock show?

- (F) 1:35
- (G) 2:35
- (H) 7:05
- (J) 12:35

9. What is another way to write the number 4?

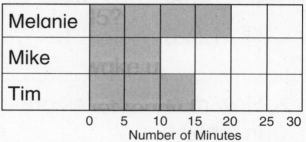

(A) IIII   (B) 卌   (C) 卌I   (D) 卌II

Use the graph below to answer items 10–12.

Saturday Morning Bike Rides

Melanie						
Mike						
Tim						

0   5   10   15   20   25   30
Number of Minutes

10. How many minutes in all do the friends ride?

(F) 60   (G) 55   (H) 50   (J) 45

11. Mike rides his bike for 10 minutes more. Which shows how much time he rides all together?

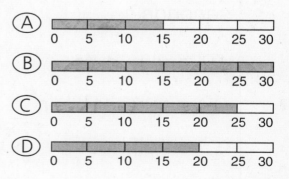

(A) 0 5 10 15 20 25 30
(B) 0 5 10 15 20 25 30
(C) 0 5 10 15 20 25 30
(D) 0 5 10 15 20 25 30

GO ON

12. Tim rides his bike for 15 minutes more. Which shows how much time he rides all together?

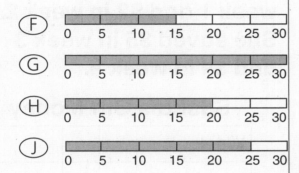

Ⓕ 0 5 10 15 20 25 30

Ⓖ 0 5 10 15 20 25 30

Ⓗ 0 5 10 15 20 25 30

Ⓙ 0 5 10 15 20 25 30

Use the tally chart and graph to answer items 13–15.

Favorite Snacks

Apples	𝍷𝍷𝍷𝍷𝍷 𝍷𝍷𝍷
Carrots	𝍷𝍷𝍷
Crackers	𝍷𝍷𝍷𝍷
Popcorn	𝍷𝍷𝍷𝍷𝍷 𝍷𝍷𝍷𝍷𝍷

Favorite Snacks

Apples	o o o o o o o o
Carrots	o o o
Crackers	o o o o
Popcorn	o o o o o o o o o o

13. How many more children voted for popcorn than apples?

Ⓐ 4

Ⓑ 3

Ⓒ 2

Ⓓ 1

14. Which snack received 8 votes?

Ⓕ Apples

Ⓖ Carrots

Ⓗ Crackers

Ⓙ Popcorn

15. What is the range of the numbers?

Ⓐ 7

Ⓑ 6

Ⓒ 5

Ⓓ 1

GO ON

16. What is the mode of the numbers?

Ⓕ 7   Ⓗ 5

Ⓖ 6   Ⓙ 2

---

17. Mrs. Ahart's class puts on puppet shows. Each show is 30 minutes long. How many minutes does it take to put on 2 puppet shows?

Ⓐ 30 minutes

Ⓑ 40 minutes

Ⓒ 50 minutes

Ⓓ 60 minutes

---

18. The students eat lunch at 12:30. They finish 30 minutes later. At what time do they finish?

Ⓕ 12:00   Ⓗ 1:00

Ⓖ 12:30   Ⓙ 1:30

Fill in the table. Then answer items 19–20.

Sasha is saving money for a gift. She saved $3 in week 1 and $2 in week 2. She saved $5 in week 3 and $4 in week 4.

Sasha's Gift Money

Week				
How Much				

19. How much more money does Sasha save in week 3 than in week 1?

Ⓐ $9   Ⓒ $5

Ⓑ $6   Ⓓ $2

---

20. How much money did Sasha save in all?

Ⓕ $15   Ⓗ $11

Ⓖ $14   Ⓙ $8

STOP

Read each question carefully. Write or circle your answer in the space provided.

1. What time does the clock show?

:
_____ _____

Use the calendar to answer exercises 4–5.

June 2002						
Sun	Mon	Tues	Wed	Thurs	Fri	Sat
					1	2
3	4	5	6	7	8	9
10	11	12	13	14	15	16
17	18	19	20	21	22	23
24	25	26	27	28	29	30

2. How many minutes are in one hour?

_____ minutes

4. What is the date of the third Thursday in June?

_____

3. Circle the time that is the same as 15 minutes.

one minute

a quarter hour

a half hour

one hour

5. How many days are there between June 16 and June 27?

_____ days

GO ON

6. It is morning. What time does the clock show?

_____ : _____

7. How many hours have passed?

_____ hours

8. What time does the clock show?

_____ : _____

9. What is another way to write the number 6?

_____

_____

Use the graph below to answer items 10–12.

Playtime on Swing Set

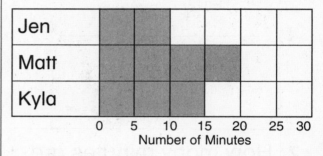

Number of Minutes

10. How many minutes in all do the friends swing?

_____ minutes

11. Kyla swings for 5 minutes more. Circle the bar that shows how much time she swings all together.

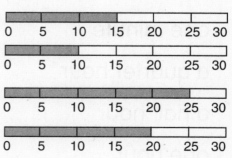

12. Jen swings for 10 minutes more. Circle the bar that shows how much Jen swings all together.

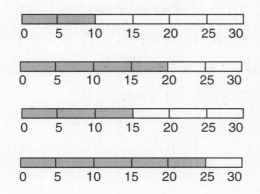

| 0 | 5 | 10 | 15 | 20 | 25 | 30 |

| 0 | 5 | 10 | 15 | 20 | 25 | 30 |

| 0 | 5 | 10 | 15 | 20 | 25 | 30 |

| 0 | 5 | 10 | 15 | 20 | 25 | 30 |

Use the tally chart and graph to answer items 13–16.

Favorite Snacks

Oranges	IIII
Grapes	ЖІ IIII
Pretzels	ЖІ I
Bananas	ЖІ II

Favorite Snacks

Oranges	o o o o
Grapes	o o o o o o o o o
Pretzels	o o o o o o
Bananas	o o o o o o o

13. How many more children voted for bananas than pretzels?

_____ more

---

14. Which snack received 6 votes?

_____

---

15. What is the range of the numbers?

_____

© Macmillan/McGraw-Hill

16. What is the mode of the numbers?

_____

_____

17. Mrs. Jackson's class puts on puppet shows. Each show is 20 minutes long. How many minutes does it take to put on 3 puppet shows?

_____ minutes

_____

18. The students eat lunch at 12:30. They finish 30 minutes later. At what time do they finish?

_____ : _____

Fill in the table. Then answer items 19–20.

Paula is saving money for a gift. She saved $1 in week 1 and $3 in week 2. She saved $8 in week 3 and $6 in week 4.

Paula's Gift Money

Week				
How Much				

19. How much more money did Paula save in week 3 than in week 2?

$ _____

_____

20. How much money did Paula save in all?

$ _____

© Macmillan/McGraw-Hill

STOP

Chapter 13 – Teacher Interview

Core Concept: *Add two 2-Digit Numbers, with and without Regrouping*

Student Activity: The student demonstrates an understanding of adding two 2-digit numbers, with and without regrouping. Have a collection of small objects, tens and ones models, pencils and paper, and a number line available for student use. Ask the student to solve 2-digit addition problems, first without regrouping and then with regrouping. You may start by having the student add 1-digit numbers to 2-digit numbers.

Teacher Question 1:

• What is the sum of 10 + 32?

Understanding Student Response	Practice and Improvement
Student cannot find the sum.	Review lessons 1 and 2 to reinforce addition facts. Find the sum together using counters. Assign practice items from lesson 2.
Student says the answer is 33.	Review lesson 2 to practice counting on tens and ones.

Teacher Question 2:

• How do I find the sum of 15 + 26?

Understanding Student Response	Practice and Improvement
Student says the answer is 311.	Review lesson 3. Remind student to regroup whenever there are 10 or more ones in the sum. Demonstrate with counters or with tens and ones models.
Student does not regroup correctly.	Review lesson 5. Use models like those in the lesson to step through the regrouping process.

Teacher Question 3:

• Use pencil and paper to find the sum of 46 + 37.

Understanding Student Response	Practice and Improvement
Student is confused by larger numbers.	Remind the student to think of simple addition facts from lessons 1. Focus on the ones first, and use addition strategies.
Student has difficulty working the problem on paper.	List the numbers in a vertical column as in the examples in lesson 5. Review the regrouping techniques taught in the lesson.

Chapter 13 – Journal Writing

Encourage students to generate their own journal entries related to math ideas in general or to concepts in this chapter. Present the following journal prompt and have students share their drawing/writing with a partner:

• The numbers 1 through 10 get together to play math-ket-ball. Miss 5 and Mister 6 are team captains. Miss 5 does not like to regroup. She will not play on a team with any number that requires her to regroup when she adds that number to herself (so 3 can be on her team, but 7 cannot). Mister 6 loves to regroup. He will only play with numbers that require regrouping when he adds them to himself. Which players will each team captain pick? Make a list of all the players on Miss 5's team and all the players on Mister 6's team. Which team will number 10 play on? Which team will number 4 play on? Are the teams even?

(Students should demonstrate an understanding that regrouping is required when the sum of the ones digits is 10 or greater. Check to make sure that the students put number 10 on 5's team, since adding 5 to 10 does not require regrouping even though it is a larger number. Number 4 could be on either team, since 4 + 5 does not require regrouping and 4 + 6 does. The teams will be even if number 4 plays on 6's team.)

FOLLOW-UP

At the end of the class, review the concept of regrouping and have the students explain when to regroup. Ask the students how they decided which team 10 and 4 should be on.

Suggest other numbers for the students to test with the regrouping rule. Ask them what would happen if numbers 35, 20, and 12 wanted to join the game, and what sums result when these numbers are added to 5 or 6. Review the regrouping procedure, reminding students to add 1 to the tens digit when regrouping in the ones digit.

Chapter 13 – Monitoring Student Progress

☐ **Form A**   ☐ **Form B**

Student Name _____ Date _____

Directions: For each item that is answered incorrectly, cross out the item number. Then record the number of correct responses in the appropriate Student Score column. If the student has not met the Criterion Score for an objective, circle the student's score. Recommended assignments are listed in the Prescription Table on the next page.

Objective	Item Numbers	Criterion Score	Student Score
A. Add a 1-digit number and a 2-digit number, with and without regrouping.	4, 10	2/3	/3
B. Add two 2-digit numbers, with and without regrouping.	1, 2, 3, 5, 6, 7	2/3	/3
C. Use strategies and skills to solve problems.	8, 9	1/2	/2
Total Test Score		6/10	/10
Total Percent Correct			%

Chapter 13 – Prescription Table

The following chart correlates the tested objectives for this chapter to supplementary materials that meet the individual needs of the students. The Reteach and Practice pages are designed for students who need further instruction in the math concepts taught in this chapter. The Enrich pages are designed for students who need advanced challenges.

Objective	Reteach	Practice	Enrich
A. Add a 1-digit number and a 2-digit number, with and without regrouping.	203, 206, 209, 215	204, 207, 210, 216	205, 208, 211, 217
B. Add tens to add 2-digit numbers.	200, 212	201, 213	202, 214
C. Use strategies and skills to solve problems.	218	219	220

Read each question carefully. Darken the circle for the correct answer.

1. $50 + 40 = \blacksquare$

Ⓐ 10   Ⓒ 70

Ⓑ 30   Ⓓ 90

---

2. $70 + 10 = \blacksquare$

Ⓕ 60   Ⓗ 80

Ⓖ 70   Ⓙ 90

---

3. $20 + 50 = \blacksquare$

Ⓐ 30   Ⓒ 70

Ⓑ 60   Ⓓ 80

4.
$$\begin{array}{r} 84 \\ + \ 2 \\ \hline \end{array}$$

Ⓕ 82   Ⓗ 92

Ⓖ 86   Ⓙ 96

5.
$$\begin{array}{r} 56 \\ + 30 \\ \hline \end{array}$$

Ⓐ 96   Ⓒ 36

Ⓑ 86   Ⓓ 26

6.
$$\begin{array}{r} 61 \\ + 21 \\ \hline \end{array}$$

Ⓕ 40   Ⓗ 82

Ⓖ 81   Ⓙ 92

7.
$$\begin{array}{r} 76 \\ + 16 \\ \hline \end{array}$$

Ⓐ 92   Ⓒ 70

Ⓑ 82   Ⓓ 60

GO ON

Use this story for questions 8–9.

The second grade class needs to make money for their spring party. The class voted on what they can do, and the winning vote went to a car wash.

8. What problem does the second grade class have?

   (F) They are having a spring party.

   (G) They don't have enough math books.

   (H) They need money for their spring party.

   (J) They don't have enough chalk.

9. What did the class decide was the best solution for their problem?

   (A) Have a car wash.

   (B) Have a bake sale.

   (C) Sell sandwiches.

   (D) Put on a magic show.

10. $$29 + 7$$

   (F) 37

   (G) 36

   (H) 35

   (J) 22

STOP

Read each question carefully. Write your answer on the line.

1. $20 + 40 =$ _____

2. $10 + 10 =$ _____

3. $10 + 80 =$ _____

4.
$$\begin{array}{r} 32 \\ +\ \ 2 \\ \hline \end{array}$$

5.
$$\begin{array}{r} 60 \\ + 30 \\ \hline \end{array}$$

6.
$$\begin{array}{r} 23 \\ + 72 \\ \hline \end{array}$$

7.
$$\begin{array}{r} 48 \\ + 16 \\ \hline \end{array}$$

GO ON

Use this story for questions 8–9.

Toby's mother was getting ready to run the dishwasher. She realized she didn't have any dish soap. She could not run the dishwasher without it. She asked her husband to pick some up on his way home from work. After he got home, she was able to run the dishwasher.

8. What problem did Toby's mother have?

_____

_____

_____

9. What did she decide was the best solution for their problem?

_____

_____

_____

10.
$$19 + 8$$

STOP

Chapter 14 – Teacher Interview

Core Concept: *Practice and Apply 2-Digit Addition*

Student Activity: The student demonstrates an understanding of adding two 2-digit numbers and three 2-digit numbers, with and without regrouping. Have a collection of small objects, tens models and ones models, and a number line available for student use. Ask the student questions such as, "What is the sum of 17 + 25?"

Teacher Question 1:

• What is the sum of 17 + 25?

Understanding Student Response	Practice and Improvement
Student finds an incorrect sum.	Review lesson 2 to reinforce addition facts. Find the sum together using counters. Assign practice from lesson 2.
Student does not know how to regroup, or does not regroup correctly.	Review lesson 3, Chapter 13 to show how to use place-value models to add ones. Ask the student to trade ten ones for a ten and then put it in the tens place to be counted.

Teacher Question 2:

• There are 19 boys and 17 girls in Ms. Rivera's room. How many students does she have in all?

Understanding Student Response	Practice and Improvement
Student does not know how to proceed.	Review lesson 1 to help student choose the correct procedure (addition) for solving the problem. Use counters or a number line to arrive at the total.
Student does not realize regrouping is necessary, or does not know how to carry it out.	Review regrouping from lessons 3–5, chapter 13. Have the student put 19 red counters and 17 green counters in 1 pile and then separate them into groups of 10. Count and write the number 36.

Teacher Question 3:

• What is the sum of 27 + 30 + 15?

Understanding Student Response	Practice and Improvement
Student cannot add three numbers.	Review lesson 5 and then use counters or the number line to perform the addition.
Student is confused with regrouping because of dealing with three addends.	Review lesson 5 and then use counters or the number line to perform the addition.

Chapter 14 – Journal Writing

Encourage students to generate their own journal entries related to math ideas in general or to concepts in this chapter. Present the following journal prompt and have students share their drawing/writing with a partner:

- Mr. Salimi's class went on a nature hike at the reservoir. They saw 12 birds, 8 turtles, and 16 fish. How many animals did they see in all? Explain how to estimate the number first and then find the exact answer. Was your estimate close?

(Responses should describe rounding to the nearest ten and adding mentally. Students may want to sketch the animals first and then do an exact count, but encourage them to estimate and then report on how near they came to the exact count.)

FOLLOW-UP

To follow up, review the concept of adding 2 digit numbers and regrouping. Ask students to think of any time that day when they had to add groups of items (for example, the cost of buying two snacks at lunchtime).

Have the student pretend that they will be going on a field trip tomorrow with another 2nd–grade class. They will need to bring 58 sandwiches, 18 bananas, 17 oranges, 23 peaches, 28 boxes of apple juice, 13 boxes of grape juice, and 17 boxes of fruit punch. Have the students answer how many pieces of fruit they will be bringing, how many boxes of juice they will be bringing, and how many items they will be bringing in all. Ask them to write about what they noticed with the sums. Students can then use the information to add in some other healthy snacks to bring on the trip.

Chapter 14 – Monitoring Student Progress

☐ **Form A**   ☐ **Form B**

Student Name _____ Date _____

Directions: For each item that is answered incorrectly, cross out the item number. Then record the number of correct responses in the appropriate Student Score column. If the student has not met the Criterion Score for an objective, circle the student's score. Recommended assignments are listed in the Prescription Table on the next page.

Objective	Item Numbers	Criterion Score	Student Score
A. Add 2-digit numbers, with and without regrouping.	1, 2, 3, 4	3/4	/4
B. Estimate sums.	5	1/1	/1
C. Add three 2-digit numbers.	6, 7, 8	2/3	/3
D. Use strategies and skills to solve problems.	9, 10	1/2	/2
Total Test Score		7/10	/10
Total Percent Correct			%

Chapter 14 – Prescription Table

The following chart correlates the tested objectives for this chapter to supplementary materials that meet the individual needs of the students. The Reteach and Practice pages are designed for students who need further instruction in the math concepts taught in this chapter. The Enrich pages are designed for students who need advanced challenges.

Objective	Reteach	Practice	Enrich
A. Add 2-digit numbers, with and without regrouping.	221, 224, 227	222, 225, 228	223, 226, 229
B. Estimate sums.	230	231	232
C. Add three 2-digit numbers.	233	234	235
D. Use strategies and skills to solve problems.	236, 237	238	

Read each question carefully. Darken the circle for the correct answer.

1. $37 + 34 = $ ▢

  Ⓐ 57   Ⓒ 67

  Ⓑ 61   Ⓓ 71

2. $\begin{array}{r} 24 \\ +\ 13 \\ \hline \end{array}$

  Ⓕ 11

  Ⓖ 17

  Ⓗ 37

  Ⓙ 47

3. $\begin{array}{r} 54 \\ +\ 19 \\ \hline \end{array}$

  Ⓐ 73

  Ⓑ 69

  Ⓒ 64

  Ⓓ 63

4. $48 + 20 = $ ▢

  Ⓕ 18   Ⓗ 58

  Ⓖ 28   Ⓙ 68

5. Estimate.

   $\begin{array}{r} 52 \\ +\ 39 \\ \hline \end{array}$

  Ⓐ 90   Ⓒ 70

  Ⓑ 80   Ⓓ 60

6. $\begin{array}{r} 25 \\ 25 \\ +\ 12 \\ \hline \end{array}$

  Ⓕ 50   Ⓗ 72

  Ⓖ 62   Ⓙ 89

GO ON

7.
```
   27
   36
 + 23
```

Ⓐ 76

Ⓑ 86

Ⓒ 87

Ⓓ 93

8.
```
   10
   20
 + 30
```

Ⓕ 30

Ⓖ 40

Ⓗ 50

Ⓙ 60

9. There are 19 students in Mrs. Black's class. There are 23 students in Miss Fry's class. Mrs. Barnaby has 22 students in her class. How many students are in all three classes?

Ⓐ 41

Ⓑ 42

Ⓒ 45

Ⓓ 64

10. Team Green scored 19 runs all season. Team Blue scored 24 runs all season. Team Purple scored 29 runs all season. How many runs did the three teams score in all?

Ⓕ 43　　Ⓗ 53

Ⓖ 48　　Ⓙ 72

STOP

Read each question carefully. Write your answer in the space provided.

1. $57 + 19 =$ _____

4. $57 + 40 =$ _____

2.
$$\begin{array}{r} 48 \\ + 13 \\ \hline \end{array}$$

5. Estimate.
$$\begin{array}{r} 38 \\ + 17 \\ \hline \end{array}$$

3.
$$\begin{array}{r} 38 \\ + 18 \\ \hline \end{array}$$

6.
$$\begin{array}{r} 27 \\ 43 \\ + 15 \\ \hline \end{array}$$

GO ON

7.
$$
\begin{array}{r}
44 \\
16 \\
+\ 20 \\
\hline
\end{array}
$$

8.
$$
\begin{array}{r}
20 \\
40 \\
+\ 60 \\
\hline
\end{array}
$$

9. The fish department took an inventory. There were 47 goldfish. They counted 19 Oscar fish, and they counted 39 guppies. How many fish were there in all?

_____

10. There are three teams in the baseball league in town. Team A has 24 members, Team B has 28 members, and Team C has 22 members. How many members are on all three teams?

_____

STOP

Chapter 15 – Teacher Interview

Core Concept: *Subtract 2-Digit Numbers, with and without Regrouping*

Student Activity: The student will correctly subtract two 2-digit numbers, with and without regrouping. Have a collection of small objects, tens models and ones models, and a number line available for student use. Ask the student to perform various 2-digit subtraction problems using the aids available. You may start by asking the student to subtract a 1-digit number from a 2-digit number.

Teacher Question 1:

• By how much is 13 less than 28?

Understanding Student Response	Practice and Improvement
Student guesses at the answer.	Review lessons 1–2, reminding student to count back to find the answer. Use counters to act out the problem.
Student tries to regroup.	Review lesson 3, showing student that regrouping is not always necessary. Ask student to check the ones digits before subtracting.

Teacher Question 2:

• What is the difference between 23 and 16?

Understanding Student Response	Practice and Improvement
Student does not know that difference means subtraction.	Review lesson 1 to review what "difference" means. If the student does not know subtraction facts, assign practice from lesson 1 and/or use number line.
Student does not know when to regroup, or does not regroup correctly.	Review lessons 3, 4, and 5. Have the student make the number 23 with 2 tens models and 3 ones models. Next, have the student exchange 1 tens model for 10 ones models. The student should remove 16 and count what is left to arrive at 7.

Teacher Question 3:

• How can you tell when regrouping will be needed in subtraction? Give an example.

Understanding Student Response	Practice and Improvement
Student knows when regrouping is required, but does not know how to carry it out.	Review lessons 5 and 6. Use models to help student visualize the regrouping.
Student cannot give an example.	Review lesson 3 and show examples of the ones place in the subtrahend being greater then the ones in the minuend.

Chapter 15 – Journal Writing

Encourage students to generate their own journal entries related to math ideas in general or to concepts in this chapter. Present the following journal prompt and have students share their drawing/writing with a partner:

- Frankie read 36 pages of a book last week and Johnny read 19 pages. How many more pages did Frankie read? Tell how to solve this problem and then do the work. Write or draw your solution.

  (Responses should state that subtraction is the process required. Students may do the solution graphically.)

FOLLOW-UP

At the end of the day, review the concept of subtraction. Ask the students to think of any times that day when you or they had to use subtraction (for example, subtracting objects for a science experiment).

For the next few days, have the class help take attendance. Each day write the number of students enrolled in the class. See how many students are absent. In their math journals, have the students construct a number sentence for the problem and solve it.

Chapter 15 – Monitoring Student Progress

☐ **Form A**   ☐ **Form B**

Student Name _____ Date _____

Directions: For each item that is answered incorrectly, cross out the item number. Then record the number of correct responses in the appropriate Student Score column. If the student has not met the Criterion Score for an objective, circle the student's score. Recommended assignments are listed in the Prescription Table on the next page.

Objective	Item Numbers	Criterion Score	Student Score
A. Subtract a 1-digit number from a 2-digit number, with and without regrouping.	3, 4	1/2	/2
B. Subtract 2-digit numbers, with and without regrouping.	1, 2, 5, 6, 9, 10	5/6	/6
C. Use strategies and skills to solve problems.	7, 8	1/2	/2
Total Test Score		7/10	/10
Total Percent Correct			%

Chapter 15 – Prescription Table

The following chart correlates the tested objectives for this chapter to supplementary materials that meet the individual needs of the students. The Reteach and Practice pages are designed for students who need further instruction in the math concepts taught in this chapter. The Enrich pages are designed for students who need advanced challenges.

Objective	Reteach	Practice	Enrich
A. Subtract a 1-digit number from a 2-digit number, with and without regrouping.	242, 245, 248, 254	243, 246, 249, 255	244, 247, 250, 256
B. Subtract 2-digit numbers, with and without regrouping.	239, 242, 251, 254	240, 243, 252, 255	241, 244, 253, 256
C. Use strategies and skills to solve problems.	257	258	259

Read each question carefully. Darken the circle for the correct answer.

1. 50 − 40 = ⬛

- Ⓐ 10
- Ⓑ 20
- Ⓒ 30
- Ⓓ 40

2. 70 − 10 = ⬛

- Ⓕ 60
- Ⓗ 40
- Ⓖ 50
- Ⓙ 30

3.
$$\begin{array}{r} 42 \\ -9 \\ \hline \end{array}$$

- Ⓐ 33
- Ⓑ 50
- Ⓒ 51
- Ⓓ 411

4.
$$\begin{array}{r} 84 \\ -2 \\ \hline \end{array}$$

- Ⓕ 82
- Ⓖ 86
- Ⓗ 92
- Ⓙ 96

5.
$$\begin{array}{r} 56 \\ -30 \\ \hline \end{array}$$

- Ⓐ 36
- Ⓑ 34
- Ⓒ 26
- Ⓓ 24

GO ON

6.   52
      − 17

Ⓕ 49   Ⓗ 39

Ⓖ 45   Ⓙ 35

7. There are 28 fish for sale. There are 19 sold. How many fish are left?

Ⓐ 47   Ⓒ 11

Ⓑ 19   Ⓓ 9

8. Karla grew tomatoes in her garden. Over the summer, she harvested a total of 87 tomatoes. Karla gave away 39 tomatoes. How many tomatoes did she NOT give away?

Ⓕ 126   Ⓗ 52

Ⓖ 58   Ⓙ 48

9. $74 - 14 =$ ▢

Ⓐ 40

Ⓑ 50

Ⓒ 60

Ⓓ 70

10. $90 - 80 =$ ▢

Ⓕ 10

Ⓖ 20

Ⓗ 80

Ⓙ 170

STOP

Read each question carefully. Write your answer in the space provided.

1. $70 - 40 =$ _____

2. $70 - 60 =$ _____

3.
$$\begin{array}{r} 31 \\ -\ 4 \\ \hline \end{array}$$

4.
$$\begin{array}{r} 80 \\ -\ 16 \\ \hline \end{array}$$

5.
$$\begin{array}{r} 63 \\ -\ 34 \\ \hline \end{array}$$

GO ON

6.   92
      $-$ 17
      _____

7. There are 34 birds for sale. There are 17 sold. How many birds are left?

_____

8. Jimmy made 23 snowman decorations for winter. He gave 7 to friends and family. How many did he keep?

_____

9. $65 - 17 =$ _____

10. $90 - 40 =$ _____

STOP

Chapter 16 – Teacher Interview

Core Concept: *Practice and Apply 2-Digit Subtraction*

Student Activity: The student demonstrates an understanding of subtracting two 2-digit numbers, and the ability to apply techniques such as estimation and answer checking. Have a collection of small objects, tens models and ones models, and a number line available for student use. Ask the student to solve 2-digit subtraction problems.

Teacher Question 1:

- There are 36 chickens in the barnyard. Rachel put 19 of the chickens into the chicken coop. How many chickens are left in the barnyard?

Understanding Student Response	Practice and Improvement
Student does not recognize the problem as a subtraction problem.	Review examples from lessons 1 and 2. Use counters to demonstrate the problem.
Student does not know how to set up and solve the problem.	Review lesson 1 to practice rewriting and solving subtraction problems. Assign practice from lesson 1.

Teacher Question 2:

- Mark says the difference between 47 and 23 is 16. How can he check his answer?

Understanding Student Response	Practice and Improvement
Student does not know how to check the answer to a subtraction problem.	Review lesson 3, reminding student that addition can be used to check subtraction.
Student knows that addition is needed, but is unsure of which numbers to add.	Review problems in lesson 3, showing that the answer added to the bottom number should yield the top number. Act out the problem using counters, and assign practice from lesson 3 if more review is needed.

Teacher Question 3:

- There are 63 cows and 29 horses at the farm. Estimate how many more cows there are than horses.

Understanding Student Response	Practice and Improvement
Student estimates by guessing.	Review lesson 4, reminding student to round each number before subtracting to find an estimate.
Student does not round numbers correctly.	Review lesson 4. Remind student that rounding means finding the nearest ten. Use a number line to practice rounding numbers, and assign practice from lesson 4.

Chapter 16 – Journal Writing

Encourage students to generate their own journal entries related to math ideas in general or to concepts in this chapter. Present the following journal prompt and have students share their drawing/writing with a partner:

- Joel and Lorena collect Space Battle trading cards. Joel has 48 cards and Lorena has 73 cards. How many more cards does Lorena have? Estimate the answer first, then solve the problem and show how you did it.

  (Students should identify the problem as a subtraction problem and demonstrate the ability to perform 2-digit subtraction with regrouping. They should estimate the answer by rounding each number to the nearest ten and subtracting.)

FOLLOW-UP

At the end of the day, review the concept of subtraction. Ask the students how they knew which number to subtract from which, and how they knew whether regrouping was necessary.

Ask the following question as an extension:

Jose started collecting Space Battle trading cards as well. Lorena gave him 19 of her cards to help get him started. How many cards does Lorena have now?

Have the students create their own subtraction problems using the information from these problems. The students can give their problems to a partner to solve.

Chapter 16 – Monitoring Student Progress

☐ **Form A**   ☐ **Form B**

Student Name _____ Date _____

Directions: For each item that is answered incorrectly, cross out the item number. Then record the number of correct responses in the appropriate Student Score column. If the student has not met the Criterion Score for an objective, circle the student's score. Recommended assignments are listed in the Prescription Table on the next page.

Objective	Item Numbers	Criterion Score	Student Score
A. Subtract 2-digit numbers, with and without regrouping.	1, 2, 3, 4	3/4	/4
B. Estimate differences.	6, 7	1/2	/2
C. Check subtraction.	5	1/1	/1
D. Use strategies and skills to solve problems.	8, 9, 10	2/3	/3
Total Test Score		7/10	/10
Total Percent Correct			%

Chapter 16 – Prescription Table

The following chart correlates the tested objectives for this chapter to supplementary materials that meet the individual needs of the students. The Reteach and Practice pages are designed for students who need further instruction in the math concepts taught in this chapter. The Enrich pages are designed for students who need advanced challenges.

Objective	Reteach	Practice	Enrich
A. Subtract 2-digit numbers, with and without regrouping.	260, 263	261, 264	262, 265
B. Estimate differences.	269	270	271
C. Check subtraction.	266	267	268
D. Use strategies and skills to solve problems.	272, 275, 278	273, 276, 279	274, 277, 280

Read each question carefully. Darken the circle for the correct answer.

1. $78 - 20 =$ ▨

   Ⓐ 58   Ⓒ 48

   Ⓑ 52   Ⓓ 42

2. $39 - 18 =$ ▨

   Ⓕ 29   Ⓗ 19

   Ⓖ 21   Ⓙ 11

3.
$$\begin{array}{r} 72 \\ -\ 47 \\ \hline \end{array}$$

▨

   Ⓐ 35

   Ⓑ 34

   Ⓒ 25

   Ⓓ 24

4.
$$\begin{array}{r} 42 \\ -\ \ 5 \\ \hline \end{array}$$

▨

   Ⓕ 27

   Ⓖ 33

   Ⓗ 36

   Ⓙ 37

5. How would you check this subtraction?

$$\begin{array}{r} 76 \\ -\ 22 \\ \hline 54 \end{array}$$

   Ⓐ $76 + 22 = 54$

   Ⓑ $22 + 76 = 54$

   Ⓒ $54 + 22 = 76$

   Ⓓ $76 + 54 = 22$

GO ON ➡

6. Estimate.

52
− 39

F 10
G 20
H 30
J 40

7. Estimate.

59
− 38

A 10
B 20
C 30
D 40

Choose the answer that shows how you could solve each problem.

8. There are 48 children in the second grade. The music teacher calls all 27 boys out of class. How many girls are left in class?

F $48 - 27 = 19$

G $48 - 27 = 21$

H $48 + 27 = 65$

J $48 + 27 = 75$

9. The school play had 74 people try out for the show. The director can only choose 45 people. How many people will not be in the show?

A $74 + 45 = 119$

B $74 + 45 = 129$

C $74 - 45 = 31$

D $74 - 45 = 29$

10. Tommy went to 63 baseball games in the summer. He then got to go to 19 more games on the weekends in the fall. How many baseball games did he go to?

F $63 - 19 = 44$

G $63 - 19 = 56$

H $63 + 19 = 72$

J $63 + 19 = 82$

STOP

Read each question carefully. Write your answer in the space provided.

1. $56 - 10 =$ _____

2. $47 - 28 =$ _____

3. $\begin{array}{r} 62 \\ -\ 45 \\ \hline \end{array}$

4. $\begin{array}{r} 63 \\ -\ 8 \\ \hline \end{array}$

5. Check the subtraction by adding.

$\begin{array}{r} 87 \\ -\ 32 \\ \hline 55 \end{array}$

_____

_____

GO ON

6. Estimate.

$$\begin{array}{r} 49 \\ -\ 18 \\ \hline \end{array}$$

7. Estimate.

$$\begin{array}{r} 64 \\ -\ 49 \\ \hline \end{array}$$

Write how you would solve each problem.

8. There are 37 children in the second grade. The gym teacher calls all 19 girls out of class. How many boys are left in class?

_____

9. The school had 53 people try out for the soccer team. The coach can only choose 25 people. How many people will not be on the team?

_____

10. Tommy went to 26 basketball games in the winter. He went to 18 more games during the spring. How many basketball games did Tommy go to?

_____

STOP

Unit 4 Performance Assessment

At the Arcade

- *Target Skill:*   Subtract 2-digit numbers.
- *Additional Skills:*   Add 2-digit numbers; add three 2-digit numbers; regroup to subtract 2-digit numbers.

Task Description: This task requires students to select stuffed animals that cost a number of arcade coupons. They need to keep track of how many coupons they have used starting from 99.

Preparing: You may wish to have students work in pairs or alone. Students should make a chart prior to beginning. Discuss which operation they should use to find the amount spent so far and the amount left.

Materials	Group Size	Time on Task
Pencil Paper	1 to 2 students	1–2 days

Guiding: Remind students that they must pick 3 stuffed animals.

Suggest students try to leave as few coupons left at the end a possible.

Observing/ Monitoring: As you move among the students, pose the following questions:

How did you decide which stuffed animals to select?

How did you find the number of coupons left?

How did you find the number of coupons used so far?

Unit 4 Performance Assessment Scoring Rubric

At the Arcade

Score	Explanation
3	Students demonstrate an efficient strategy and a thorough approach that enables them to solve the problem completely. A satisfactory answer: • presents a completed table with the monkey, elephant, and puppy chosen; • includes correct answers for the number of coupons left and used at each step. Students are able to complete the problem quickly and have all of the above correct solutions with appropriate work shown.
2	Students demonstrate a strategy that enables them to solve most of the problem correctly. The strategy is somewhat disorganized, making it less efficient. A solution is found but errors are contained. Students may: • correctly add and subtract the number of coupons left or used; • not have used all of the coupons. Students may have some difficulty determining all solutions correctly but demonstrate an understanding of general concepts.
1	Students demonstrate a confused strategy, which leads to difficulty solving the problem. Most answers are incorrect, but students demonstrate knowledge of at least one concept being assessed. Students may: • have selected three stuffed animals, but added or subtracted incorrectly.

Unit 4 Performance Assessment
Student Activity

At the Arcade

You will need
• A pencil
• Paper for a chart

Nancy won 99 coupons at the arcade.
She wants to use as many of the coupons as possible.
Help her use them.

Make a chart like the one shown below.

Item	Coupons Used	Coupons Left

Remember to use as many of the coupons as possible.

1. Nancy wants to get at least three different stuffed
animals. Name three that she can get.

_____

2. How many coupons will Nancy have left?

_____

3. How many coupons did Nancy use?

_____

4. Is it possible to use all of the coupons?

_____

Unit 4 – Monitoring Student Progress

☐ **Form A**   ☐ **Form B**

Student Name _____ Date _____

Directions: This test targets selected objectives. For each item that is answered incorrectly, cross out the item number. Then record the number of correct responses in the column labeled **Number of Correct Responses.** Add to find the **Total Number of Correct Responses** and record the total. Use this total to determine the **Total Test Score** and the **Total Percent Correct.**

Strand • Objective(s)	Item Numbers	Number of Correct Responses
Number Sense, Concepts, and Operations • Add a 1-digit number and a 2-digit number, with and without regrouping. • Add two 2-digit numbers, with and without regrouping. • Estimate sums. • Add three 2-digit numbers. • Subtract a 1-digit number from a 2-digit number, with and without regrouping. • Subtract 2-digit numbers, with and without regrouping. • Estimate differences. • Check subtraction. • Use strategies and skills to solve problems.	1, 2, 3, 4, 5, 6, 7, 8, 9, 10, 11, 12, 13, 14, 15, 16, 17, 18, 19, 20	/20
Total Number of Correct Responses		
Total Test Score		/20
Total Percent Correct		%

Name ______________________________

UNIT 4 TEST
FORM A
PAGE 1

Read each question carefully. Darken the circle for the correct answer.

1. 46 + 20 = ☐

Ⓐ 26

Ⓑ 60

Ⓒ 66

Ⓓ 70

2.

$$\begin{array}{r} 27 \\ 23 \\ +\ 31 \\ \hline \end{array}$$

Ⓕ 70

Ⓖ 71

Ⓗ 81

Ⓙ 91

3. Estimate.

37 + 41

Ⓐ 60 Ⓒ 80

Ⓑ 70 Ⓓ 90

4.

$$\begin{array}{r} 42 \\ 38 \\ +\ 19 \\ \hline \end{array}$$

Ⓕ 87

Ⓖ 89

Ⓗ 98

Ⓙ 99

5.

$$\begin{array}{r} 18 \\ +\ 29 \\ \hline \end{array}$$

Ⓐ 37

Ⓑ 38

Ⓒ 47

Ⓓ 48

GO ON

Name ______________________

6.

$$\begin{array}{r} 15 \\ 36 \\ +\ 25 \\ \hline \end{array}$$

Ⓕ 66

Ⓖ 76

Ⓗ 86

Ⓙ 96

7.

$$\begin{array}{r} 25 \\ +\ \ 6 \\ \hline \end{array}$$

Ⓐ 21

Ⓑ 28

Ⓒ 31

Ⓓ 32

8.

$$\begin{array}{r} 47 \\ +\ 33 \\ \hline \end{array}$$

Ⓕ 70 Ⓗ 80

Ⓖ 74 Ⓙ 84

9.

$$\begin{array}{r} 83¢ \\ -\ 27¢ \\ \hline \end{array}$$

Ⓐ 56¢

Ⓑ 64¢

Ⓒ 66¢

Ⓓ 90¢

10. 80 − 30 = ▢

Ⓕ 20

Ⓖ 40

Ⓗ 50

Ⓙ 60

GO ON

11.   50¢
        – 25¢

    Ⓐ 24¢

    Ⓑ 25¢

    Ⓒ 35¢

    Ⓓ 75¢

12. For which number sentence do you need to regroup?

    Ⓕ 86 – 6 = 80

    Ⓖ 78 – 5 = 73

    Ⓗ 64 – 6 = 58

    Ⓙ 56 – 2 = 4

13.   74
        – 27

    Ⓐ 47   Ⓒ 57

    Ⓑ 53   Ⓓ 93

14. How can you add to check 83 – 57 = 26?

    Ⓕ 26 + 57 = 83

    Ⓖ 30 + 53 = 83

    Ⓗ 83 – 26 = 57

    Ⓙ 32 + 51 = 83

15. Estimate.

58 – 39

    Ⓐ 10

    Ⓑ 20

    Ⓒ 30

    Ⓓ 40

16.   34¢
        – 8¢

    Ⓕ 26¢   Ⓗ 36¢

    Ⓖ 32¢   Ⓙ 42¢

GO ON

17. On Tuesday, 18 boys and 16 girls visit the library. How many children visit the library in all?

    (A) 22 children

    (B) 27 children

    (C) 34 children

    (D) 40 children

18. Mr. Smith is at the store. He buys 12 red apples and 19 green apples. How many apples does he buy in all?

    (F) 20 apples

    (G) 21 apples

    (H) 27 apples

    (J) 31 apples

19. There are 24 crackers on a plate. Then 7 crackers are eaten. Which number sentence shows how many crackers are left?

    (A) $7 + 17 = 24$

    (B) $27 + 7 = 34$

    (C) $24 - 7 = 17$

    (D) $7 + 7 = 14$

20. There are 15 children in Mr. Brown's class who say red is their favorite color. There are 18 children who say blue is their favorite color. How many more children like blue than red?

    (F) 3 children

    (G) 15 children

    (H) 18 children

    (J) 33 children

STOP

Read each question carefully. Write or circle your answer in the space provided.

1. $52 + 20 =$ _____

2.
$$
\begin{array}{r}
46 \\
23 \\
+\ 17 \\
\hline
\end{array}
$$

3. Estimate.

$43 + 51 =$ _____

4.
$$
\begin{array}{r}
35 \\
29 \\
+\ 15 \\
\hline
\end{array}
$$

5.
$$
\begin{array}{r}
17 \\
+\ 18 \\
\hline
\end{array}
$$

GO ON

6.
```
   16
   25
+ 35
_____
```

7.
```
   22
+  7
_____
```

8.
```
   64
+ 19
_____
```

9.
```
   63¢
-  28¢
_____
```

10. 90 − 20 = _____

GO ON

Name ____________________

11.
$$\begin{array}{r} 50¢ \\ -\ 15¢ \\ \hline \end{array}$$

12. For which number sentence do you need to regroup?

Circle the answer.

65 − 3 = 62

89 − 8 = 81

57 − 6 = 51

74 − 7 = 67

13.
$$\begin{array}{r} 86 \\ -\ 39 \\ \hline \end{array}$$

14. Show how you can add to check 92 − 48 = 44.

____

15. Estimate.

87 − 49

16.
$$\begin{array}{r} 43¢ \\ -\ 7¢ \\ \hline \end{array}$$

GO ON

17. On Friday, 19 boys and 15 girls visit the library. How many children are at the library?

_____ children

18. Mr. Smith is at the store. He buys 15 red apples and 28 green apples. How many apples does he buy in all?

_____ apples

19. There are 32 crackers on a plate. Then 9 crackers are eaten. Circle the number sentence that shows how many crackers are on the plate now?

$32 - 9 = 23$

$23 - 9 = 14$

$23 + 9 = 32$

$9 - 9 = 0$

20. There are 20 children in Mr. Chester's class who say green is their favorite color. There are 15 children who picked yellow. How many more like green than yellow?

_____ children

STOP

Chapter 17 – Teacher Interview

Core Concept: *Length*

Student Activity: The student demonstrates an understanding of measuring length using nonstandard units as well as customary and metric units. Ask the student questions such as "Order the following units from least to greatest: foot, inch, yard."

Teacher Question 1:

• Order the following units from least to greatest: foot, inch, yard.

Understanding Student Response	Practice and Improvement
Student answers "yard, foot, inch."	Review lesson 3 and prompt the student to order the units from least to greatest.
Student does not know how to order the units.	Review lesson 3 to help the student learn the sizes of customary units of length.

Teacher Question 2:

• Which is a greater length: 50 centimeters or 1 meter?

Understanding Student Response	Practice and Improvement
Student answers 50 centimeters.	Review lesson 4 to reinforce to the student that 100 centimeters = 1 meter.
Student says the lengths are equal.	Review lesson 4 to help the student learn about lengths in the metric system.

Teacher Question 3:

• How can you use counters to measure the length of your math book?

Understanding Student Response	Practice and Improvement
Student fails to mention using the counters from end to end.	Review lesson 1 to help the student learn that to measure length it is necessary to start at one end and measure to the other.
Student measures end to end, but does not know that the counters all have to be the same size.	Review lesson 1 to help the student to measure in one unit.

Chapter 17 – Journal Writing

Encourage students to generate their own journal entries related to math ideas in general or to concepts in this chapter. Present the following journal prompt and have students share their drawing/writing with a partner:

- How good are you at estimating length? Estimate the length of three classroom items and have your math partner measure them with a ruler. Record your estimates and the measurements. Then have your partner estimate the length of three other items, while you measure them. Record these estimates and measurements, too. How could you improve your estimates?

  (Make some common items available to students, such as crayons, chalk, board erasers, paper clips, books, etc. Students should record the discrepancies between their estimates and actual measurements in their journals. Vary the units of measurement between metric and customary units, and ask students which are easiest to use and why.)

FOLLOW-UP

At the end of the day, review the basic measurement concepts, such as beginning measurement with the end of the ruler, measuring to the nearest whole (or half) unit, using successive measurements to measure something longer than the ruler, etc. Ask students to label their measurements appropriately in inches, centimeters, etc.

Ask students to think of when estimates of linear measures are sufficient, and when accuracy is required. Students should share their writing and drawing with a math partner.

Chapter 17 – Monitoring Student Progress

☐ **Form A**   ☐ **Form B**

Student Name _____ Date _____

Directions: For each item that is answered incorrectly, cross out the item number. Then record the number of correct responses in the appropriate Student Score column. If the student has not met the Criterion Score for an objective, circle the student's score. Recommended assignments are listed in the Prescription Table on the next page.

Objective	Item Numbers	Criterion Score	Student Score
A. Measure length in customary and metric units.	1, 2, 3, 4, 5, 6, 8	6/7	/7
B. Use strategies and skills to solve problems.	7, 9, 10	2/3	/3
Total Test Score		8/10	/10
Total Percent Correct			%

Chapter 17 – Prescription Table

The following chart correlates the tested objectives for this chapter to supplementary materials that meet the individual needs of the students. The Reteach and Practice pages are designed for students who need further instruction in the math concepts taught in this chapter. The Enrich pages are designed for students who need advanced challenges.

Objective	Reteach	Practice	Enrich
A. Measure length in customary and metric units.	280, 283, 286, 289	281, 284, 287, 290	282, 285, 288, 291
B. Use skills and strategies to solve problems.	292	293	294

Read each question carefully. Darken the circle for the correct answer.

1. Use an inch ruler to measure.

How long is the line?

Ⓐ 1 inch

Ⓑ 2 inches

Ⓒ 3 inches

Ⓓ 4 inches

2. What is the width of this book using a small paper clip to measure?

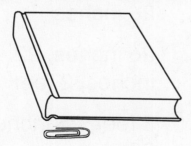

Ⓕ about 2 paper clips

Ⓖ about 3 paper clips

Ⓗ about 4 paper clips

Ⓙ about 5 paper clips

3. How many inches are in 2 feet?

Ⓐ 6   Ⓒ 24

Ⓑ 12   Ⓓ 36

4. Use a centimeter ruler to measure.

How long is the line?

Ⓕ 6 centimeters

Ⓖ 5 centimeters

Ⓗ 4 centimeters

Ⓙ 3 centimeters

5. Which object is about 1 yard long?

Ⓐ eraser

Ⓑ calculator

Ⓒ desk top

Ⓓ pencil

6. How many meters are there in 100 centimeters?

Ⓕ 100

Ⓖ 50

Ⓗ 10

Ⓙ 1

7. Which length would you measure in meters?

Ⓐ a pen

Ⓑ a CD

Ⓒ a book

Ⓓ your school

8. Estimate the length of this page.

Ⓕ about 1 inch

Ⓖ about 1 foot

Ⓗ about 1 yard

Ⓙ about 1 meter

9. Josie is 48 inches tall. How much taller is she than a yard?

Ⓐ 12 inches

Ⓑ 24 inches

Ⓒ 36 inches

Ⓓ 48 inches

10. Which is in order from longest to shortest?

Ⓕ 22 inches, 2 feet, 26 inches

Ⓖ 26 inches, 22 inches, 2 feet

Ⓗ 2 feet, 26 inches, 22 inches

Ⓙ 26 inches, 2 feet, 22 inches

STOP

Read each question carefully. Write or circle your answer in the space provided.

1. Use an inch ruler to measure.
How many inches long is the line?

|———————————————|

_____ inches

_____

2. What is the length of this book using a large paper clip to measure?

_____

_____

3. How many inches are in 3 feet?

_____ inches

4. Use a centimeter ruler to measure.
How many centimeters long is the line?

|———————————————————|

_____ centimeters

_____

5. Circle the correct unit.
The door is about l

_____ wide?

inch

foot

yard

GO ON

6. How many centimeters are there in 1 meter?

_____ centimeters

7. Name something in the classroom that you would measure in meters.

_____

_____

8. Estimate the length of a pencil.
A pencil is about _____ inches long?

9. Juan's painting is 31 inches long. How many inches shorter than a yard is it?

_____ inches

10. Order from longest to shortest.

34 inches,
38 inches,
3 feet

_____

_____

_____

STOP

Chapter 18 – Teacher Interview

Core Concept: *Capacity, Weight, and Temperature*

Student Activity: The student will demonstrate an understanding of measuring capacity, weight, and temperature. Have pencils and paper available for student use. Ask the student questions such as, "What is the best tool to use to measure the weight of your family dog?"

Teacher Question 1:

• Sam and Rose have put 3 cups of water into a bottle. Does the bottle hold more than a pint?

Understanding Student Response	Practice and Improvement
Student says there is not enough information to tell.	Review lesson 2 to compare cups and pints. Ask the student if more information is needed. Point out that 2 cups = 1 pint, so the bottle must hold more than 1 pint. Assign examples like those following lesson 3.
Student says that the bottle does not hold more than a pint.	Review lesson 2, in which it is noted that 2 cups = 1 pint. Point out that if Sam and Rose have put more than 2 cups into it, it must hold more than a pint.

Teacher Question 2:

• What is the best tool to use to measure the weight of your family's dog?

Understanding Student Response	Practice and Improvement
Student identifies an inappropriate tool (such as thermometer or measuring cup).	Review lesson 3 and the concept of weight. Assign practice from items at end of lesson 3.
Student identifies an inappropriate tool for measuring weight (such as a jeweler's balance).	Review lesson 5 and give examples of what you may measure in grams (coins) or in pounds (fruit). Point out that it is better to use a measuring tool suitable to the weight of the object to be measured, such as a bathroom scale.

Chapter 18 – Journal Writing

Encourage students to generate their own journal entries related to math ideas in general or to concepts in this chapter. Present the following journal prompt and have students share their drawing/writing with a partner:

- Cleo is making a sports beverage from powder. She is making 8 quarts of the drink for her track team. How many gallons of the sports beverage can she make? Explain how you found your answer in your journal.

  (Responses should indicate that Cleo made 2 gallons of the drink because there are 4 quarts in one gallon. Student explanations may come up with more than one way to the solution such as adding 4 + 4 or skip-counting by 4s. Encourage them to see how they can use more than one way to find the answer.)

FOLLOW-UP

At the end of the class, review the basic capacity measurements, such as using fluid ounces, cups, pints, quarts, and gallons for customary capacity and milliliters and liters for metric capacity.

Ask students to write about items that they use that are measured in customary units and other items that are measured in metric units. Students should draw a picture of an item that they use in both customary and metric units, and share their writing and drawing with a math partner.

Chapter 18 – Monitoring Student Progress

☐ **Form A**   ☐ **Form B**

Student Name _____ Date _____

Directions: For each item that is answered incorrectly, cross out the item number. Then record the number of correct responses in the appropriate Student Score column. If the student has not met the Criterion Score for an objective, circle the student's score. Recommended assignments are listed in the Prescription Table on the next page.

Objective	Item Numbers	Criterion Score	Student Score
A. Estimate and measure capacity and weight in customary and metric units.	1, 2, 3, 4	3/4	/4
B. Read temperatures.	5, 6, 7	2/3	/3
C. Use strategies and skills to solve problems.	8, 9, 10	2/3	/3
Total Test Score		7/10	/10
Total Percent Correct			%

Chapter 18 – Prescription Table

The following chart correlates the tested objectives for this chapter to supplementary materials that meet the individual needs of the students. The Reteach and Practice pages are designed for students who need further instruction in the math concepts taught in this chapter. The Enrich pages are designed for students who need advanced challenges.

Objective	Reteach	Practice	Enrich
A. Estimate and measure capacity and weight in customary and metric units.	295, 298, 301, 304, 307	296, 299, 302, 305, 308	297, 300, 303, 306, 309
B. Read temperatures.	310	311	312
C. Use strategies and skills to solve problems.	313, 314	315	

Read each question carefully. Darken the circle for the correct answer.

1. Which would weigh more than one pound?

Ⓐ

Ⓑ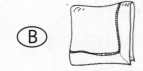

Ⓒ

Ⓓ

2. Which of these would hold more than one quart of water?

Ⓕ    Ⓗ

Ⓖ   Ⓙ

3. How many quarts in a gallon?

Ⓐ 1   Ⓒ 3

Ⓑ 2   Ⓓ 4

4. How many grams in one kilogram?

Ⓕ 1,000   Ⓗ 10

Ⓖ 100   Ⓙ 1

5. What temperature does this thermometer show?

Ⓐ 59° C

Ⓑ 59° F

Ⓒ 58° F

Ⓓ 58° C

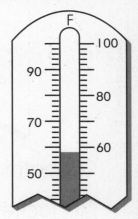

GO ON

6. What temperature does this thermometer show?

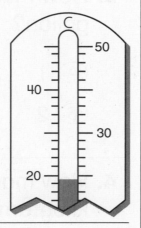

Ⓕ 21°C

Ⓖ 20°C

Ⓗ 19°C

Ⓙ 18°C

7. What would be the best clothing for this temperature?

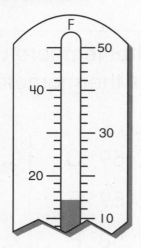

Ⓐ bathing suit

Ⓑ jacket

Ⓒ T-shirt

Ⓓ coat and gloves

8. Veronica is making cookies. Which of these would be best to use to measure out the flour?

Ⓕ balance scale

Ⓖ gallon jug

Ⓗ measuring cup

Ⓙ thermometer

9. Which of these would be best for using a gallon jug to fill?

Ⓐ tea cup

Ⓑ baby bottle

Ⓒ small fish tank

Ⓓ swimming pool

10. What tool would you use to measure the weight of a rock?

Ⓕ cup

Ⓖ ruler

Ⓗ scale

Ⓙ thermometer

STOP

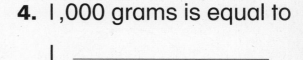
Read each question carefully. Write or circle your answer in the space provided.

1. A brick weighs
more/less
than a pound.

_____

2. A bottle of soda is
more/less
than a gallon of milk.

_____

3. A bicycle weighs
more/less
than a pound.

_____

4. 1,000 grams is equal to

1 _____

_____

5. What is the temperature on this thermometer?

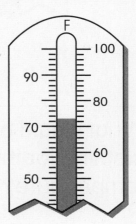

_____

GO ON

6. What temperature does this thermometer show?

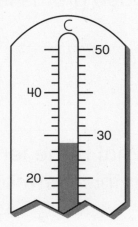

_____

7. What would be the best clothing for this temperature?

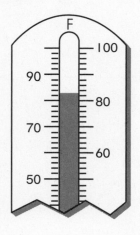

_____

_____

8. Lin is filling her large fish tank. Circle the best tool to fill the tank.

9. Tell something you could use this tool for.

_____

_____

10. What tool would you use to measure the amount of milk you put in your cereal bowl? Circle the best tool.

STOP

Chapter 19 – Teacher Interview

Core Concept: *Identifying and Describing Geometric Shapes*

Student Activity: The student will demonstrate an ability to identify common 2-dimensional shapes and 3-dimensional figures. Have pencils and paper available for student use, along with several geometric shapes and solids.

Teacher Question 1:

• What is the difference between a circle and a sphere?

Understanding Student Response	Practice and Improvement
Student does not realize that a circle is 2-dimensional and a sphere is 3-dimensional.	Review lessons 1 and 2 to clarify the differences between 2-dimensional shapes and 3-dimensional figures.
Student misidentifies the circle and/or the sphere.	Review lessons 1 and 2. Go over the characteristics and properties of the shape and figure, and how to identify them.

Teacher Question 2:

• If you take 2 squares of the same size and place them next to each other, what shape results?

Understanding Student Response	Practice and Improvement
Student says a square.	Review the definition of "square" and "rectangle" as found in lesson 2. Have the student use manipulatives to work out the idea that a rectangle will result.
Student guesses a shape other than a rectangle.	Review all of lesson 2, working with manipulatives or having student sketch figures on paper. Have the student practice with all the shapes discussed in lesson 2.

Teacher Question 3:

• How are the number of sides and the number of angles of triangles, squares, and other plane figures related?

Understanding Student Response	Practice and Improvement
Student does not know the shapes of various plane figures.	Review shapes shown in lesson 2. Have the student sketch various plane figures, counting the sides and the angles in each. Reinforce with manipulatives.
Student states that there is no relationship, or gives another incorrect response.	Use lesson 2 to prompt the student to examine sides and angles of figures as the basis of comparison.

Chapter 19 – Journal Writing

Encourage students to generate their own journal entries related to math ideas in general or to concepts in this chapter. Present the following journal prompt and have students share their drawing/writing with a partner:

- Draw one of each of these shapes in your journal: triangle, rectangle, pentagon, hexagon, octagon, trapezoid, and parallelogram. Think about your school, your home, and your town, and find examples of as many of those shapes as you can in those places. Work with your math partner and write these down.

  (Responses should be fairly accurate. Some further prompting may be needed. Students may also look for examples in magazine advertisements, cut them out, and paste them in their journals.)

FOLLOW-UP

At an appropriate time, have students discuss ways in which knowledge of shapes in the environment has value, such as in the shapes of traffic signs. Reinforce use of correct terminology in naming shapes.

Other activities may include combining or partitioning various shapes to form other shapes, such as flipping a trapezoid to form a hexagon, and counting the number of triangles formed by drawing diagonals of a square (there are 6!).

Chapter 19 – Monitoring Student Progress

☐ **Form A**   ☐ **Form B**

Student Name _____ Date _____

Directions: For each item that is answered incorrectly, cross out the item number. Then record the number of correct responses in the appropriate Student Score column. If the student has not met the Criterion Score for an objective, circle the student's score. Recommended assignments are listed in the Prescription Table on the next page.

Objective	Item Numbers	Criterion Score	Student Score
A. Identify 3-dimensional figures and their attributes.	1, 2, 7, 8	3/4	/4
B. Identify 2-dimensional shapes and their attributes.	3, 4, 5	2/3	/3
C. Identify and translate shape patterns.	6	1/1	/1
D. Use strategies and skills to solve problems.	9, 10	1/2	/2
Total Test Score		7/10	/10
Total Percent Correct			%

Chapter 19 – Prescription Table

The following chart correlates the tested objectives for this chapter to supplementary materials that meet the individual needs of the students. The Reteach and Practice pages are designed for students who need further instruction in the math concepts taught in this chapter. The Enrich pages are designed for students who need advanced challenges.

Objective	Reteach	Practice	Enrich
A. Identify 3-dimensional figures and their attributes.	316, 322	317, 323	318, 324
B. Identify 2-dimensional shapes and their attributes.	319, 322	320, 323	321, 324
C. Identify and translate shape patterns.	328	329	330
D. Use strategies and skills to solve problems.	331	332	333

Read each question carefully.
Darken the circle for the correct answer.

1. Which is a 3-dimensional figure?

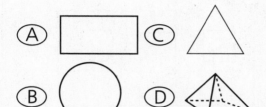

Ⓐ   Ⓒ   Ⓑ   Ⓓ

2. How many faces does a rectangular prism have?

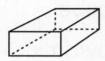

Ⓕ 6   Ⓗ 4

Ⓖ 5   Ⓙ 3

3. Which 2-dimensional shape has 5 sides and 5 angles?

Ⓐ triangle

Ⓑ square

Ⓒ rectangle

Ⓓ pentagon

4. Which 2-dimensional shape could you make if you traced this 3-dimensional figure?

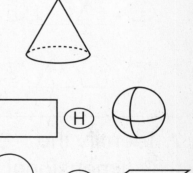

Ⓕ   Ⓗ   Ⓖ   Ⓙ

5. What shape do you get if you put these two triangles together?

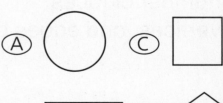

Ⓐ   Ⓒ   Ⓑ   Ⓓ

GO ON

6. What are the next two shapes?

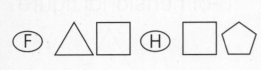

⒡

⒢

⒣

⒥

7. Identify the 3-dimensional figure.

Ⓐ cylinder Ⓒ cone

Ⓑ circle Ⓓ cube

8. A cube has the same number of faces, vertices, and edges as a _____.

⒡ pyramid

⒢ sphere

⒣ rectangular prism

⒥ cone

Use the picture for exercises 9–10.

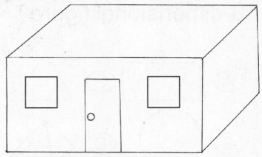

9. Which 3-dimensional figure is used in the drawing of the building?

Ⓐ cube

Ⓑ pyramid

Ⓒ rectangular prism

Ⓓ cylinder

10. Which 2-dimensional shape is NOT used in the drawing of the building?

⒡ triangle

⒢ rectangle

⒣ square

⒥ circle

STOP

Read each question carefully. Write or draw your answer in the space provided.

1. Identify the 3-dimensional figure.

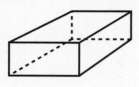

_____

_____

2. How many faces does a cube have?

_____

3. What 2-dimensional shape has 3 sides and 3 angles?

_____

4. What 2-dimensional shape could you make if you traced this 3-dimensional figure?

_____

5. Draw the shape you get if you put these two figures together?

GO ON

6. What are the next two shapes?

 _____ _____

_____

7. Identify the 3-dimensional figure.

_____

8. A rectangular prism has the same number of faces, vertices, and edges as a

_____ .

Use the picture for exercises 9–10.

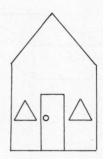

9. The door is shaped like which 2-dimensional shape?

_____

10. What 2-dimensional shape is the drawing of the house?

_____

© Macmillan/McGraw-Hill

STOP

Chapter 20 – Teacher Interview

Core Concept: *Spatial Sense*

Student Activity: The student will demonstrate an understanding of distinguishing congruent and symmetrical shapes; using slides, flips, and turns of geometric shapes, and knowing how to find the perimeter and area of a shape. Ask the student questions such as, "What is the perimeter of a rectangle that has sides of 2 inches, 3 inches, 2 inches, and 3 inches?"

Teacher Question 1:

• What is the perimeter of a rectangle that has sides of 2 inches, 3 inches, 2 inches, and 3 inches?

Understanding Student Response	Practice and Improvement
Student says 12 square units or some other value, indicating an attempt to calculate area.	Review lesson 4 to help the student learn that perimeter is the measure of the distance outside of a shape and is measured in units, such as inches.
Student does not answer "10 inches."	Review lesson 4 to help the student learn that perimeter is the measure of the distance outside of a shape.

Teacher Question 2:

• How do you find the perimeter of your classroom?

Understanding Student Response	Practice and Improvement
Student answers, "Find the length and the width of the classroom."	Prompt the student by asking is that it? Review lesson 4 to reinforce that the perimeter is the measure of the outside of all the sides of a shape.
Student does not know how to find the perimeter.	Review lesson 4 to help the student learn that perimeter is the measure of the distance outside of a shape.

Teacher Question 3:

• What does it mean for a shape to have symmetry? Give an example.

Understanding Student Response	Practice and Improvement
Student cannot define symmetry.	Review lesson 2 to point out that symmetry requires that the two parts of a shape match exactly.
Student understands the definition of symmetry, but does not give an example of a symmetrical shape.	Review lesson 2 to point out that symmetry requires that the two parts of a shape match exactly.

Chapter 20 – Journal Writing

Encourage students to generate their own journal entries related to math ideas in general or to concepts in this chapter. Present the following journal prompt and have students share their drawing/writing with a partner:

- Draw a triangle with sides of 2 cm, 2 cm, and a bottom of 3 cm; draw a trapezoid with a top of 3 cm, sides of 4 cm, and a bottom of 5 cm. What is the perimeter of each shape? Draw a line of symmetry for each one. Now slide the triangle so that it sits on the trapezoid. What happens? What is the perimeter of the new shape?

  (Responses should include the perimeters of the three shapes: 7 cm for the small triangle; 16 cm for the trapezoid, and 17 cm for the resulting triangle. Students should discover that the two figures together make a bigger triangle, and that the lines of symmetry line up. Some students will see this more easily if they use cut-outs to slide the triangle over the trapezoid, and some will need to redraw the shapes.)

FOLLOW-UP

During the discussion of shapes, have students discuss whether or not different objects have symmetry. Ask them how they know for sure.

Ask students to draw and cut out triangles, squares, rectangles, pentagons, hexagons and other shapes. Allow students to test the shapes for symmetry by folding them. When they find a line of symmetry, have them color the fold on their shape. Encourage students to keep looking after they find a shape's first line.

Chapter 20 – Monitoring Student Progress

☐ **Form A**　　　☐ **Form B**

Student Name _____　Date _____

Directions: For each item that is answered incorrectly, cross out the item number. Then record the number of correct responses in the appropriate Student Score column. If the student has not met the Criterion Score for an objective, circle the student's score. Recommended assignments are listed in the Prescription Table on the next page.

Objective	Item Numbers	Criterion Score	Student Score
A. Identify congruent and symmetrical shapes.	3, 4	1/2	/2
B. Identify slides, flips, and turns.	6, 7, 8	2/3	/3
C. Find the perimeter and area of a shape.	1, 2, 9, 10	3/4	/4
D. Use strategies and skills to solve problems.	5	1/1	/1
Total Test Score		7/10	/10
Total Percent Correct			%

Chapter 20 – Prescription Table

The following chart correlates the tested objectives for this chapter to supplementary materials that meet the individual needs of the students. The Reteach andPractice pages are designed for students who need further instruction in the math concepts taught in this chapter. The Enrich pages are designed for students who need advanced challenges.

Objective	Reteach	Practice	Enrich
A. Identify congruent and symmetrical shapes.	334	335	336
B. Identify slides, flips, and turns.	340	341	342
C. Find the perimeter and area of a shape.	343, 346	344, 347	345,348
D. Use strategies and skills to solve probllems.	349, 350	351	

Name_____

Read each question carefully.
Darken the circle for the correct answer.

1. Find the perimeter.

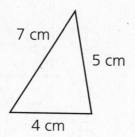

7 cm
5 cm
4 cm

(A) 9 cm   (C) 12 cm

(B) 11 cm   (D) 16 cm

2. Find the number of square units in this rectangle.

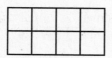

(F) 4   (G) 6   (H) 8   (J) 12

3. Which shape is congruent to this shape?

(A)   (C)

(B)   (D)

4. Which shows a line of symmetry?

(F)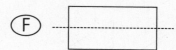

(G)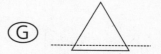

(H)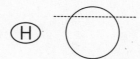

(J)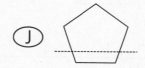

5. The perimeter of a square garden is 20 meters. How long is each side of the garden?

(A) 2 meters

(B) 4 meters

(C) 5 meters

(D) 10 meters

GO ON

© Macmillan/McGraw-Hill

6. Which shows a slide?

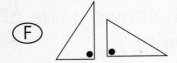

F

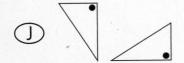

G

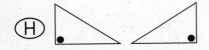

H

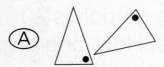

J

7. Which shows a flip?

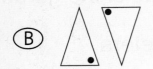

A

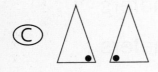

B

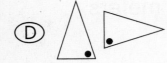

C

D

8. Which shows a turn?

F

G

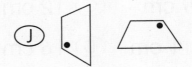

H

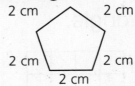

J

9. What is the perimeter of the pentagon?

2 cm   2 cm

2 cm   2 cm

2 cm

Ⓐ 2 cm   Ⓒ 10 cm

Ⓑ 8 cm   Ⓓ 12 cm

10. Which shows an area of 10 square units?

Ⓕ    Ⓗ

Ⓖ   Ⓙ

STOP

Read each question carefully. Fill in your answer in the space provided.

1. Find the perimeter.

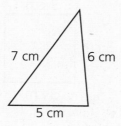

7 cm   6 cm

5 cm

_____ centimeters

2. Find the number of square units in this rectangle.

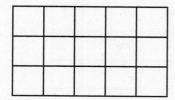

_____ square units

3. Draw a shape that is congruent to this shape? Use a ruler.

4. Draw a line of symmetry.

5. The perimeter of a square garden is 24 meters. How long is each side of the garden?

_____ meters

GO ON

Circle the correct answer.

6.

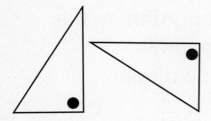

Slide

Flip

Turn

7.

Slide

Flip

Turn

8.

Slide

Flip

Turn

9. What is the perimeter of the square?

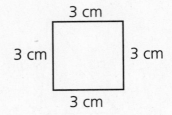

3 cm

3 cm   3 cm

3 cm

_____ centimeters

10. What is the area of the rectangle?

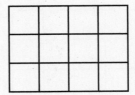

_____ square units

STOP

Unit 5 Performance Assessment

Pop Pop's Perimeter

- **Target Skill:**   Find the perimeter of a figure.
- **Additional Skills:**   Measure length in customary units, identify 2-dimensional shapes and their attributes.

Task Description: This task requires students to measure a garden using a centimeter ruler, find the perimeter, and identify the shape of the garden.

Preparing: Discuss the difference between perimeter and area. You may wish to have students give an example of when each is used.

Materials	Group Size	Time on Task
Centimeter Ruler Pencil	1 to 2 students	1–2 days

Guiding: Remind students that to measure length using a ruler, start at the left of the ruler, not at 1. Make sure students are using a centimeter ruler and not a customary ruler.

Observing/ Monitoring: As you move among the students, pose the following questions:

How did you measure each of the sides?

How do you find the perimeter of an item?

How do you know the shape of the garden?

Unit 5 Performance Assessment Scoring Rubric

Pop Pop's Perimeter

Score	Explanation
3	Students demonstrate an efficient strategy and a thorough approach that enables them to solve the problem completely. A satisfactory answer: • states that 24 meters of fence need to be bought; • correctly finds the perimeter of the picture of the garden; • states the garden is rectangular. Students are able to complete the problem quickly and have all of the above correct solutions with appropriate work shown.
2	Students demonstrate a strategy that enables them to solve most of the problem correctly. The strategy is somewhat disorganized, making it less efficient. A solution is found but errors are contained. Students may: • have found the perimeter, but may have measured incorrectly. Students may have some difficulty determining all solutions correctly but demonstrate an understanding of general concepts.
1	Students demonstrate a confused strategy, which leads to difficulty solving the problem. Most answers are incorrect, but students demonstrate knowledge of at least one concept being assessed, such as finding the perimeter of an object.

Unit 5 Performance Assessment
Student Activity

Pop Pop's Perimeter

You will need
- A centimeter ruler
- Pencil

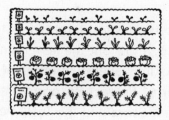

Pop Pop is planting a flower garden. To keep his dog out of the garden, Pop Pop is putting up a fence. He needs to know how much fence to buy. Help Pop Pop do this.

1. What is the measure of each long side to the nearest centimeter?

_____ centimeters

2. What is the measure of each short side to the nearest centimeter?

_____ centimeters

3. What is the perimeter of the picture of the garden?

_____ centimeters

4. 1 centimeter in the picture stands for 1 meter for the garden. How many meters of fence does Pop Pop need to buy?

_____ meters

5. What shape is the garden?

_____

Unit 5 – Monitoring Student Progress

☐ **Form A**   ☐ **Form B**

Student Name ——————————————— Date ——————

Directions: This test targets selected objectives. For each item that is answered incorrectly, cross out the item number. Then record the number of correct responses in the column labeled **Number of Correct Responses.** Add to find the **Total Number of Correct Responses** and record the total. Use this total to determine the **Total Test Score** and the **Total Percent Correct.**

Strand • Objective(s)	Item Numbers	Number of Correct Responses
Measurement • Measure length in customary and metric units. • Estimate and measure capacity and weight in customary and metric units. • Read temperatures. • Use strategies and skills to solve problems.	1, 2, 3, 4, 5, 6, 17, 18	/8
Geometry and Spatial Sense • Identify 3-dimensional figures and their attributes. • Identify 2-dimensional shapes and their attributes. • Identify and translate shape patterns. • Identify congruent and symmetrical shapes. • Identify slides, flips, and turns. • Find the perimeter and area of a shape. • Use strategies and skills to solve problems.	7, 8, 9, 10, 11, 12, 13, 14, 15, 16, 19, 20	/12
Total Number of Correct Responses		
Total Test Score		/20
Total Percent Correct		%

Read each question carefully. Darken the circle for the correct answer.

Find the length.

1.

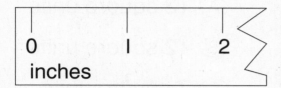

| 0 | I | 2 |
inches

- Ⓐ 4 inches
- Ⓑ 3 inches
- Ⓒ 2 inches
- Ⓓ I inch

2.

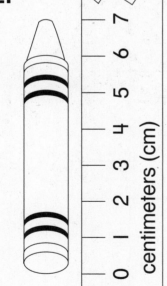

- Ⓕ 10 cm   Ⓗ 8 cm
- Ⓖ 9 cm   Ⓙ 7 cm

Choose the best estimate.

3.

- Ⓐ 2 quarts   Ⓒ 2 pints
- Ⓑ I quart   Ⓓ I cup

4.

- Ⓕ heavier than I kilogram
- Ⓖ about I kilogram
- Ⓗ lighter than I gram
- Ⓙ about I gram

5.

- Ⓐ about 15 liters
- Ⓑ about 2 liters
- Ⓒ about I liter
- Ⓓ less than I liter

GO ON

6. What is the temperature?

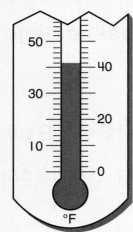

°F

Ⓕ 52°F

Ⓖ 42°F

Ⓗ 50°F

Ⓙ 32°F

7. Find the perimeter.

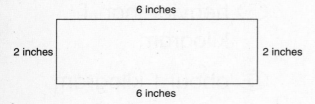

6 inches

2 inches   2 inches

6 inches

Ⓐ 20 inches

Ⓑ 18 inches

Ⓒ 16 inches

Ⓓ 8 inches

8. Name the solid figure.

Ⓕ cone   Ⓗ cylinder

Ⓖ cube   Ⓙ pyramid

9. Find the area.

Ⓐ 13 square units

Ⓑ 12 square units

Ⓒ 7 square units

Ⓓ 3 square units

10. Which shapes are congruent?

Ⓕ

Ⓖ

Ⓗ

Ⓙ

GO ON

11. Which of these figures is a quadrilateral?

Ⓐ

Ⓑ

Ⓒ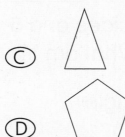

Ⓓ

12. What is a matching part for the figure?

Ⓕ  Ⓗ

Ⓖ  Ⓙ

13. Which shows a line of symmetry?

Ⓐ Ⓒ

Ⓑ Ⓓ

14. What is this figure?

Ⓕ triangle

Ⓖ trapezoid

Ⓗ parallelogram

Ⓙ pentagon

15. How many edges does this solid figure have?

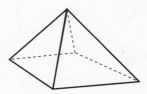

Ⓐ 10 edges

Ⓑ 8 edges

Ⓒ 6 edges

Ⓓ 4 edges

GO ON

16. How many angles does this figure have?

(F) 6   (H) 4

(G) 5   (J) 3

17. How long is the path?

(A) 2

(B) 3

(C) 4

(D) 5

2 units

1 unit

1 unit

Use this picture to answer 18.

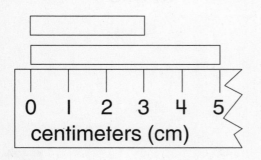

0   1   2   3   4   5
centimeters (cm)

18. How much longer was one piece of ribbon than the other?

(F) 1 cm   (H) 3 cm

(G) 2 cm   (J) 4 cm

19. I have 5 sides and 5 angles. What am I?

(A) rectangle

(B) hexagon

(C) pentagon

(D) trapezoid

20. How many of the little squares does it take to make the big square?

(F) 4

(G) 3

(H) 2

(J) 1

STOP

Read each question carefully. Write or circle your answer in the space provided.

Write the length.

1.

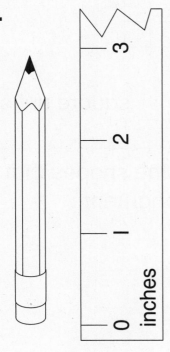

_____ inches

2.

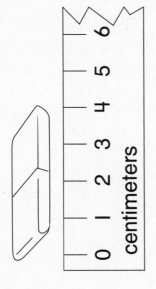

_____ centimeters

Circle the best estimate.

3.

4 quarts   I pint

I quart   I cup

4.

heavier than I kilogram

about I kilogram

lighter than I kilogram

about I gram

5.

about I0 liters

about 2 liters

about I liter

less than I liter

6. Write the temperature.

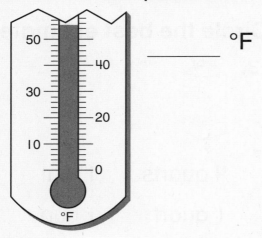

_____ °F

_____

7. What is the perimeter?

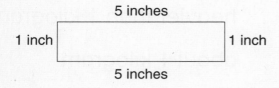

5 inches

1 inch   1 inch

5 inches

_____ inches

_____

8. Name the solid figure.

_____

9. What is the area?

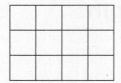

_____ square units

_____

10. Circle the shapes that are congruent.

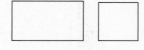

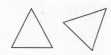

GO ON

11. Circle the quadrilateral.

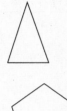

12. Circle the matching part for the figure.

13. Which shows a line of symmetry? Circle the figure.

14. What is this figure?

_____

15. How many edges does this solid figure have?

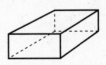

_____ edges

GO ON

16. How many angles does this figure have?

_____ angles

---

17. How long is the path?

1 unit

3 units

_____ units

---

18. How much longer is one piece than the other?

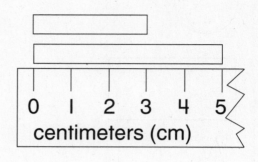

centimeters (cm)

_____ cm

---

19. I have 4 sides and 4 angles. What plane figure am I?

_____

---

20. How many of these triangles does it take to make this figure?

_____ triangles

STOP

Chapter 21 – Teacher Interview

Core Concept: *Place Value to Thousands*

Student Activity: The student demonstrates an understanding of reading, writing, comparing, and ordering numbers to 1,000, as well as identifying number patterns to 1,000. Have plenty of beans or counters, some hundreds models, tens models, and ones models, and plenty of graph paper for the student. Ask the student questions such as, "What is the biggest number you can write using the digits 1, 3, and 9?"

Teacher Question 1:
• Write the number that is 8 more than 798.

Understanding Student Response	Practice and Improvement
Student regroups in the ones place but not in the tens place, obtaining a result like 796.	Review lessons in Chapter 4. Put the 10 tens models together to make a hundred square, and move it to the hundreds place. Point out that no tens are left.
Student does not regroup in the hundreds place, obtaining a result like 706.	Use the same procedure as above, with the place-value models. Point out because 8 and 798 are being added, the sum must be greater than 798.

Teacher Question 2:
• What is the greatest number you can write using the digits 1, 3, and 9?

Understanding Student Response	Practice and Improvement
Student says 139, perhaps because that is the order in which the digits are given.	Review lesson 3 to reinforce that we write and read numbers from left to right, with the greatest value to the left or in the hundreds place. Therefore, the greatest digit must be in the hundreds place, the next greatest in the tens, and finally the least in the ones. Use items in lesson 3 for practice.
Student says 913.	Use lesson 3 to have the student put 913 and 931 in expanded form and then compare the numbers to see which is greater.

Teacher Question 3:
• Think about the number 518. How many hundreds, tens and ones are in 518?

Understanding Student Response	Practice and Improvement
Student refers to 51 tens or eighteen ones.	Review lesson 3 to reinforce place value. Demonstrate how ten ones form a group of ten and ten tens form a group of a hundred. Assign practice items from lesson 3.
Student confuses the places.	Review lesson 2. Use models to show how their answer is different from 518.

Chapter 21 – Journal Writing

Encourage students to generate their own journal entries related to math ideas in general or to concepts in this chapter. Present the following journal prompt and have students share their drawing/writing with a partner:

- How is it helpful to show a number in expanded form? Make up some 3-digit numbers, and write them in expanded form. Write the name of each number. Ask your math partner to check your work, while you check your partner's work.

  (Responses should state expanded form makes it easier to see what each digit in the number stands for—hundreds, tens, or ones.)

FOLLOW-UP

At the end of the day, ask students to read several 3-digit numbers. Ask for responses to what the number would be if a number of ones or tens or hundreds were added. Students should grasp the concept that when a number is written in expanded form, the separate parts are added to get the number in its common form.

Have students practice going to expanded form and back with numbers having zeros in the ones or tens place, and blank in the hundreds place. Students should write these equations in their journal and share their work with a math partner.

Chapter 21 – Monitoring Student Progress

☐ Form A   ☐ Form B

Student Name _____ Date _____

Directions: For each item that is answered incorrectly, cross out the item number. Then record the number of correct responses in the appropriate Student Score column. If the student has not met the Criterion Score for an objective, circle the student's score. Recommended assignments are listed in the Prescription Table on the next page.

Objective	Item Numbers	Criterion Score	Student Score
A. Count, read, write, and represent numbers to 1,000.	1, 2, 3, 4	3/4	/4
B. Identify place value for each digit for numbers to 1,000.	5, 6, 7, 8, 9	4/5	/5
C. Use strategies and skills to solve problems.	10	1/1	/1
Total Test Score		8/10	/10
Total Percent Correct			%

Chapter 21 – Prescription Table

The following chart correlates the tested objectives for this chapter to supplementary materials that meet the individual needs of the students. The Reteach and Practice pages are designed for students who need further instruction in the math concepts taught in this chapter. The Enrich pages are designed for students who need advanced challenges.

Objective	Reteach	Practice	Enrich
A. Count, read, write, and represent numbers to 1,000.	353	354	355
B. Identify place value for each digit for numbers to 1,000.	356, 359, 362	357, 360, 363	358, 361, 364
C. Use strategies and skills to solve problems.	365	366	367

Read each question carefully. Darken the circle for the correct answer.

1. 20 tens = ▮ hundreds

   Ⓐ 2

   Ⓑ 20

   Ⓒ 200

   Ⓓ 400

2. 40 tens = ▮ hundreds

   Ⓕ 400

   Ⓖ 40

   Ⓗ 4

   Ⓙ 1

3. 900 ones = ▮ tens

   Ⓐ 900

   Ⓑ 90

   Ⓒ 10

   Ⓓ 9

4. 20 hundreds = ▮ thousands

   Ⓕ 2,000

   Ⓖ 200

   Ⓗ 20

   Ⓙ 2

5. How many tens in 593?

   Ⓐ 90

   Ⓑ 50

   Ⓒ 9

   Ⓓ 3

6. Which number has 5 tens?

   Ⓕ 534   Ⓗ 352

   Ⓖ 495   Ⓙ 205

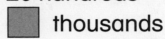

GO ON

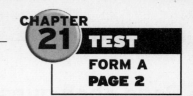

7. Which number is the same as 6 hundreds, 3 tens, and 9 ones?

Ⓐ 600309

Ⓑ 6391

Ⓒ 6309

Ⓓ 639

8. Which is the same as 7 hundreds, 9 tens, and 9 ones?

Ⓕ 997   Ⓗ 799

Ⓖ 979   Ⓙ 79

9. What is the value of the zero in 1,909?

Ⓐ 0 thousands

Ⓑ 0 hundreds

Ⓒ 0 tens

Ⓓ 0 ones

Use the story to answer question 10.

Mario likes to paint. He saves his allowance so that he can buy brushes. He has 3 big brushes, 2 medium brushes, and 4 small brushes. Mario uses all of his brushes when he paints.

10. What is the main idea of this story?

Ⓕ Mario has 4 small brushes.

Ⓖ Mario saves his allowance.

Ⓗ Mario has 9 brushes in all.

Ⓙ Mario likes to paint.

STOP

Read each question carefully. Write your answer on the line.

1. 60 tens =

_____ hundreds

4. 30 hundreds =

_____ thousands

2. 90 tens =

_____ hundreds

5. How many tens in 397?

_____

3. 400 ones =

_____ tens

6. How many hundreds in 2,436?

_____

GO ON

7. Write a number that is the same as 1 hundred, 3 tens, and 7 ones.

_____

8. Write the number for 5 hundreds, 1 ten, and 9 ones?

_____

9. How many ones in 890?

_____

Use the story to answer question 10.

Sophie has a large family. She has 4 brothers, 2 sisters, and 16 cousins. Sophie likes having a big family because there is always someone to play with.

10. What is the main idea of the story?

_____

_____

_____

STOP

Chapter 22 – Teacher Interview

Core Concept: *Compare and Order Numbers to 1,000*

Student Activity: The student demonstrates an understanding of comparing and ordering numbers to 1,000 and knowing number patterns such as counting forward or backward by 100. Ask the student questions such as, "Which is the greatest number: 725, 527, or 752?"

Teacher Question 1:

• Which number is between 452 and 454?

Understanding Student Response	Practice and Improvement
Student answers 451 or 455.	Review lesson 2 to help the student learn that "between" is different than "before" and "after."
Student gives an inappropriate answer.	Review lesson 2 to help the student use a number line to order numbers.

Teacher Question 2:

• Which is the greatest number: 725, 527, or 752?

Understanding Student Response	Practice and Improvement
Student says 527.	Review lesson 3 and prompt the student to name the greatest number. Explain that to compare numbers all in the hundreds, look at the hundreds place first.
Student says 725.	Review lesson 3 to help the student learn to look at the tens place if the numbers in the hundreds place are the same.

Teacher Question 3:

• Listen to these numbers and tell me if I am counting by ones, tens, or hundreds: 357, 367, 377, (etc.).

Understanding Student Response	Practice and Improvement
Student does not detect any pattern.	Review lessons 4 and 5 to help the student write the numbers in order to detect a pattern.
Student answers ones or hundreds.	Review lessons 4 and 5 to help the student learn to look for similarities in the numbers before looking for what was changed.

Chapter 22 – Journal Writing

Encourage students to generate their own journal entries related to math ideas in general or to concepts in this chapter. Present the following journal prompt and have students share their drawing/writing with a partner:

- Ed lifts weights in his basement every night. First he lifts 220 pounds. Next, he lifts 230 pounds and then 240 pounds. If the pattern continues, what will he lift next? What will he lift after that? Ask your math partner to check your work, while you check your partner's work.

  (Responses should include the correct answers, 250 pounds and 260 pounds, and should reflect an understanding that 10 more pounds are lifted each time. Students should see that the hundreds and ones places stayed the same while the tens place increased by 1 with each lift. Use place-value models if needed.)

FOLLOW-UP

At the end of the class, review the ideas of comparing and ordering three-digit numbers. Ask the students to think of times where they would need to compare and order numbers.

Have students describe the process they use to compare and order three-digit numbers. Then students should explain how a pattern of counting by tens and another one by hundreds works. Students should write these explanations in their journals and share their work with a math partner.

Chapter 22 – Monitoring Student Progress

☐ **Form A**   ☐ **Form B**

Student Name _____ Date _____

Directions: For each item that is answered incorrectly, cross out the item number. Then record the number of correct responses in the appropriate Student Score column. If the student has not met the Criterion Score for an objective, circle the student's score. Recommended assignments are listed in the Prescription Table on the next page.

Objective	Item Numbers	Criterion Score	Student Score
A. Compare and order numbers to 1,000.	1, 2, 3, 4	3/4	/4
B. Identify number patterns.	5, 8, 9, 10	3/4	/4
C. Use strategies and skills to solve problems.	6, 7	1/2	/2
Total Test Score		7/10	/10
Total Percent Correct			%

Chapter 22 – Prescription Table

The following chart correlates the tested objectives for this chapter to supplementary materials that meet the individual needs of the students. The Reteach and Practice pages are designed for students who need further instruction in the math concepts taught in this chapter. The Enrich pages are designed for students who need advanced challenges.

Objective	Reteach	Practice	Enrich
A. Compare and order numbers to 1,000.	368, 371, 374	369, 372, 375	370, 373, 376
B. Identify number patterns.	377, 380	378, 381	379, 382
C. Use strategies and skills to solve problems.	383, 384	385	

Read each question carefully.
Darken the circle for the correct answer.

1. ▢ > 794

   Ⓐ 637

   Ⓑ 695

   Ⓒ 793

   Ⓓ 796

2. 252 > ▢

   Ⓕ 273

   Ⓖ 261

   Ⓗ 255

   Ⓙ 250

Use this number line for items 3 and 4.

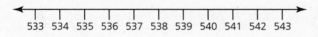

533 534 535 536 537 538 539 540 541 542 543

3. What number is between 539 and 541?

   Ⓐ 538

   Ⓑ 540

   Ⓒ 542

   Ⓓ 543

4. What number is just before 537?

   Ⓕ 535

   Ⓖ 536

   Ⓗ 538

   Ⓙ 539

5. What number is missing?

210, ▢, 230, 240, 250

   Ⓐ 211

   Ⓑ 215

   Ⓒ 218

   Ⓓ 220

GO ON

6. Kasey puts a nickel in her piggy bank every week. How much can she save in 5 weeks?

(F) 5¢   (H) 25¢

(G) 10¢   (J) 50¢

7. Paul can fit 4 baseball caps on a shelf. How many shelves will he need for 28 caps?

(A) 112 shelves

(B) 28 shelves

(C) 7 shelves

(D) 4 shelves

8. What number is missing?

480, 490, 500, ▮, 520, 530, 540

(F) 501   (H) 510

(G) 505   (J) 515

9. What number is next?

333, 433, 533, ▮, 733, 833, 933

(A) 534

(B) 593

(C) 630

(D) 633

10. Count backwards by 50. What number is missing?

850, 800, 750, ▮, 650, 600, 550

(F) 700

(G) 675

(H) 660

(J) 655

STOP

Chapter 23 – Teacher Interview

Core Concept: *3-Digit Addition*

Student Activity: The student will demonstrate an understanding of adding 3-digit numbers with and without regrouping, including money amounts. Have manipulative materials such as place-value models and place-value mats for the student. Ask the student questions such as, "What is the sum of 545 and 369?"

Teacher Question 1:

• How do you regroup ones in 545 + 369?

Understanding Student Response	Practice and Improvement
Student does not know when to regroup ones.	Review lesson 2 to help the student review that ones are regrouped into tens when the sum of the ones column is 10 or greater.
Student regroups the tens instead of the ones.	Review lesson 2 to help the student review that ones are regrouped into tens when the sum of the ones column is 10 or greater.

Teacher Question 2:

• Which places need to be regrouped in 545 + 369?

Understanding Student Response	Practice and Improvement
Student answers ones only.	Review lesson 3 to help the student understand when to regroup tens.
Student answers tens only.	Review lesson 2 to help the student understand when to regroup ones.
Student says regrouping is not necessary.	Review lessons 2 and 3 to help the student learn when to regroup to a particular place.

Teacher Question 3:

• What is the sum of 545 and 369?

Understanding Student Response	Practice and Improvement
Student answers 804 or 904.	Review lesson 2 to help the student learn how to regroup ones and lesson 3 to help the student review how to regroup tens.
Student regroups correctly but still gets an answer other than 914.	Review lesson 2 and 3 and have the student explain their steps to check that the student knows the steps, but is perhaps computing incorrectly.

Chapter 23 – Journal Writing

- Ari and Leah are saving their change to buy their mother a birthday present. Ari has saved $1.86 and Leah has saved $2.77. How much have the children saved together? In your journal, tell how you found the answer.

  (Responses should include the correct answer, $4.63, and should reflect an understanding that dollars and cents amounts can be seen as 3-digit numbers. Students should also realize that they can regroup ones to tens and tens to hundreds in the same problem. Some students may require prompting to see these ideas. Encourage the use of workmats, if needed.)

FOLLOW-UP

At the end of the class, review the ideas of adding 3-digit numbers and regrouping. Ask the students to make up a few addition problems that require regrouping, and solve them in their journals.

Have students write a word problem using 3-digit numbers on one page in their journal, and write the solution on another. Have them trade problems with a math partner, and ask each partner to solve the other's problem without looking at the answer. Have the two partners get back together to check each other's answers.

Chapter 23 – Monitoring Student Progress

☐ **Form A**   ☐ **Form B**

Student Name _____ Date _____

Directions: For each item that is answered incorrectly, cross out the item number. Then record the number of correct responses in the appropriate Student Score column. If the student has not met the Criterion Score for an objective, circle the student's score. Recommended assignments are listed in the Prescription Table on the next page.

Objective	Item Numbers	Criterion Score	Student Score
A. Regroup ones or tens to add 3-digit numbers.	1, 2, 3, 4, 5, 6, 7, 8, 9	8/9	/9
B. Use strategies and skills to solve problems.	10	1/1	/1
Total Test Score		9/10	/10
Total Percent Correct			%

Chapter 23 – Prescription Table

The following chart correlates the tested objectives for this chapter to supplementary materials that meet the individual needs of the students. The Reteach and Practice pages are designed for students who need further instruction in the math concepts taught in this chapter. The Enrich pages are designed for students who need advanced challenges.

Objective	Reteach	Practice	Enrich
A. Regroup ones or tens to add 3-digit numbers.	386, 389, 392	387, 390, 393	388, 391 394
B. Use strategies and skills to solve problems	395	396	397

Read each question carefully. Darken the circle for the correct answer.

1. $200 + 400 =$ ⬛

    (A) 200

    (B) 300

    (C) 500

    (D) 600

2.
$$\begin{array}{r} 271 \\ + \ 164 \\ \hline \end{array}$$

    (F) 435   (H) 235

    (G) 335   (J) 135

3.
$$\begin{array}{r} 157 \\ + \ 136 \\ \hline \end{array}$$

    (A) 293

    (B) 283

    (C) 193

    (D) 183

4. $659 + 300 =$ ⬛

    (F) 359

    (G) 689

    (H) 900

    (J) 959

5. $195 + 404 =$ ⬛

    (A) 594

    (B) 599

    (C) 604

    (D) 609

GO ON

6.   624
    + 263

F) 887   H) 877
G) 878   J) 788

7.   369
    + 475

A) 734   C) 834
B) 744   D) 844

8.   729
    + 175

F) 804
G) 894
H) 904
J) 994

9.   268
    + 534

A) 702   C) 802
B) 792   D) 892

10. Students in Mrs. Govan's class make paintings every Monday. Today, they did not make paintings. What can you tell from this story?

F) The students made paintings today.

G) Today is not Monday.

H) Mrs. Govan does not paint.

J) Monday is Mrs. Govan's birthday.

STOP

Read each question carefully. Write your answer in the space provided.

1. $500 + 400 =$ _____

4. $799 + 200 =$ _____

2.
$$\begin{array}{r} 371 \\ + \ 567 \\ \hline \end{array}$$

5. $392 + 403 =$ _____

3.
$$\begin{array}{r} 198 \\ + \ 248 \\ \hline \end{array}$$

GO ON ➡

6. 437
   + 312

7. 157
   + 368

8. 819
   + 119

9. 647
   + 216

10. Students in Mrs. Levine's class have a milk box with each snack. The class has two snacks a day. What can you tell about students in the class?

   _____

   _____

   _____

STOP

Chapter 24 – Teacher Interview

Core Concept: 3-digit Subtraction

Student Activity: The student will demonstrate an understanding of adding and subtracting 3-digit numbers with and without regrouping, including money amounts. Have manipulative materials such as place-value models and place-value mats available for the student. You may also have beans or counters and cups available. Ask the student questions such as, "Find the difference between 728 and 300 by counting back by hundreds."

Teacher Question 1:

• Marcus got autographs from two professional football players. One of the football players weighed 268 pounds, and the other weighed 325 pounds. Calculate the difference in weight.

Understanding Student Response	Practice and Improvement
Student adds the weight to get an exact amount.	Review estimating from lesson 5 and remind the student that they were asked to estimate the weight. Observe whether they find the nearest hundreds correctly, and review using a number line if needed.
Student does not know how to find the nearest hundreds.	Review estimating sums from lesson 5. Point out that this is a good way to check for reasonableness.

Teacher Question 2:

• Find the difference between 728 − 300 by counting back by hundreds.

Understanding Student Response	Practice and Improvement
Student does not know how to count back by hundreds.	Practice counting back by hundreds using items like **Try It** in lesson 1. Use a number line to help the student understand.
Student drops the tens and ones while counting back.	Review lesson 1 and then ask the student to put 728 in expanded form. Then count back by hundreds, and finally combine the tens and ones to make 428.

Teacher Question 3:

• Abby spent $5.85 on a CD and $3.50 on food. How much did she spend all together?

Understanding Student Response	Practice and Improvement
Student does not know whether to add or to subtract.	Review lesson 4. Remind the student that addition is required because of the "all together." Assign **Facts Practice** if needed.
Student does not line up numbers on the decimal point.	Review that to the left of the decimal is the dollar amount and to the right is the change. Assign money items from **Concepts and Skills** in Chapter Review for practice.

Chapter 24 – Journal Writing

Encourage students to generate their own journal entries related to math ideas in general or to concepts in this chapter. Present the following journal prompt and have students share their drawing/writing with a partner:

- The city library received a donation of 736 books. Of those, 347 were children's books. How many of the books were not children's books? In your journal, tell how to solve this problem, solve it, and check your work by addition. Explain why this process checks your work. Then explain how you could also check by estimating.

    (Responses should indicate that subtraction is the process to use in solving the problem. The correct result is 389. This difference is added back to 347 to check-if you add back what you first took away, you should come back to the same starting point. If one found the nearest hundreds, one could subtract 700 − 300 = 400, which is reasonably close to 389.)

FOLLOW-UP

Ask students to reflect on the process of checking subtraction by addition. Have them make up a few subtraction problems that they will solve, and then check by addition, in their journals. These should be 3-digit numbers, and should include some with zeros in the ones and tens place.

Have students write two word problems using 3-digit numbers. One should use addition and the other should use subtraction. Trade with a partner and solve each other's word problems. Remind students to use addition or estimation to check their work. When they are done, they should share their work with a math partner.

Chapter 24 – Monitoring Student Progress

☐ **Form A**   ☐ **Form B**

Student Name _____ Date _____

Directions: For each item that is answered incorrectly, cross out the item number. Then record the number of correct responses in the appropriate Student Score column. If the student has not met the Criterion Score for an objective, circle the student's score. Recommended assignments are listed in the Prescription Table on the next page.

Objective	Item Numbers	Criterion Score	Student Score
A. Regroup tens or hundreds to subtract 3-digit numbers.	1, 2, 3, 4, 5	4/5	/5
B. Add and subtract money amounts.	6, 7, 10	2/3	/3
C. Use strategies and skills to solve problems.	8, 9	1/2	/2
Total Test Score		7/10	/10
Total Percent Correct			%

Chapter 24 – Prescription Table

The following chart correlates the tested objectives for this chapter to supplementary materials that meet the individual needs of the students. The Reteach and Practice pages are designed for students who need further instruction in the math concepts taught in this chapter. The Enrich pages are designed for students who need advanced challenges.

Objective	Reteach	Practice	Enrich
A. Regroup tens or hundreds to subtract 3-digit numbers.	398, 401, 404	399, 402, 405	400, 403, 406
B. Add and subtract money amounts.	407	408	409
C. Use strategies and skills to solve problems.	410, 411	412	

Read each question carefully.
Darken the circle for the correct answer.

Subtract.

1.

hundreds	tens	ones
	☐	☐
3	3	2
− 2	1	3

(A) 19 (C) 129

(B) 119 (D) 545

2.

hundreds	tens	ones
☐	☐	
6	1	2
− 4	4	1

(F) 171 (H) 271

(G) 261 (J) 1,053

3.

hundreds	tens	ones
☐	☐	
3	2	5
− 2	3	3

(A) 558 (C) 92

(B) 192 (D) 82

4.

hundreds	tens	ones
	☐	☐
4	8	5
− 1	5	7

(F) 742

(G) 642

(H) 328

(J) 228

5.

hundreds	tens	ones
☐	☐	
5	2	1
− 2	3	1

(A) 752

(B) 652

(C) 390

(D) 290

GO ON

6. $5.09
  − $3.25

Ⓕ $1.74   Ⓗ $8.24

Ⓖ $1.84   Ⓙ $8.34

7. $7.28
  + $4.36

Ⓐ $2.82

Ⓑ $2.92

Ⓒ $11.64

Ⓓ $12.64

8. Maggie bought a book for $5.29. She got $4.71 in change. How much did she pay with?

Ⓕ $8.00

Ⓖ $9.00

Ⓗ $10.00

Ⓙ $11.00

9. There are 48 days of school left. The children have already gone 132 days. How many days of school are there total?

Ⓐ 160

Ⓑ 180

Ⓒ 190

Ⓓ 200

10. $5.78
  −$2.43

Ⓕ $3.25

Ⓖ $3.35

Ⓗ $8.11

Ⓙ $8.21

STOP

Read each question carefully. Write your answer in the space provided.

Subtract.

1.

hundreds	tens	ones
	☐	☐
5	4	1
− 2	2	2

_____

2.

hundreds	tens	ones
☐	☐	
7	4	5
− 6	7	1

_____

3.

hundreds	tens	ones
☐	☐	
9	1	3
− 6	2	1

_____

4.

hundreds	tens	ones
	☐	☐
5	7	4
− 1	6	7

_____

5.

hundreds	tens	ones
☐	☐	
7	1	9
− 4	7	1

_____

GO ON

6. $6.89
      − $4.75

7. $6.89
      + $5.09

8. Preston bought a game for $6.42. He was given $3.58 in change. How much did he pay the cashier?

$ _____

9. Cienna passed out 187 pennants for the game. She still has 58 left to pass out. How many pennants did she start with?

_____ pennants

10. $7.81
       − $2.43

STOP

Unit 6 Performance Assessment

Card Collections

- *Target Skill:*   Add 3-digit numbers.
- *Additional Skills:* Subtract 3-digit numbers, regroup tens and hundreds to subtract 3-digit numbers, solve problems by choosing an operation, estimate sums.

Task Description: This task requires students to add and subtract 3-digit numbers. Then the students have to estimate to find the total number of cards.

Preparing: Discuss with students about card collections, whether they be sports cards or cards used to play games. Have students talk about the cards they have.

Materials	Group Size	Time on Task
Paper Pencil	1 to 2 students	1–2 days

Guiding: Remind students that words *how many more* usually indicate subtraction and *in all* usually indicate addition.

Observing/ Monitoring: As you move among the students, pose the following questions:

How did you choose which operation to use?

How do you regroup if there are not enough tens?

Unit 6 Performance Assessment Scoring Rubric

Card Collections

Score	Explanation
3	Students demonstrate an efficient strategy and a thorough approach that enables them to solve the problem completely. A satisfactory answer: • correctly answers the addition and subtraction questions: 186; 855; 864; 9; • gives a reasonable estimate for the total number of cards: accept 1,600 or 1,720. Students are able to complete the problem quickly and have all of the above correct solutions with appropriate work shown.
2	Students demonstrate a strategy that enables them to solve most of the problem correctly. The strategy is somewhat disorganized, making it less efficient. A solution is found but errors are contained. Students may: • correctly add or subtract but use the incorrect operation; • find a reasonable estimate. Students may have some difficulty determining all solutions correctly but demonstrate an understanding of general concepts.
1	Students demonstrate a confused strategy, which leads to difficulty solving the problem. Most answers are incorrect, but students demonstrate knowledge of at least one concept being assessed. Students may: • correctly add or subtract some of the questions; • make an estimate.

Unit 6 Performance Assessment Student Activity

Card Collections

You will need
- Paper
- Pencil

Four friends are comparing their card collections. Use the chart to answer the questions.

Card Collections	
Sue	525
Mark	413
Mike	442
Karen	339

1. How many more cards does Sue have than Karen?
_____ cards

2. How many cards do the boys have in all?
_____ cards

3. How many cards do the girls have in all?
_____ cards

4. How many more cards do the girls have than the boys? _____ cards

5. About how many cards do the four friends have?
_____ cards

Unit 6 – Monitoring Student Progress

☐ **Form A**   ☐ **Form B**

Student Name _____ Date _____

Directions: This test targets selected objectives. For each item that is answered incorrectly, cross out the item number. Then record the number of correct responses in the column labeled **Number of Correct Responses.** Add to find the **Total Number of Correct Responses** and record the total. Use this total to determine the **Total Test Score** and the **Total Percent Correct.**

Strand • Objective(s)	Item Numbers	Number of Correct Responses
Number Sense, Concepts, and Operations • Count, read, write, and represent numbers to 1,000. • Identify place value for each digit for numbers to 1,000. • Compare and order numbers to 1,000 • Identify number patterns. • Regroup ones or tens to add 3-digit numbers. • Regroup tens or hundreds to subtract 3-digit numbers. • Add and subtract money amounts. • Use strategies and skills to solve problems.	1, 2, 3, 4, 5, 6, 7, 8, 9, 10, 11, 12, 13, 14, 15, 16, 17, 18, 19, 20	/20
Total Number of Correct Responses		
Total Test Score		/20
Total Percent Correct		%

Read each question carefully. Darken the circle for the correct answer.

1. What number is shown?

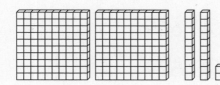

Ⓐ 332   Ⓒ 232

Ⓑ 322   Ⓓ 222

2. Which is true?

Ⓕ 935 > 940

Ⓖ 962 > 753

Ⓗ 412 > 420

Ⓙ 424 > 447

3. What is the word name for 651?

Ⓐ six hundred fifty-one

Ⓑ six hundred fifteen

Ⓒ five hundred sixty-one

Ⓓ one hundred fifty-six

4. What is the value of the 2 in 284?

Ⓕ 2 hundreds

Ⓖ 2 tens

Ⓗ 2 ones

Ⓙ 28 ones

5. Which number comes just before 469?

Ⓐ 460   Ⓒ 470

Ⓑ 468   Ⓓ 467

6. Which number comes between 830 and 832?

Ⓕ 381

Ⓖ 820

Ⓗ 829

Ⓙ 831

GO ON

Find the missing number in each pattern.

7. 145, 245, 345,

    Ⓐ 346

    Ⓑ 355

    Ⓒ 440

    Ⓓ 445

8. 432, ▓, 434, 435

    Ⓕ 431

    Ⓖ 433

    Ⓗ 436

    Ⓙ 439

9.   326
  + 243

    Ⓐ 669

    Ⓑ 579

    Ⓒ 569

    Ⓓ 529

10.   648
  + 137

    Ⓕ 785

    Ⓖ 775

    Ⓗ 771

    Ⓙ 512

GO ON

11. 535
        + 386

(A) 931   (C) 831

(B) 921   (D) 821

12. 600
        − 300

(F) 500   (H) 300

(G) 400   (J) 200

13. 642
        − 137

(A) 579   (C) 506

(B) 519   (D) 505

14. 324
        − 256

(F) 580

(G) 132

(H) 68

(J) 58

15. $9.37
        − 6.54

(A) $15.91

(B) $3.23

(C) $2.84

(D) $2.83

GO ON

16. $7.81
      + 1.59

  Ⓕ $9.50 Ⓗ $8.40

  Ⓖ $9.40 Ⓙ $6.40

---

17. There are 257 people in line to buy tickets to the football game. Sam is the last person in line. How many people are in front of Sam?

  Ⓐ 256 Ⓒ 258

  Ⓑ 257 Ⓓ 260

---

18. How many pennies does Alex have?

  Ⓕ 600 Ⓗ 800

  Ⓖ 700 Ⓙ 900

---

19. Fran has 4 pencils. She buys 8 more. How many pencils does she have altogether?

  Ⓐ $8 + 6 = 15$

  Ⓑ $12 - 8 = 4$

  Ⓒ $4 + 8 = 12$

  Ⓓ $12 - 4 = 8$

---

20. There were 15 cookies on a plate. Tim puts all but 9 of them in his lunchbox. How many cookies did Tim put in his lunchbox?

  Ⓕ 9

  Ⓖ 8

  Ⓗ 7

  Ⓙ 6

STOP

Read each question carefully. Write your answer in the space provided.

1. What number is shown?

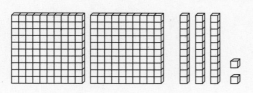

_____

2. Use >, <, or 5 to compare.

542 ◯ 513

_____

3. What is the word name for 745?

_____

4. What is the value of the 7 in 371?

_____

5. Which number comes just after 333?

_____

6. Which number comes between 634 and 636?

_____

GO ON

Write the missing number in each pattern.

7. 235, 335, 435, _____

8. 234, _____, 236, 237

9. $\begin{array}{r} 627 \\ +\ 149 \\ \hline \end{array}$

10. $\begin{array}{r} 385 \\ +\ 61 \\ \hline \end{array}$

GO ON

11.   577
     + 259
_____

12.   700
     − 300
_____

13.   451
     − 246
_____

14.   437
     − 288
_____

15. $8.29
     − 6.47
_____

GO ON

16. $4.72
     +   3.68
   _____

17. There are 324 people in line to buy tickets to the football game. How many people are in front of the last person in line?

_____ people

18. How many pennies does Amanda have?

_____ pennies

19. Theo's class collects 283 cans of dog food for the dogs at the animal shelter. Brad's class collects 325 cans of dog food. How many cans do they collect in all?

_____ cans

20. Sima has $8.50. She spends $7.15 on a birthday present for her dad. How much change does she have left?

$ _____

STOP

Chapter 25 – Teacher Interview

Core Concept: *Fractions*

Student Activity: The student demonstrates an understanding of fractions as parts of a whole and fractional parts of a group. Have a collection of small objects such as coins, beans, or colored counters available for the student.

Teacher Question 1:

• What does the fraction "one fourth" mean?

Understanding Student Response	Practice and Improvement
Student says it stands for a part of a whole, but cannot say into how many parts the whole has been divided.	Review lesson 1. Lay out a group of 4 objects and ask the student to gather one fourth of the group together. Use items like those following lesson 1 for further practice.
Student knows that the whole is divided into four parts, but does not specify that the parts must be equal.	Use the procedure above, reinforcing the idea from lesson 1 that the fractional parts must be equal. Using collections of objects, have student show other fractions such as $\frac{1}{3}$ and $\frac{1}{6}$.

Teacher Question 2:

• Which is greater: $\frac{1}{8}$ or $\frac{1}{4}$? How do you know?

Understanding Student Response	Practice and Improvement
Student says $\frac{1}{8}$, because 8 is greater than 4.	Review lesson 1. Lay out 8 objects and ask the student to gather one eighth of the group together and count how many. Repeat for $\frac{1}{4}$. Have the student compare the results and amend the answer with an explanation.
Student says $\frac{1}{4}$ is greater, but is unable to explain why.	Follow a procedure similar to the one above. Have the student practice drawing and visualizing all of the fractions covered in lesson 1.

Teacher Question 3:

• Which is greater: $\frac{3}{8}$ or $\frac{1}{2}$? How do you know?

Understanding Student Response	Practice and Improvement
Student says $\frac{3}{8}$.	Review lesson 1. Follow a procedure similar to the one in Question 2. Have student practice visualizing and drawing fractions on lesson 1.
Student says that they are equal.	Review lesson 1. Follow a procedure similar to the one in Question 2. Explain that $\frac{3}{6}$, not $\frac{3}{8}$, is equal to $\frac{1}{2}$

Chapter 25 – Journal Writing

Encourage students to generate their own journal entries related to math ideas in general or to concepts in this chapter. Present the following journal prompt and have students share their drawing/writing with a partner:

- What does it mean to say that you have $\frac{3}{4}$ of something?

- Draw a circle and color $\frac{3}{4}$ of it. Then draw a square and color $\frac{3}{4}$ of it. How much of each one is not colored?

*(Responses should state that the fraction represents three of four **equal** parts. Students should see that the uncolored part is $\frac{1}{4}$ of the whole.)*

FOLLOW-UP

At the end of the day, review the concept of fractions. You do not have to use the terms numerator or denominator, but students should understand that the "bottom number" shows the number of equal parts into which the whole is divided and the "top number" tells how many of those equal parts one has. Ask students to think about what it might mean if the bottom number and the top number were the same.

Have students think of situations where they use fractions in ordinary conversation, like "quarter to three" or "half-pint of milk." They may draw representations of these and similar expressions in their journals and then share their work with a math partner.

Chapter 25 – Monitoring Student Progress

☐ **Form A** ☐ **Form B**

Student Name _____ Date _____

Directions: For each item that is answered incorrectly, cross out the item number. Then record the number of correct responses in the appropriate Student Score column. If the student has not met the Criterion Score for an objective, circle the student's score. Recommended assignments are listed in the Prescription Table on the next page.

Objective	Item Numbers	Criterion Score	Student Score
A. Identify fractional parts of a whole.	1, 2, 3	2/3	/3
B. Identify fractions as a part of a group.	4, 5, 6	2/3	/3
C. Compare fractions.	7, 8, 9	2/3	/3
D. Use strategies and skills to solve problems.	10	1/1	/1
Total Test Score		7/10	/10
Total Percent Correct			%

Chapter 25 – Prescription Table

The following chart correlates the tested objectives for this chapter to supplementary materials that meet the individual needs of the students. The Reteach and Practice pages are designed for students who need further instruction in the math concepts taught in this chapter. The Enrich pages are designed for students who need advanced challenges.

Objective	Reteach	Practice	Enrich
A. Identify fractional parts of a whole.	414, 417	415, 418	416, 419
B. Identify fractions as a part of a group.	420, 423, 426	421, 424, 427	422, 425, 428
C. Compare fractions.	429	430	431
D. Use strategies amd skills to solve problems.	432	433	434

Read each question carefully. Darken the circle for the correct answer.

What is the fraction for the shaded part?

1.

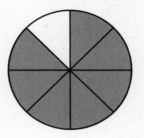

Ⓐ $\dfrac{1}{8}$ Ⓒ $\dfrac{7}{8}$

Ⓑ $\dfrac{2}{8}$ Ⓓ $\dfrac{8}{8}$

2.

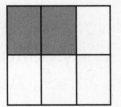

Ⓕ $\dfrac{6}{6}$ Ⓗ $\dfrac{2}{6}$

Ⓖ $\dfrac{4}{6}$ Ⓙ $\dfrac{1}{6}$

3.

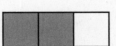

Ⓐ $\dfrac{3}{3}$ Ⓒ $\dfrac{2}{4}$

Ⓑ $\dfrac{2}{3}$ Ⓓ $\dfrac{1}{3}$

4.

Ⓕ $\dfrac{9}{12}$ Ⓗ $\dfrac{7}{12}$

Ⓖ $\dfrac{8}{12}$ Ⓙ $\dfrac{5}{12}$

5.

Ⓐ $\dfrac{6}{6}$ Ⓒ $\dfrac{2}{4}$

Ⓑ $\dfrac{2}{3}$ Ⓓ $\dfrac{1}{3}$

GO ON

6.

(F) $\frac{1}{10}$ (H) $\frac{9}{10}$

(G) $\frac{5}{10}$ (J) $\frac{10}{10}$

---

7. Which fraction is greater than the area shaded?

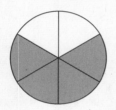

(A) $\frac{2}{6}$ (C) $\frac{4}{6}$

(B) $\frac{3}{6}$ (D) $\frac{5}{6}$

---

8. Which fraction is less than the area shaded?

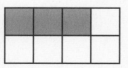

(F) $\frac{7}{8}$ (H) $\frac{3}{8}$

(G) $\frac{5}{8}$ (J) $\frac{1}{8}$

---

9. Which fraction is equal to the shaded area?

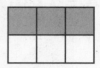

(A)

(B)

(C)

(D)

---

10. Derek and Jeremy went to the fair. They bought hot dogs for lunch. After eating, Derek watched the horse show, but Jeremy got another hot dog. Why did Jeremy get another hot dog?

(F) Jeremy felt sick.

(G) Jeremy is scared of heights.

(H) Jeremy was hungry.

(J) Jeremy doesn't like hot dogs.

STOP

Read each question carefully. Fill in your answer in the space provided.

What is the fraction for the shaded part?

1.

_____

2.

_____

3. Draw a shape that is $\frac{1}{3}$ shaded.

4.

_____

5. Draw a group of items that show $\frac{3}{5}$ shaded.

GO ON

6. Draw a group of items that shows $\frac{3}{4}$ shaded.

_____

7. Write a fraction that is greater than the area shaded.

_____

8. Color a fraction that is less than the fraction shaded.

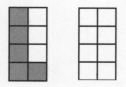

_____

9. Color a fraction that is equal to the shaded area.

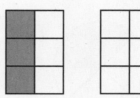

_____

10. Kelly, Tina, and Geena went to the movies. Kelly wanted to see *Space Voyagers*. Tina wanted to see *Lost at Sea*. Geena agreed to see anything except *Zombie Night*. Why might Geena have not wanted to see that movie?

_____

_____

_____

STOP

Chapter 26 – Teacher Interview

Core Concept: *Probability*

Student Activity: The student will demonstrate an understanding of probability in determining which events are more *certain likely, equally likely, less likely,* and *impossible.* Have a collection of small objects such as coins, beans, or colored counters available for the student.

Teacher Question 1:

• There are 6 pennies, 2 quarters, and a dime inside a bag. What is the probability of picking a coin: *certain, likely,* or *impossible?*

Understanding Student Response	Practice and Improvement
Student answers "likely."	Review lesson 1 to help the student understand that if a bag is filled with coins, it is *certain* that a coin will be picked.
Student answers "impossible."	Review lesson 1 to help the student understand that an *impossible* event is one that cannot happen and a *certain* event is one that will happen.

Teacher Question 2:

• What is the probability of picking a penny from the bag: *more likely, equally likely,* or *less likely?*

Understanding Student Response	Practice and Improvement
Student answers "equally likely."	Review lesson 2 to help the student understand that if the first event has more of a chance to occur than a second event, than the probability of the first event happening is *more likely*.
Student answers "less likely."	Review lesson 2 to help the student learn that for an event to be *less likely* than another, there are to be less of a chance of it happening.

Teacher Question 3:

• If you toss a coin 20 times, how many times do you think you will get heads?

Understanding Student Response	Practice and Improvement
Student answers 0 or 20.	Review lessons 1-3 to reinforce to students that when two events are *equally likely*, the chances of each of the events occurring is equally likely.
Student does not have a prediction.	Review lesson 3 to help the student learn how to make a prediction based on a probability.

Chapter 26 – Journal Writing

Encourage students to generate their own journal entries related to math ideas in general or to concepts in this chapter. Present the following journal prompt and have students share their drawing/writing with a partner:

- If you make 2-digit numbers from three 1-digit numbers, how many 2-digit numbers can you make if each digit does not have to be different? Make a plan, then draw or write an explanation in your journal.

  (Responses should indicate that each digit can be combined with any of the three digits, so that three different 2-digit numbers can be formed starting with each digit. The total is 9 different 2-digit numbers.)

FOLLOW-UP

At the end of the class, review the concepts of *equally likely, less likely,* and *more likely*. Ask students a real-life question about predicting the outcome of an event. For example, if in your refrigerator there is a bag of grapes, 20 of them green grapes and 20 of them red grapes, is the first grape you pick out *more likely, less likely,* or *equally likely* to be red?

Have students write in their journals about an event that is *certain*, an event that is *likely*, and an event that is *impossible*. Have them share their work with a math partner.

Chapter 26 – Monitoring Student Progress

☐ Form A   ☐ Form B

Student Name _____ Date _____

Directions: For each item that is answered incorrectly, cross out the item number. Then record the number of correct responses in the appropriate Student Score column. If the student has not met the Criterion Score for an objective, circle the student's score. Recommended assignments are listed in the Prescription Table on the next page.

Objective	Item Numbers	Criterion Score	Student Score
A. Identify the likelihood of events to occur.	2, 3, 4, 5, 8, 9	5/6	/6
B. Make predictions.	1	1/1	/1
C. Use strategies and skills to solve problems.	6, 7	1/2	/2
Total Test Score		7/9	/9
Total Percent Correct			%

Chapter 26 – Prescription Table

The following chart correlates the tested objectives for this chapter to supplementary materials that meet the individual needs of the students. The Reteach and Practice pages are designed for students who need further instruction in the math concepts taught in this chapter. The Enrich pages are designed for students who need advanced challenges.

Objective	Reteach	Practice	Enrich
A. Identify the likelihood of events to occur.	435	436	437
B. Make predictions.	438, 441	439, 442	440, 443
C. Use strategies and skills to solve problems.	444, 445	446	

Read each question carefully. Darken the circle for the correct answer.

1. You toss a coin 10 times. How many times should you get heads?

Ⓐ 0   Ⓑ 1   Ⓒ 5   Ⓓ 10

2. Which color is it impossible for the spinner to stop on?

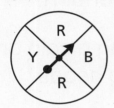

Ⓕ blue   Ⓗ red

Ⓖ green   Ⓙ yellow

3. Anthony put these cubes in a bag. Which color is he certain to pick out?

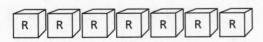

Ⓐ blue   Ⓒ red

Ⓑ green   Ⓓ yellow

Use this picture for questions 4 and 5.

Olga put these shapes into a bag.

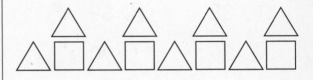

4. Which shape is she more likely to pick?

Ⓕ circle

Ⓖ hexagon

Ⓗ square

Ⓙ triangle

5. Of the shapes in the bag, which is she less likely to pick?

Ⓐ circle

Ⓑ hexagon

Ⓒ square

Ⓓ triangle

6. Derrick used the numbers 3, 8, and 9 to make different 2-digit numbers. Which number would NOT be on his list of 2-digit numbers?

(F) 38   (H) 89

(G) 39   (J) 90

7. Marie was making color combinations with her fabric pieces. She used red, blue, and orange fabric. Which of these could be one of her color combinations?

(A) blue and green

(B) red and yellow

(C) orange and blue

(D) blue and pink

8. Which spinner is most likely to land on blue?

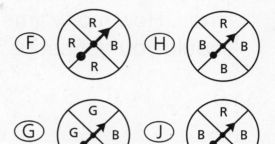

9. Which is certain?

(A) Tossing a coin and getting heads.

(B) Picking a red marble out of a bag of blue marbles.

(C) A spinner with red, white, and blue landing on blue.

(D) Tossing a 1– 6 number cube and getting a number less than 7.

© Macmillan/McGraw-Hill

STOP

Read each question carefully. Write your answer on the line.

1. You toss a coin 10 times. How many times should you get tails?

_____

_____

_____

2. Which color is it impossible for the spinner to stop on?

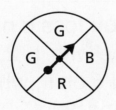

_____

3. Nancy put these cubes in a bag. Which color is she certain to pick out?

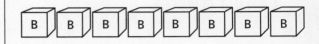

_____

Use this picture for questions 4 and 5.

Kaylie puts these shapes into a bag.

4. Which shape is she more likely to pick?

_____

5. Which shape is she less likely to pick?

_____

GO ON

6. Joseph used the numbers 2, 7, and 5 to make different 2-digit numbers. Write all the 2-digit numbers he could make.

_____

_____

7. Steven was making color combinations to choose 2 new class colors. He used green, purple, and orange markers. Which combinations of 2 colors could he use?

_____

_____

8. Draw a spinner that would most likely land on blue.

9. If you toss a number cube with 1, 2, 3, 4, 5, and 6 on it, what is impossible?

_____

_____

STOP

Chapter 27 – Teacher Interview

Core Concept: *Interpreting Data*

Student Activity: The student demonstrates an understanding of reading graphs, and identifying the median, range, and mode. Ask questions such as, "A graph shows that Larry got 6 votes, Marianne got 7 votes, Bobby got 5 votes, Nancy got 5 votes, and Ricky got 8 votes. What is the range of the votes?"

Teacher Question 1:

• What is the range of the votes?

Understanding Student Response	Practice and Improvement
Student answers 5 or 6.	Review lessons 1 and 2 to help the student learn the difference between the range, the mode, and the median.
Student answers 5–8.	Review lesson 1 and remind the student that the range is the difference between the greatest and least numbers in a data set.

Teacher Question 2:

• What is the median of the votes?

Understanding Student Response	Practice and Improvement
Student answers 3.	Review lessons 1 and 2 to help the student understand the difference between the median and the range.
Student answers 5.	Review lessons 1 and 2 to help the student understand the difference between the mode and the median.

Teacher Question 3:

• What is the mode of the votes?

Understanding Student Response	Practice and Improvement
Student answers 6.	Review lessons 1 and 2 to help the student understand the difference between the mode and the median.
Student answers 3.	Review lessons 1 and 2 to help the student understand the difference between the mode and the range.

Chapter 27 – Journal Writing

Encourage students to generate their own journal entries related to math ideas in general or to concepts in this chapter. Present the following journal prompt and have students share their drawing/writing with a partner:

- Bruce listened to 4 CDs on Monday, 5 CDs on Tuesday, 5 CDs on Wednesday, 3 CDs on Thursday, and 2 CDs on Friday. What is the range, median, and mode of the number of CDs Bruce listened to?

  (Responses should list the range as 3 CDs, the median as 4 CDs, and the mode as 5 CDs. Students should explain that the range is the least number subtracted from the greatest number, the median is the middle number when the set is ordered, and the mode is the number that occurs most often.)

FOLLOW-UP

At the end of the class, review the different types of graphs with students. Ask students what type of information various graphs display.

Have students ask an adult at home to think of where they have used different types of graphs. Have students share the stories that they were told and then draw the graphs with a math partner.

Chapter 27 – Monitoring Student Progress

☐ Form A   ☐ Form B

Student Name _____ Date _____

Directions: For each item that is answered incorrectly, cross out the item number. Then record the number of correct responses in the appropriate Student Score column. If the student has not met the Criterion Score for an objective, circle the student's score. Recommended assignments are listed in the Prescription Table on the next page.

Objective	Item Numbers	Criterion Score	Student Score
A. Identify range, mode, and median.	1, 2, 3, 6, 7, 8	5/6	/6
B. Read a coordinate graph.	4, 5	1/2	/2
C. Use strategies and skills to solve problems.	9, 10	1/2	/2
Total Test Score		7/10	/10
Total Percent Correct			%

Chapter 27 – Prescription Table

The following chart correlates the tested objectives for this chapter to supplementary materials that meet the individual needs of the students. The Reteach and Practice pages are designed for students who need further instruction in the math concepts taught in this chapter. The Enrich pages are designed for students who need advanced challenges.

Objective	Reteach	Practice	Enrich
A. Identify, range, mode, and median.	447, 450	448, 451	449, 452
B. Read a coordinate graph.	453, 456	454, 457	455, 458
C. Use strategies and skills to solve problems.	459	460	461

Read each question carefully.
Darken the circle for the correct answer.

Use the following sequence of numbers for exercises 1–3.

3, 3, 3, 5, 7, 8, 8

1. What is the range of the data?

Ⓐ 3   Ⓒ 5

Ⓑ 4   Ⓓ 6

2. What is the median of the data?

Ⓕ 3   Ⓗ 7

Ⓖ 5   Ⓙ 8

3. What is the mode of the data?

Ⓐ 3   Ⓒ 7

Ⓑ 5   Ⓓ 8

Use the coordinate graph for exercises 4 and 5.

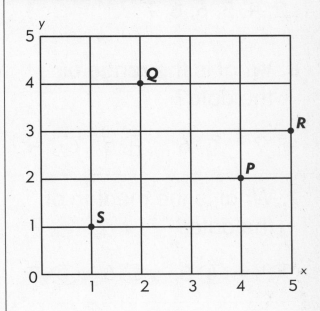

4. Which coordinates represent point *R*?

Ⓕ (1, 1)   Ⓗ (4, 2)

Ⓖ (2, 4)   Ⓙ (5, 3)

5. Which point is represented by (2, 4)?

Ⓐ *P*   Ⓒ *R*

Ⓑ *Q*   Ⓓ *S*

GO ON ▶

Use the following sequence of numbers for exercises 6–8.

1, 2, 4, 5, 6, 6, 7

6. What is the range of the data?

Ⓕ 7   Ⓖ 6   Ⓗ 5   Ⓙ 4

7. What is the median of the data?

Ⓐ 4   Ⓑ 5   Ⓒ 6   Ⓓ 7

8. What is the mode of the data?

Ⓕ 1   Ⓗ 2   Ⓖ 6   Ⓙ 7

Use the information below for exercises 9–10.

The school is selling concert tickets for $7 each. 23 students are in the concert, and 30 students are selling tickets. The concert is on March 25.

9. What is important in determining the amount the school makes?

Ⓐ the day of the concert

Ⓑ the number of students in all

Ⓒ the number of tickets sold

10. What is NOT important in determining the average amount of money each student collected?

Ⓕ the total number of tickets sold

Ⓖ the number of students in the concert

Ⓗ the amount charged for each ticket

© Macmillan/McGraw-Hill

STOP

Read each question carefully. Write your answer on the line.

Use the following sequence of numbers for exercises 1–3.

5, 8, 8, 11, 14, 14, 14

1. What is the range of the data?

_____

2. What is the median of the data?

_____

3. What is the mode of the data?

_____

Use the coordinate graph for exercises 4 and 5.

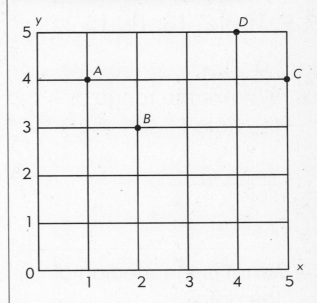

4. What coordinates represent point *A*?

_____

5. What point represents the coordinates (4, 5)?

_____

GO ON

Use the following sequence of numbers for exercises 6–8.

9, 9, 10, 12, 13, 14, 15

6. What is the range of the data?

_____

7. What is the median of the data?

_____

8. What is the mode of the data?

_____

Use the information below for exercises 9–10.

The French club is raising money for a trip to Paris. In September, they raised $300. In October, they raised $500. In November, they had a bake sale.

9. What information is missing to determine the amount of money raised during September, October, and November?

_____

_____

10. What information is NOT important in determining the number of plane tickets the club will purchase?

_____

_____

STOP

Chapter 28 – Teacher Interview

Core Concept: *Exporing Multiplication and Division*

Student Activity: The student demonstrates an understanding of multiplying and dividing, with and without remainders. Have manipulative materials, such as place-value models, available for the student. You may also have beans or counters and cups available.

Teacher Question 1:

- What is a multiplication sentence that means the same as 2 + 2 + 2 + 2 = 8?

Understanding Student Response	Practice and Improvement
Student is confused by the term 'multiplication sentence.'	Review lesson 2 for terminology and practice; review lesson 3 on arrays. Help student see the problem as an array.
Student writes a multiplication sentence using factors other than 4 and 2, such as 8 × 1 = 8, or an addition sentence like 6 + 2 = 8.	Point out that these are ways to get a "correct" answer, but they do not address the question. Use procedure above and assign **Facts Practice** following lesson 16.

Teacher Queston 2:

- Twelve people are going to town in 4 cars. How many will ride in each car, if each car is to carry an equal number of people?

Understanding Student Response	Practice and Improvement
Student says you should put 4 or 5 people in each car.	Review lesson 5 to remind the student that each car has an equal number of people. Have them sketch 12 people and 4 cars, then group people by 3s and assign to cars. Assign **Extra Practice** items.
Student does not place all 12 people in a car or does not divide them evenly.	Review lesson 5. Have the student use 4 cups for cars and 12 beans for people. Put a bean in each cup until all are grouped.

Teacher Question 3:

- What is the remainder when you divide 15 by 6?

Understanding Student Response	Practice and Improvement
Student is confused by the term 'remainder.'	Review lessons 4 and 5 to explain that items cannot always be grouped equally. When the equal groups have been created, the remainder is what is left ungrouped.
Student calculates a remainder other than 3.	Have the student redo calculation after reviewing remainders from lessons 4 and 5. Put 15 beans in 6 cups until no more equal groups can be formed. The remainder is 3. Use **Extra Practice** items.

Chapter 28 – Journal Writing

Encourage students to generate their own journal entries related to math ideas in general or to concepts in this chapter. Present the following journal prompt and have students share their drawing/writing with a partner:

- Multiplication is like repeated addition. Division is like repeated subtraction. Draw diagrams to show that $4 \times 6 = 24$, and that $35 \div 7 = 5$. Then draw a diagram to show the result and the remainder in $37 \div 7 = 5$ R2.

  (Responses to the multiplication prompt may show groups of 4 (or 6) added together or aligned for counting. If students show other groups, ask for clarification. Responses to the division prompt may show a group of 35 objects with 5 groups of 7 (or 7 groups of 5) circled. Responses to the last prompt should be like the previous example, with 2 objects ungrouped.)

FOLLOW-UP

At the end of the day, review ways to multiply and divide through graphic means, relating this to repetitive addition and subtraction. Ask students to make up and solve problems involving multiplication and division.

Have the students figure out how many students would be in each group if they divided the class into groups of 3, 4, 5, and 6. Have the students discuss the process that they followed. Also, have the students discuss why they may want to divide the class into groups. Have the students share their work with a math partner.

Chapter 28 – Monitoring Student Progress

☐ **Form A**   ☐ **Form B**

Student Name _____ Date _____

Directions: For each item that is answered incorrectly, cross out the item number. Then record the number of correct responses in the appropriate Student Score column. If the student has not met the Criterion Score for an objective, circle the student's score. Recommended assignments are listed in the Prescription Table on the next page.

Objective	Item Numbers	Criterion Score	Student Score
A. Use strategies to multiply.	1, 2, 3, 4, 5	4/5	/5
B. Use strategies to divide.	6, 7	1/2	/2
C. Use strategies and skills to solve problems.	8, 9, 10	2/3	/3
Total Test Score		7/10	/10
Total Percent Correct			%

Chapter 28 – Prescription Table

The following chart correlates the tested objectives for this chapter to supplementary materials that meet the individual needs of the students. The Reteach and Practice pages are designed for students who need further instruction in the math concepts taught in this chapter. The Enrich pages are designed for students who need advanced challenges.

Objective	Reteach	Practice	Enrich
A. Use strategies to multiply.	462, 465, 468	463, 466, 469	464, 467, 470
B. Use strategies to divide.	471, 474	472, 475	473, 476
C. Use strategies and skills to solve problems.	477, 478	479	

Read each question carefully. Darken the circle for the correct answer.

Skip-count to find the total.

1.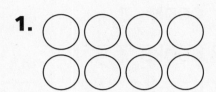

Ⓐ 2   Ⓒ 2

Ⓑ 4   Ⓓ 8

2.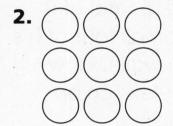

Ⓕ 3   Ⓗ 9

Ⓖ 6   Ⓙ 12

3.

Ⓐ 14   Ⓒ 10

Ⓑ 12   Ⓓ 8

4. How many groups of 2 are there?

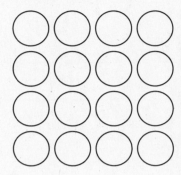

Ⓕ 4   Ⓗ 12

Ⓖ 8   Ⓙ 16

5. How many groups of 5 are there?

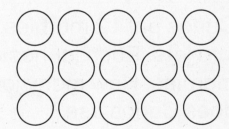

Ⓐ 3   Ⓒ 5

Ⓑ 4   Ⓓ 6

GO ON

6. How many groups of 2 can you make from 10 counters?

   F 1

   G 2

   H 5

   J 10

7. How many groups of 5 can you make from 20 counters?

   A 1   C 2

   B 3   D 4

8. Carlos put 12 marbles into jars. Each jar has 6 marbles. How many jars does Carlos use?

   F 1 jar

   G 2 jars

   H 3 jars

   J 6 jars

9. Maria places 18 books on 3 shelves. How many books go on each shelf?

   A 1 book

   B 3 books

   C 6 books

   D 9 books

10. Josh puts a total of 8 posters on all four of his bedroom walls. How many posters go on each wall?

   F 2 posters

   G 3 posters

   H 4 posters

   J 5 posters

STOP

Read each question carefully.
Write your answer on the line.

Skip-count to find the total.

1.

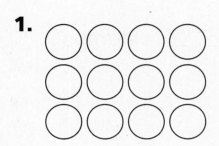

_____

2.

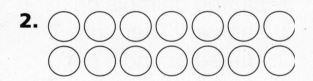

_____

3.

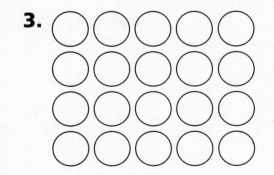

_____

4. How many groups of 6 are there?

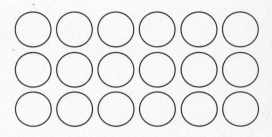

_____

5. How many groups of 3 are there?

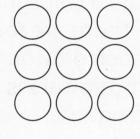

_____

GO ON

6. How many groups of 4 can you make from 24 counters?

_____

7. How many groups of 3 can you make from 15 counters?

_____

8. James puts 8 shirts in drawers. There are four shirts in each drawer. How many drawers is James using?

_____ drawers

9. Marcus puts 30 stamps in 3 stamp albums. How many stamps are in each album?

_____ stamps

10. Teresa places 14 stuffed animals on shelves. There are 7 stuffed animals per shelf. How many shelves is Teresa using?

_____ shelves

STOP

Unit 7 Performance Assessment

Playoffs

- *Target Skill:*   Identify range, mode, and median.
- *Additional Skills:* Compare and order numbers to 100; subtract 2-digit numbers.

Task Description: This task requires students to order 5 numbers from least to greatest, then find the range, mode, and median.

Preparing: Tell students that at events the attendance is often recorded. It is usually either the number of people at the event or the number of tickets sold.

Materials	Group Size	Time on Task
Paper Pencil	1 to 2 students	1 day

Guiding: Remind students that *range* is the difference between the greatest and least numbers in a set, *mode* is the number that occurs most frequently, and *median* is the middle number in an ordered set.

Observing/ Monitoring: As you move among the students, pose the following questions:

How did you find the range?

How did you find the mode?

How did you find the median?

Unit 7 Performance Assessment Scoring Rubric

Playoffs

Score	Explanation
3	Students demonstrate an efficient strategy and a thorough approach that enables them to solve the problem completely. A satisfactory answer: • correctly orders the attendance from least to greatest; • correctly finds the range, mode, and median.13, 46, 46. Students are able to complete the problem quickly and have all of the above correct solutions with appropriate work shown.
2	Students demonstrate a strategy that enables them to solve most of the problem correctly. The strategy is somewhat disorganized, making it less efficient. A solution is found but errors are contained. Students may: • correctly order the attendance; • incorrectly name one of the three central measures. Students may have some difficulty determining all solutions correctly but demonstrate an understanding of general concepts.
1	Students demonstrate a confused strategy, which leads to difficulty solving the problem. Most answers are incorrect, but students demonstrate knowledge of at least one concept being assessed. Students may: • order the numbers from least to greatest; • find the range.

Unit 7 Performance Assessment
Student Activity

Playoffs

You will need
- Paper
- Pencil

The Terriers and the Pioneers
met in a 5-game playoff series.
The attendance for each
game is shown below.
Use the chart to answer
the questions.

Playoff Attendance	
Game 1	46
Game 2	43
Game 3	42
Game 4	55
Game 5	46

1. Order the attendance from least to greatest.

_____

2. What is the range of the attendance? _____

3. What is the mode of the attendance? _____

4. What is the median of the attendance? _____

Unit 7 – Monitoring Student Progress

☐ **Form A**   ☐ **Form B**

Student Name _____ Date _____

Directions: This test targets selected objectives. For each item that is answered incorrectly, cross out the item number. Then record the number of correct responses in the column labeled **Number of Correct Responses.** Add to find the **Total Number of Correct Responses** and record the total. Use this total to determine the **Total Test Score** and the **Total Percent Correct.**

Strand • Objective(s)	Item Numbers	Number of Correct Responses
Number Sense, Concepts, and Operations • Identify fractional parts of a whole. • Identify fractions as a part of a group. • Compare fractions. • Use strategies to multiply. • Use strategies to divide. • Use strategies and skills to solve problems.	1, 2, 3, 4, 5, 6, 12, 13, 14, 15, 16, 17, 18, 19, 20	/15
Data Analysis and Probability • Identify the likelihood of events to occur. • Make predictions. • Identify range, mode, and median. • Read a coordinate graph. • Use strategies and skills to solve problems.	7, 8, 9, 10, 11	/5
Total Number of Correct Responses		
Total Test Score		/20
Total Percent Correct		%

Read each question carefully. Darken the circle for the correct answer.

What is the fraction for the shaded part?

1.

- Ⓐ $\frac{3}{4}$
- Ⓒ $\frac{1}{3}$
- Ⓑ $\frac{1}{4}$
- Ⓓ $\frac{1}{8}$

2.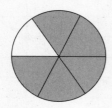

- Ⓕ $\frac{5}{6}$
- Ⓗ $\frac{2}{5}$
- Ⓖ $\frac{2}{4}$
- Ⓙ $\frac{1}{8}$

3. Which fraction is greater than $\frac{1}{3}$?

- Ⓐ $\frac{1}{2}$
- Ⓒ $\frac{1}{5}$
- Ⓑ $\frac{1}{4}$
- Ⓓ $\frac{1}{6}$

4. Which shows $\frac{1}{3}$ shaded?

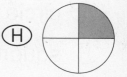
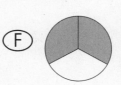

- Ⓕ
- Ⓗ
- Ⓖ
- Ⓙ

Use the picture for items 5–6.

5. Which shape is the most likely to be picked?

- Ⓐ triangle
- Ⓑ circle
- Ⓒ square
- Ⓓ rectangle

GO ON

6. Which shape is the least likely to be picked?

   (F) triangle

   (G) circle

   (H) square

   (J) rectangle

Use the information to answer questions 7–9.

Nancy went golfing 5 times and got the following scores:

    78, 75, 82, 80, 80

7. What is the range?

  (A) 5   (C) 3

  (B) 4   (D) 2

8. What is the median?

  (F) 75   (H) 80

  (G) 78   (J) 82

9. What is the mode?

  (A) 75   (C) 80

  (B) 78   (D) 82

Use the graph for problems 10–11.

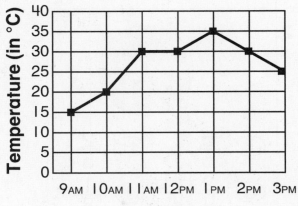

Los Angeles Summer Temperatures

10. At 11 A.M., what is the temperature?

  (F) 15°C   (H) 25°C

  (G) 20°C   (J) 30°C

GO ON

11. When was the lowest recorded temperature?

 (A) 9 A.M.

 (B) 10 A.M.

 (C) 1 P.M.

 (D) 2 P.M.

12. Divide.

 15 into 6 equal groups is _____.

 (F) 3 in each group, 0 left over

 (G) 3 in each group, 3 left over

 (H) 2 in each group, 1 left over

 (J) 2 in each group, 3 left over

13. Make equal groups. There are 2 baskets. There are 10 apples. How many apples in each basket?

 (A) 4 (C) 6

 (B) 5 (D) 12

14. Make equal groups. There are 2 children. There are 18 grapes. How many grapes for each child?

 (F) 18 (H) 9

 (G) 12 (J) 3

15. $4 \times 5 =$ ▢

 (A) 25 (C) 9

 (B) 20 (D) 7

GO ON

16.
$$\begin{array}{r} 2 \\ \times\ 9 \\ \hline \end{array}$$

Ⓕ 20   Ⓗ 11

Ⓖ 18   Ⓙ 9

17. Zach has 8 shells in a basket. There are 5 pink shells and 3 gray ones. What fraction of the shells are pink?

Ⓐ $\frac{6}{8}$ Ⓒ $\frac{3}{8}$

Ⓑ $\frac{5}{8}$ Ⓓ $\frac{3}{5}$

18. Erika has 6 grapes in a cup. There are 5 red grapes and 1 green one. What fraction of Erika's grapes are red?

Ⓕ $\frac{7}{8}$ Ⓗ $\frac{1}{5}$

Ⓖ $\frac{5}{6}$ Ⓙ $\frac{1}{6}$

19. Each of 7 scouts sells 2 boxes of cookies. How many boxes do they sell in all?

Ⓐ 21 boxes

Ⓑ 14 boxes

Ⓒ 7 boxes

Ⓓ 2 boxes

20. There are 5 balloons in each bag. Terry buys 3 bags of balloons. How many balloons does Terry buy in all?

Ⓕ 20 balloons

Ⓖ 15 balloons

Ⓗ 10 balloons

Ⓙ 5 balloons

STOP

Read each question carefully. Write or circle your answer in the space provided.

Write the fraction for the shaded part?

1.

_____

2.

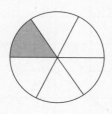

_____

3. Compare.
Write >, <, or =.

$\frac{2}{3}$ ◯ $\frac{2}{4}$

4. Which shows $\frac{1}{4}$ shaded?
Circle the figure.

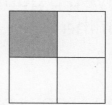 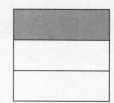

Use the picture for items 5–6.

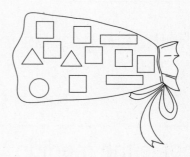

5. Which is the most likely to be picked?

_____

GO ON

6. Which is the least likely to be picked?

_____

Use the information to answer questions 7–9.

Darryl went played 5 games of darts and got the following scores:

97, 101, 104, 109, 109

7. What is the range?

_____

8. What is the median?

_____

9. What is the mode?

_____

Use the graph for problems 10–11.

New York Summer Temperatures

10. At 10 A.M., what is the temperature?

_____

GO ON

11. When was the highest recorded temperature?

_____

_____

12. Divide.

18 into 4 equal groups is

_____ in each group,

_____ left over.

_____

13. Make equal groups. There are 14 crayons. There are 2 boxes. How many crayons in each box?

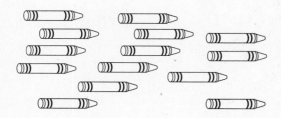

_____ crayons

14. Make equal groups. There are 3 students. There are 15 markers. How many markers for each student?

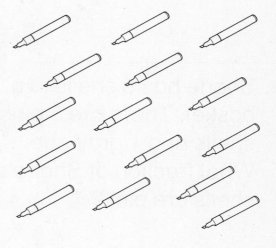

_____ markers

_____

15. $10 \times 3 =$ _____

GO ON

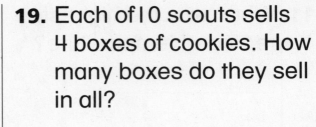

16. $\begin{array}{r} 3 \\ \times\ 5 \\ \hline \end{array}$

17. Shane has 6 shells in a basket. There are 5 pink shells and 1 gray one. What fraction of Shane's shells are pink?

_____

18. Shanelle has 8 grapes in a cup. There are 3 red grapes and 5 green ones. What fraction of Shanelle's grapes are red?

_____

19. Each of 10 scouts sells 4 boxes of cookies. How many boxes do they sell in all?

_____ boxes

20. There are 7 balloons in each bag. Derrick buys 5 bags of balloons. How many balloons does Derrick buy in all?

_____ balloons

STOP

Final Test – Monitoring Student Progress

☐ **Form A**   ☐ **Form B**

Student Name _____ Date _____

Directions: This test targets selected objectives. For each item that is answered incorrectly, cross out the item number. Then record the number of correct responses for each strand in the column labeled **Number of Correct Responses.** Add to find the **Total Number of Correct Responses** and record the total. Use this total to determine the **Total Test Score** and the **Total Percent Correct.**

Strand • Objective(s)	Item Numbers	Number of Correct Responses
Number Sense, Concepts, and Operations • Use fact families to add and subtract. • Compare and order numbers to 100. • Identify coins and their values. • Add three 2-digit numbers. • Estimate sums. • Add 3-digit numbers. • Subtract 3-digit numbers. • Identify fractional parts of a whole. • Compare fractions. • Use strategies to multiply. • Use strategies and skills to solve problems.	1, 2, 3, 4, 5, 7, 8, 9, 16, 17, 18, 19	
Measurement and Geometry • Tell and write time to 5–minute intervals. • Find elapsed time. • Measure length in customary and metric units. • Measure weight, mass, and capacity in customary and metric units. • Identify 3-dimensional figures and their attributes. • Identify 2-dimensional shapes and their attributes. • Use strategies and skills to solve problems.	6, 12, 13, 14, 15, 20	
Statistics, Data, and Probability • Read, interpret, and create graphs. • Identify range, mode, median. • Use strategies and skills to solve problems.	10, 11	
Total Number of Correct Responses		
Total Test Score		/20
Total Percent Correct		%

Read each question carefully. Darken the circle for the correct answer.

1. There are 12 people in line. Nanette is sixth. How many people are behind Nanette?

(A) 7   (C) 5

(B) 6   (D) 4

2. Estimate 48 + 33.

(F) 60

(G) 80

(H) 90

(J) 100

3. Which does not belong to the fact family?

(A) 9 + 8 = 17

(B) 17 − 10 = 7

(C) 17 − 9 = 8

(D) 8 + 9 = 17

4. Compare.

65 ◯ 57

(F) <   (G) >   (H) =

5. How much money is shown?

(A) 63¢   (C) 75¢

(B) 66¢   (D) 90¢

6. What time does the clock show?

(F) 4:07   (H) 5:07

(G) 4:35   (J) 5:35

GO ON ➡

7. What part is shaded?

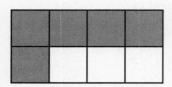

(A) $\frac{5}{6}$ (C) $\frac{3}{6}$

(B) $\frac{5}{8}$ (D) $\frac{3}{8}$

8.   253
      + 325

(F) 478   (H) 578

(G) 568   (J) 678

9.   788
      − 617

(A) 161   (C) 181

(B) 171   (D) 271

Anna's class collected pet food for the animal shelter. Use the pictograph to answer items 10–11.

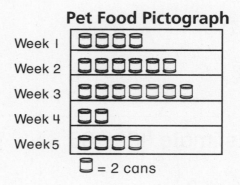

Pet Food Pictograph

$\square$ = 2 cans

10. How many more cans were collected in week 3 than in week 4?

(F) 4 cans   (H) 8 cans

(G) 5 cans   (J) 10 cans

11. What is the mode of the number of cans collected each week?

(A) 5 cans   (C) 10 cans

(B) 8 cans   (D) 14 cans

GO ON

12. Name the 3-dimensional figure.

- Ⓕ cylinder
- Ⓖ cone
- Ⓗ cube
- Ⓙ rectangular prism

13. How much time has passed?

- Ⓐ 4 hours
- Ⓒ 6 hours
- Ⓑ 5 hours
- Ⓓ 7 hours

14. Find the length in inches.

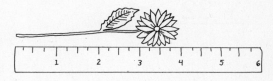

- Ⓕ 4
- Ⓗ 2
- Ⓖ 3
- Ⓙ 1

15. Which shape has 5 sides?

- Ⓐ pentagon
- Ⓑ square
- Ⓒ triangle
- Ⓓ parallelogram

GO ON

16.
$$\begin{array}{r} 37 \\ 24 \\ +\ 32 \\ \hline \end{array}$$

   (F) 103   (H) 83

   (G) 93   (J) 73

17. Compare.

$\dfrac{1}{3}$ ◯ $\dfrac{1}{4}$

   (A) <

   (B) >

   (C) =

18. There are 3 cookies in each pack. Sasha has 5 packs. How many cookies does Sasha have?

   (F) 16 cookies

   (G) 15 cookies

   (H) 8 cookies

   (J) 2 cookies

19. Make equal groups. You have 20 boxes. You can put 4 boxes in each wagon. How many wagons do you need?

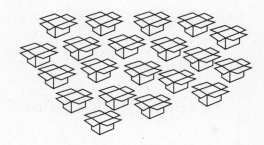

   (A) 80 wagons

   (B) 16 wagons

   (C) 5 wagons

   (D) 4 wagons

20. How many pints are in a quart?

   (F) 1 pint

   (G) 2 pints

   (H) 3 pints

   (J) 4 pints

STOP

Read each question carefully. Write your answer in the space provided.

1. Neil is seventh in line. How many people are in front of him?

_____ people

2. Estimate

37 + 22

_____

3. What subtraction fact is related to 7 + 6 = 13?

_____

4. Compare. Write <, > , or = .

42  53

5. How much money is shown?

_____ ¢

6. What time does the clock show?

_____

GO ON

7. What part is shaded?

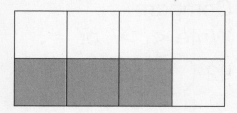

_____

8. 128
    + 311

_____

9. 824
    − 303

Anna's class collected pet food for the animal shelter. Use the pictograph to answer items 10–11.

Pet Food Pictograph

Week 1

Week 2

Week 3

Week 4

🥫 = 2 cans

10. How many more cans were collected in week 2 than in week 1?

_____ cans

11. What is the range of the number of cans collected each week?

_____ cans

© Macmillan/McGraw-Hill

GO ON ▶

12. Name the 3-dimensional figure?

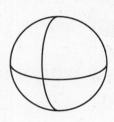

_____

13. How much time has passed?

_____ hours

14. Find the length in inches.

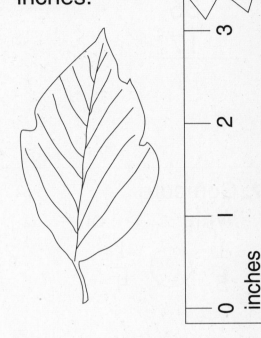

_____ inches

15. Which shape has 3 sides?

_____

GO ON

16.   42
     36
   + 17
   _____

17. Compare.
Write <, >, or = .

$\dfrac{1}{5}$ ◯ $\dfrac{1}{4}$

18. There are 4 brownies in each pack. Steve has 5 packs. How many brownies does Steve have?

_____

19. Make equal groups. You have 15 boxes. You can put 5 boxes in each wagon.

How many wagons do you need?

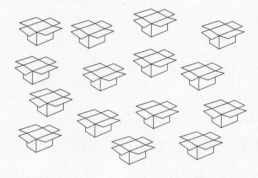

_____ wagons

20. How many cups are in a quart?

_____ cups

STOP

Inventory

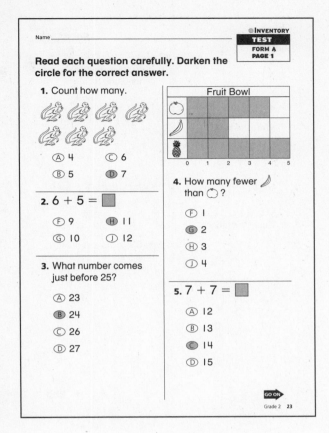

Read each question carefully. Darken the circle for the correct answer.

1. Count how many.

- Ⓐ 4
- Ⓒ 6
- Ⓑ 5
- Ⓓ 7

2. $6 + 5 = \boxed{}$

- Ⓕ 9
- Ⓗ 11
- Ⓖ 10
- Ⓙ 12

3. What number comes just before 25?

- Ⓐ 23
- Ⓑ 24
- Ⓒ 26
- Ⓓ 27

Fruit Bowl

4. How many fewer 🍌 than 🍎?

- Ⓕ 1
- Ⓖ 2
- Ⓗ 3
- Ⓙ 4

5. $7 + 7 = \boxed{}$

- Ⓐ 12
- Ⓑ 13
- Ⓒ 14
- Ⓓ 15

GO ON

Grade 2 **23**

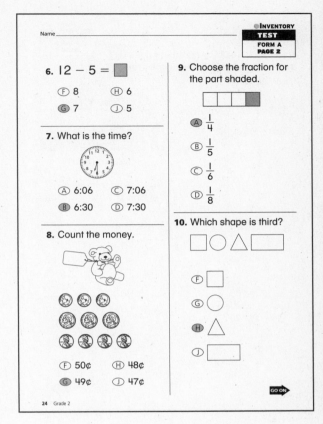

6. $12 - 5 = \boxed{}$

- Ⓕ 8
- Ⓗ 6
- Ⓖ 7
- Ⓙ 5

7. What is the time?

- Ⓐ 6:06
- Ⓒ 7:06
- Ⓑ 6:30
- Ⓓ 7:30

8. Count the money.

- Ⓕ 50¢
- Ⓗ 48¢
- Ⓖ 49¢
- Ⓙ 47¢

9. Choose the fraction for the part shaded.

- Ⓐ $\frac{1}{4}$
- Ⓑ $\frac{1}{5}$
- Ⓒ $\frac{1}{6}$
- Ⓓ $\frac{1}{8}$

10. Which shape is third?

- Ⓕ ▢
- Ⓖ ◯
- Ⓗ △
- Ⓙ ▭

GO ON

24 Grade 2

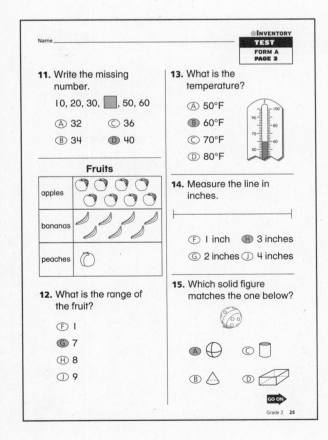

11. Write the missing number.

10, 20, 30, ▢, 50, 60

- Ⓐ 32
- Ⓒ 36
- Ⓑ 34
- Ⓓ 40

Fruits

apples	🍎🍎🍎🍎🍎🍎🍎🍎
bananas	🍌🍌🍌🍌🍌
peaches	🍑

12. What is the range of the fruit?

- Ⓕ 1
- Ⓖ 7
- Ⓗ 8
- Ⓙ 9

13. What is the temperature?

- Ⓐ 50°F
- Ⓑ 60°F
- Ⓒ 70°F
- Ⓓ 80°F

14. Measure the line in inches.

- Ⓕ 1 inch
- Ⓗ 3 inches
- Ⓖ 2 inches
- Ⓙ 4 inches

15. Which solid figure matches the one below?

- Ⓐ
- Ⓒ
- Ⓑ
- Ⓓ

GO ON

Grade 2 **25**

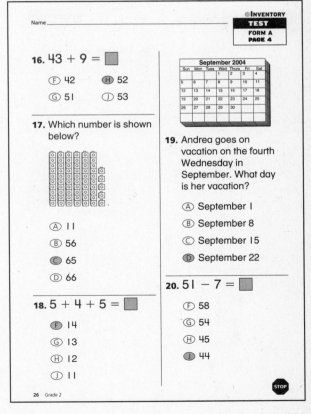

16. $43 + 9 = \boxed{}$

- Ⓕ 42
- Ⓗ 52
- Ⓖ 51
- Ⓙ 53

17. Which number is shown below?

- Ⓐ 11
- Ⓑ 56
- Ⓒ 65
- Ⓓ 66

18. $5 + 4 + 5 = \boxed{}$

- Ⓕ 14
- Ⓖ 13
- Ⓗ 12
- Ⓙ 11

September 2004

19. Andrea goes on vacation on the fourth Wednesday in September. What day is her vacation?

- Ⓐ September 1
- Ⓑ September 8
- Ⓒ September 15
- Ⓓ September 22

20. $51 - 7 = \boxed{}$

- Ⓕ 58
- Ⓖ 54
- Ⓗ 45
- Ⓙ 44

STOP

26 Grade 2

Inventory

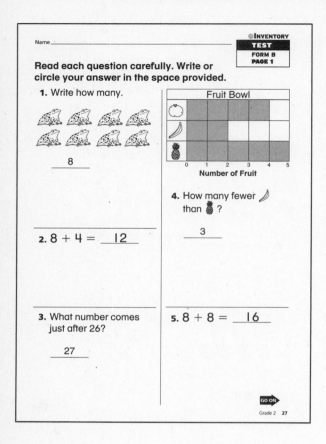

Read each question carefully. Write or circle your answer in the space provided.

1. Write how many.

8

Fruit Bowl

Number of Fruit

4. How many fewer 🍌 than 🍍 ?

3

2. $8 + 4 = \underline{12}$

5. $8 + 8 = \underline{16}$

3. What number comes just after 26?

27

GO ON
Grade 2   27

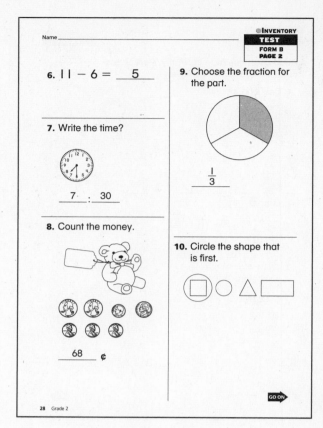

6. $11 - 6 = \underline{5}$

7. Write the time?

$\underline{7}$: $\underline{30}$

8. Count the money.

$\underline{68}$ ¢

9. Choose the fraction for the part.

$\dfrac{1}{3}$

10. Circle the shape that is first.

28   Grade 2

GO ON

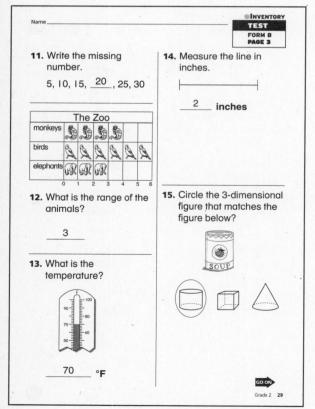

11. Write the missing number.

5, 10, 15, $\underline{20}$, 25, 30

The Zoo

monkeys

birds

elephants

12. What is the range of the animals?

3

13. What is the temperature?

$\underline{70}$ °F

14. Measure the line in inches.

$\underline{2}$ **inches**

15. Circle the 3-dimensional figure that matches the figure below?

GO ON
Grade 2   29

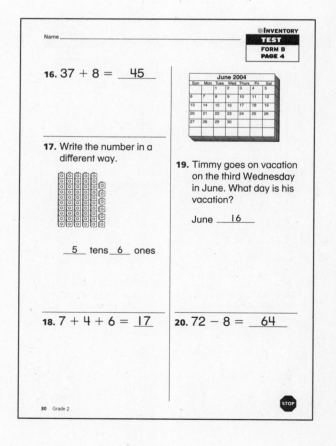

16. $37 + 8 = \underline{45}$

June 2004

Sun	Mon	Tues	Wed	Thurs	Fri	Sat
		1	2	3	4	5
6	7	8	9	10	11	12
13	14	15	16	17	18	19
20	21	22	23	24	25	26
27	28	29	30			

17. Write the number in a different way.

$\underline{5}$ tens $\underline{6}$ ones

19. Timmy goes on vacation on the third Wednesday in June. What day is his vacation?

June $\underline{16}$

18. $7 + 4 + 6 = \underline{17}$

20. $72 - 8 = \underline{64}$

30   Grade 2

STOP

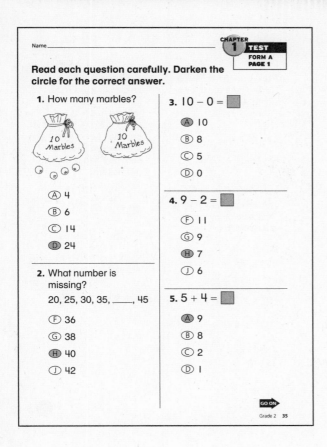

Chapter 1

Name _____

Read each question carefully. Darken the circle for the correct answer.

1. How many marbles?

10 Marbles   10 Marbles

- Ⓐ 4
- Ⓑ 6
- Ⓒ 14
- Ⓓ 24

2. What number is missing?

20, 25, 30, 35, _____, 45

- Ⓕ 36
- Ⓖ 38
- Ⓗ 40
- Ⓙ 42

3. $10 - 0 = \blacksquare$

- Ⓐ 10
- Ⓑ 8
- Ⓒ 5
- Ⓓ 0

4. $9 - 2 = \blacksquare$

- Ⓕ 11
- Ⓖ 9
- Ⓗ 7
- Ⓙ 6

5. $5 + 4 = \blacksquare$

- Ⓐ 9
- Ⓑ 8
- Ⓒ 2
- Ⓓ 1

GO ON

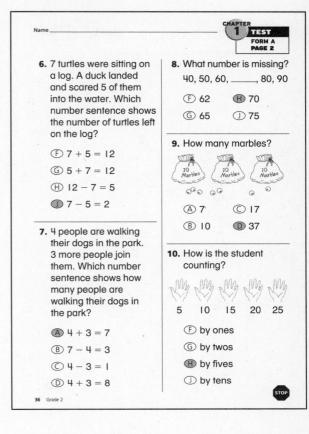

Name _____

6. 7 turtles were sitting on a log. A duck landed and scared 5 of them into the water. Which number sentence shows the number of turtles left on the log?

- Ⓕ $7 + 5 = 12$
- Ⓖ $5 + 7 = 12$
- Ⓗ $12 - 7 = 5$
- Ⓙ $7 - 5 = 2$

7. 4 people are walking their dogs in the park. 3 more people join them. Which number sentence shows how many people are walking their dogs in the park?

- Ⓐ $4 + 3 = 7$
- Ⓑ $7 - 4 = 3$
- Ⓒ $4 - 3 = 1$
- Ⓓ $4 + 3 = 8$

8. What number is missing?

40, 50, 60, _____, 80, 90

- Ⓕ 62
- Ⓖ 65
- Ⓗ 70
- Ⓙ 75

9. How many marbles?

10 Marbles   10 Marbles   10 Marbles

- Ⓐ 7
- Ⓑ 10
- Ⓒ 17
- Ⓓ 37

10. How is the student counting?

5   10   15   20   25

- Ⓕ by ones
- Ⓖ by twos
- Ⓗ by fives
- Ⓙ by tens

STOP

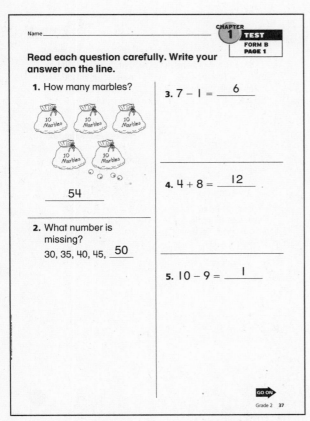

Name _____

Read each question carefully. Write your answer on the line.

1. How many marbles?

10 Marbles   10 Marbles   10 Marbles
10 Marbles   10 Marbles

54

2. What number is missing?

30, 35, 40, 45, __50__

3. $7 - 1 =$ __6__

_____

4. $4 + 8 =$ __12__

_____

5. $10 - 9 =$ __1__

GO ON

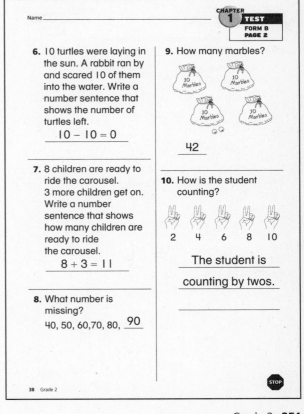

Name _____

6. 10 turtles were laying in the sun. A rabbit ran by and scared 10 of them into the water. Write a number sentence that shows the number of turtles left.

__$10 - 10 = 0$__

7. 8 children are ready to ride the carousel. 3 more children get on. Write a number sentence that shows how many children are ready to ride the carousel.

__$8 + 3 = 11$__

8. What number is missing?

40, 50, 60, 70, 80, __90__

9. How many marbles?

10 Marbles   10 Marbles
10 Marbles   10 Marbles

42

10. How is the student counting?

2   4   6   8   10

The student is counting by twos.

STOP

Chapter 2

Chapter 2

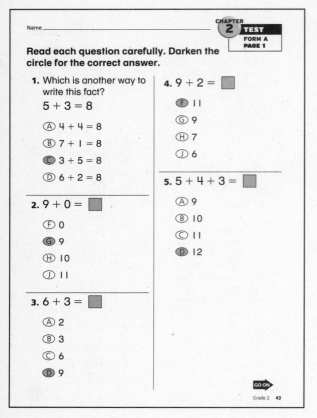

Name _____

CHAPTER 2 TEST
FORM A
PAGE 1

Read each question carefully. Darken the circle for the correct answer.

1. Which is another way to write this fact?

$5 + 3 = 8$

- Ⓐ $4 + 4 = 8$
- Ⓑ $7 + 1 = 8$
- Ⓒ $3 + 5 = 8$
- Ⓓ $6 + 2 = 8$

2. $9 + 0 = \square$

- Ⓕ 0
- Ⓖ 9
- Ⓗ 10
- Ⓙ 11

3. $6 + 3 = \square$

- Ⓐ 2
- Ⓑ 3
- Ⓒ 6
- Ⓓ 9

4. $9 + 2 = \square$

- Ⓕ 11
- Ⓖ 9
- Ⓗ 7
- Ⓙ 6

5. $5 + 4 + 3 = \square$

- Ⓐ 9
- Ⓑ 10
- Ⓒ 11
- Ⓓ 12

GO ON
Grade 2 43

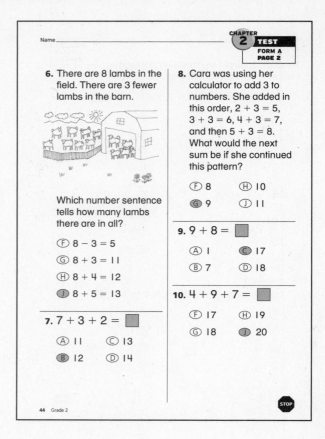

Name _____

CHAPTER 2 TEST
FORM A
PAGE 2

6. There are 8 lambs in the field. There are 3 fewer lambs in the barn.

Which number sentence tells how many lambs there are in all?

- Ⓕ $8 - 3 = 5$
- Ⓖ $8 + 3 = 11$
- Ⓗ $8 + 4 = 12$
- Ⓙ $8 + 5 = 13$

7. $7 + 3 + 2 = \square$

- Ⓐ 11
- Ⓑ 12
- Ⓒ 13
- Ⓓ 14

8. Cara was using her calculator to add 3 to numbers. She added in this order, $2 + 3 = 5$, $3 + 3 = 6$, $4 + 3 = 7$, and then $5 + 3 = 8$. What would the next sum be if she continued this pattern?

- Ⓕ 8
- Ⓖ 9
- Ⓗ 10
- Ⓙ 11

9. $9 + 8 = \square$

- Ⓐ 1
- Ⓑ 7
- Ⓒ 17
- Ⓓ 18

10. $4 + 9 + 7 = \square$

- Ⓕ 17
- Ⓖ 18
- Ⓗ 19
- Ⓙ 20

STOP
44 Grade 2

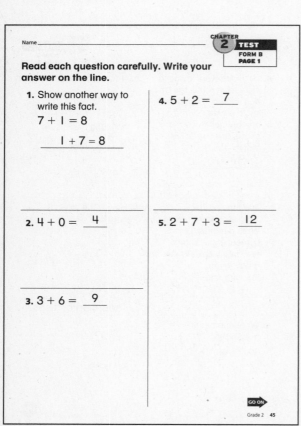

Name _____

CHAPTER 2 TEST
FORM B
PAGE 1

Read each question carefully. Write your answer on the line.

1. Show another way to write this fact.

$7 + 1 = 8$

$1 + 7 = 8$

2. $4 + 0 = \underline{4}$

3. $3 + 6 = \underline{9}$

4. $5 + 2 = \underline{7}$

5. $2 + 7 + 3 = \underline{12}$

GO ON
Grade 2 45

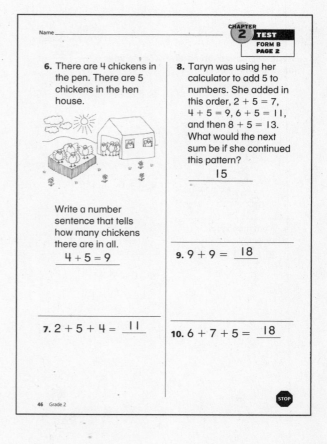

Name _____

CHAPTER 2 TEST
FORM B
PAGE 2

6. There are 4 chickens in the pen. There are 5 chickens in the hen house.

Write a number sentence that tells how many chickens there are in all.

$4 + 5 = 9$

7. $2 + 5 + 4 = \underline{11}$

8. Taryn was using her calculator to add 5 to numbers. She added in this order, $2 + 5 = 7$, $4 + 5 = 9$, $6 + 5 = 11$, and then $8 + 5 = 13$. What would the next sum be if she continued this pattern?

$\underline{15}$

9. $9 + 9 = \underline{18}$

10. $6 + 7 + 5 = \underline{18}$

STOP
46 Grade 2

Chapter 3

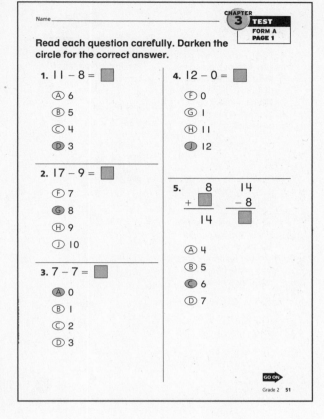

Name _____

Read each question carefully. Darken the circle for the correct answer.

1. $11 - 8 =$ ☐
   - Ⓐ 6
   - Ⓑ 5
   - Ⓒ 4
   - Ⓓ 3

2. $17 - 9 =$ ☐
   - Ⓕ 7
   - Ⓖ 8
   - Ⓗ 9
   - Ⓙ 10

3. $7 - 7 =$ ☐
   - Ⓐ 0
   - Ⓑ 1
   - Ⓒ 2
   - Ⓓ 3

4. $12 - 0 =$ ☐
   - Ⓕ 0
   - Ⓖ 1
   - Ⓗ 11
   - Ⓙ 12

5.
   $$\begin{array}{r} 8 \\ +\ ☐ \\ \hline 14 \end{array} \qquad \begin{array}{r} 14 \\ -\ 8 \\ \hline ☐ \end{array}$$
   - Ⓐ 4
   - Ⓑ 5
   - Ⓒ 6
   - Ⓓ 7

GO ON ▸

Grade 2 **51**

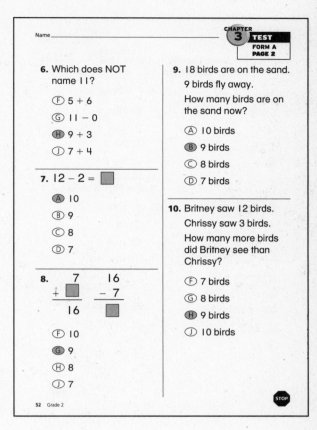

Name _____

6. Which does NOT name 11?
   - Ⓕ $5 + 6$
   - Ⓖ $11 - 0$
   - Ⓗ $9 + 3$
   - Ⓙ $7 + 4$

7. $12 - 2 =$ ☐
   - Ⓐ 10
   - Ⓑ 9
   - Ⓒ 8
   - Ⓓ 7

8.
   $$\begin{array}{r} 7 \\ +\ ☐ \\ \hline 16 \end{array} \qquad \begin{array}{r} 16 \\ -\ 7 \\ \hline ☐ \end{array}$$
   - Ⓕ 10
   - Ⓖ 9
   - Ⓗ 8
   - Ⓙ 7

9. 18 birds are on the sand.
   9 birds fly away.
   How many birds are on the sand now?
   - Ⓐ 10 birds
   - Ⓑ 9 birds
   - Ⓒ 8 birds
   - Ⓓ 7 birds

10. Britney saw 12 birds.
    Chrissy saw 3 birds.
    How many more birds did Britney see than Chrissy?
    - Ⓕ 7 birds
    - Ⓖ 8 birds
    - Ⓗ 9 birds
    - Ⓙ 10 birds

STOP

52 Grade 2

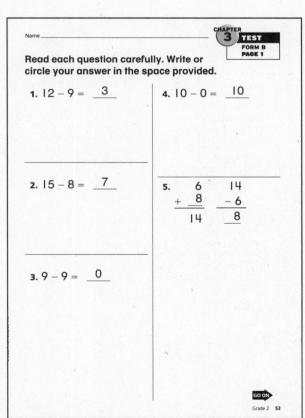

Name _____

Read each question carefully. Write or circle your answer in the space provided.

1. $12 - 9 =$ ___3___

2. $15 - 8 =$ ___7___

3. $9 - 9 =$ ___0___

4. $10 - 0 =$ ___10___

5.
   $$\begin{array}{r} 6 \\ +\ 8 \\ \hline 14 \end{array} \qquad \begin{array}{r} 14 \\ -\ 6 \\ \hline 8 \end{array}$$

GO ON ▸

Grade 2 **53**

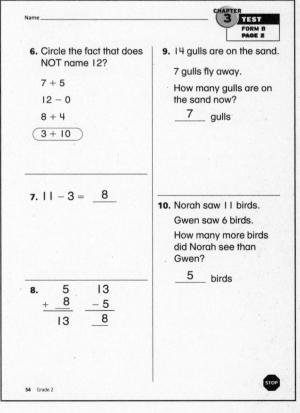

Name _____

6. Circle the fact that does NOT name 12?

   $7 + 5$

   $12 - 0$

   $8 + 4$

   (3 + 10)

7. $11 - 3 =$ ___8___

8.
   $$\begin{array}{r} 5 \\ +\ 8 \\ \hline 13 \end{array} \qquad \begin{array}{r} 13 \\ -\ 5 \\ \hline 8 \end{array}$$

9. 14 gulls are on the sand.
   7 gulls fly away.
   How many gulls are on the sand now?
   ___7___ gulls

10. Norah saw 11 birds.
    Gwen saw 6 birds.
    How many more birds did Norah see than Gwen?
    ___5___ birds

STOP

54 Grade 2

Chapter 4

Name _____

Read each question carefully. Darken the circle for the correct answer.

1. 10 − 5 =

- Ⓐ 15
- Ⓑ 10
- Ⓒ 6
- Ⓓ 5

2. What number sentence is missing from this fact family?

6 + 7 = 13   13 − 7 = 6
7 + 6 = 13

- Ⓕ 7 − 6 = 1
- Ⓖ 6 + 13 = 19
- Ⓗ 13 − 6 = 7
- Ⓙ 13 + 7 = 20

3. 9 + 2 is the same as:

- Ⓐ 10 + 1
- Ⓑ 10 + 2
- Ⓒ 9 + 3
- Ⓓ 9 + 2

4. 9 + 7 is the same as:

- Ⓕ 10 + 2
- Ⓖ 10 + 4
- Ⓗ 10 + 6
- Ⓙ 10 + 7

5. 8 + 4 is the same as:

- Ⓐ 10 + 1
- Ⓑ 10 + 2
- Ⓒ 10 + 3
- Ⓓ 10 + 4

GO ON

Name _____

6. 7 frogs were sitting on a log. A turtle jumped into the pond and scared 4 of them into the water. Which number sentence shows the number of turtles left on the log?

- Ⓕ 7 + 4 = 11
- Ⓖ 4 + 7 = 11
- Ⓗ 11 − 7 = 4
- Ⓙ 7 − 4 = 3

7. 4 people are riding their bikes. 6 more people join them. Which number sentence shows how many people are riding their bikes?

- Ⓐ 4 + 6 = 10
- Ⓑ 10 − 4 = 6
- Ⓒ 6 − 4 = 2
- Ⓓ 4 + 6 = 9

8. What number sentence is missing from this fact family?

4 + 8 = 12
8 + 4 = 12
12 − 8 = 4

- Ⓕ 8 − 4 = 4
- Ⓖ 4 + 12 = 16
- Ⓗ 12 − 4 = 8
- Ⓙ 12 + 8 = 20

9. 7 + 4 =

- Ⓐ 3   Ⓒ 11
- Ⓑ 4   Ⓓ 12

10. 9 + 3 = ▢

- Ⓕ 6   Ⓗ 12
- Ⓖ 9   Ⓙ 13

STOP

Name _____

Read each question carefully. Write your answer on the line.

1. 8 − 5 = ___3___

2. What number sentence is missing from this fact family?

2 + 6 = 8
6 + 2 = 8
8 − 6 = 2

___8 − 6 = 2___

3. 9 + 4 is the same as:

10 + ___3___

4. 9 + 8 is the same as:

10 + ___7___

5. 7 + 4 is the same as:

10 + ___1___

GO ON

Name _____

6. 2 boys were playing hockey. 8 other children joined them. Write a number sentence that shows how many children are playing hockey.

___2 + 8 = 10___

7. 6 girls are playing soccer. 3 had to go home to have dinner. Write a number sentence to show how many girls are still playing soccer.

___6 − 3 = 3___

8. What number sentence is missing from this fact family?

4 + 3 = 7
3 + 4 = 7
7 − 3 = 4

___7 − 4 = 3___

9. 7 + 6 = ___13___

10. 9 + 8 = ___17___

STOP

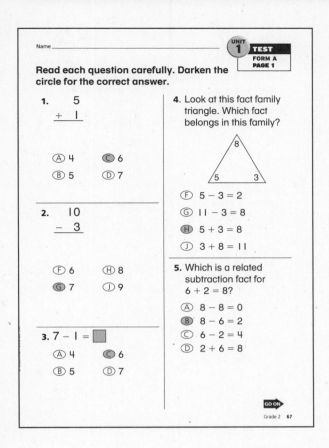

Name_____

Read each question carefully. Darken the circle for the correct answer.

1.
```
    5
  + 1
```
Ⓐ 4   Ⓒ 6
Ⓑ 5   Ⓓ 7

2.
```
   10
  - 3
```
Ⓕ 6   Ⓗ 8
Ⓖ 7   Ⓙ 9

3. $7 - 1 = \square$
Ⓐ 4   Ⓒ 6
Ⓑ 5   Ⓓ 7

4. Look at this fact family triangle. Which fact belongs in this family?

(triangle with 8 at top, 5 and 3 at bottom)

Ⓕ $5 - 3 = 2$
Ⓖ $11 - 3 = 8$
Ⓗ $5 + 3 = 8$
Ⓙ $3 + 8 = 11$

5. Which is a related subtraction fact for $6 + 2 = 8$?
Ⓐ $8 - 8 = 0$
Ⓑ $8 - 6 = 2$
Ⓒ $6 - 2 = 4$
Ⓓ $2 + 6 = 8$

GO ON
Grade 2   67

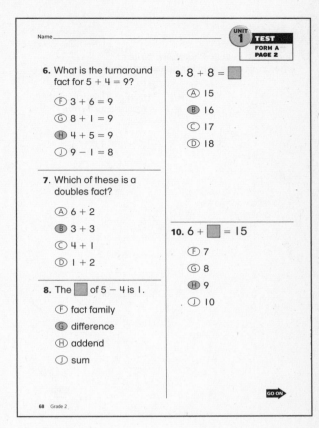

Name_____

6. What is the turnaround fact for $5 + 4 = 9$?
Ⓕ $3 + 6 = 9$
Ⓖ $8 + 1 = 9$
Ⓗ $4 + 5 = 9$
Ⓙ $9 - 1 = 8$

7. Which of these is a doubles fact?
Ⓐ $6 + 2$
Ⓑ $3 + 3$
Ⓒ $4 + 1$
Ⓓ $1 + 2$

8. The $\square$ of $5 - 4$ is 1.
Ⓕ fact family
Ⓖ difference
Ⓗ addend
Ⓙ sum

9. $8 + 8 = \square$
Ⓐ 15
Ⓑ 16
Ⓒ 17
Ⓓ 18

10. $6 + \square = 15$
Ⓕ 7
Ⓖ 8
Ⓗ 9
Ⓙ 10

GO ON
68   Grade 2

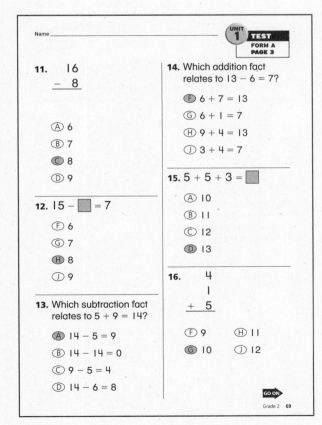

Name_____

11.
```
   16
  - 8
```
Ⓐ 6
Ⓑ 7
Ⓒ 8
Ⓓ 9

12. $15 - \square = 7$
Ⓕ 6
Ⓖ 7
Ⓗ 8
Ⓙ 9

13. Which subtraction fact relates to $5 + 9 = 14$?
Ⓐ $14 - 5 = 9$
Ⓑ $14 - 14 = 0$
Ⓒ $9 - 5 = 4$
Ⓓ $14 - 6 = 8$

14. Which addition fact relates to $13 - 6 = 7$?
Ⓕ $6 + 7 = 13$
Ⓖ $6 + 1 = 7$
Ⓗ $9 + 4 = 13$
Ⓙ $3 + 4 = 7$

15. $5 + 5 + 3 = \square$
Ⓐ 10
Ⓑ 11
Ⓒ 12
Ⓓ 13

16.
```
   4
   1
 + 5
```
Ⓕ 9   Ⓗ 11
Ⓖ 10   Ⓙ 12

GO ON
Grade 2   69

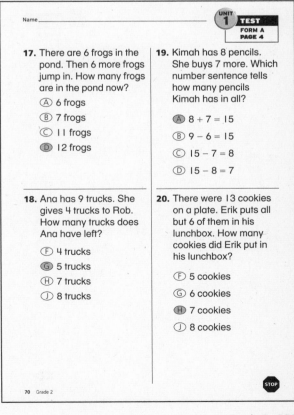

Name_____

17. There are 6 frogs in the pond. Then 6 more frogs jump in. How many frogs are in the pond now?
Ⓐ 6 frogs
Ⓑ 7 frogs
Ⓒ 11 frogs
Ⓓ 12 frogs

18. Ana has 9 trucks. She gives 4 trucks to Rob. How many trucks does Ana have left?
Ⓕ 4 trucks
Ⓖ 5 trucks
Ⓗ 7 trucks
Ⓙ 8 trucks

19. Kimah has 8 pencils. She buys 7 more. Which number sentence tells how many pencils Kimah has in all?
Ⓐ $8 + 7 = 15$
Ⓑ $9 - 6 = 15$
Ⓒ $15 - 7 = 8$
Ⓓ $15 - 8 = 7$

20. There were 13 cookies on a plate. Erik puts all but 6 of them in his lunchbox. How many cookies did Erik put in his lunchbox?
Ⓕ 5 cookies
Ⓖ 6 cookies
Ⓗ 7 cookies
Ⓙ 8 cookies

STOP
70   Grade 2

Name _____

Read each question carefully. Write or circle your answer in the space provided.

1.   4
    + 5
    ___
     9

2.   12
    − 2
    ___
    10

3.   12
    − 6
    ___
     6

4. Look at this fact family triangle. Circle the fact that belongs in this family.

3 + 3 = 6
(6 + 3 = 9)
5 + 4 = 9
6 + 6 = 12

5. Circle the related subtraction fact for 5 + 7 = 12.

7 − 5 = 2
2 + 5 = 7
7 + 5 = 12
(12 − 7 = 5)

GO ON

Name _____

6. What is the turnaround fact for 1 + 3 = 4?

3 + 1 = 4

7. Which of these is a doubles fact? Circle the answer.

7 + 1
8 + 4
(4 + 4)
9 + 3

8. Complete the sentence using one of the following: *fact family, difference, addend, sum.*

The ___sum___ of 4 + 1 is 5.

9. 9 + 6 = ___15___

10. 4 + ___8___ = 12

GO ON

Name _____

11.   14
    − 7
    ___
     7

12. 14 − ___6___ = 8

13. What is the subtraction fact that relates to 6 + 7 = 13?

13 − 7 = 6

14. What is the addition fact that relates to 16 − 7 = 9?

9 + 7 = 16

15. 6 + 3 + 4 = ___13___

16.   3
     5
    + 2
    ___
    10

GO ON

Name _____

17. There are 9 frogs in the pond. Then 2 more frogs hop in. How many frogs are in the pond?

___11___ frogs

18. Miguel has 11 fish. He gave 7 fish to his friends. How many fish does Miguel have left?

___4___ fish

19. Janell has 6 pencils. She buys 7 more. Which number sentence tells how many pencils Janell has in all?

(6 + 7 = 13)
9 − 6 = 15
15 − 7 = 8
15 − 8 = 7

20. There were 11 cookies on a plate. Michael puts all but 6 of them in his lunchbox. How many cookies did Michael put in his lunchbox?

___5___ cookies

STOP

Chapter 5

Name _____

CHAPTER **5** **TEST**
FORM A
PAGE 1

Read each question carefully.
Darken the circle for the correct answer.

1. What is another name for 50 ones?

   Ⓐ 50 tens   Ⓒ 10 ones

   Ⓑ 5 tens   Ⓓ 1 ten

2. What is another name for 7 tens?

   Ⓕ 710   Ⓗ 70

   Ⓖ 700   Ⓙ 7

3. How many tens and ones are these?

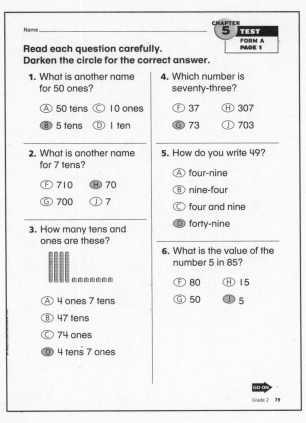

   Ⓐ 4 ones 7 tens

   Ⓑ 47 tens

   Ⓒ 74 ones

   Ⓓ 4 tens 7 ones

4. Which number is seventy-three?

   Ⓕ 37   Ⓗ 307

   Ⓖ 73   Ⓙ 703

5. How do you write 49?

   Ⓐ four-nine

   Ⓑ nine-four

   Ⓒ four and nine

   Ⓓ forty-nine

6. What is the value of the number 5 in 85?

   Ⓕ 80   Ⓗ 15

   Ⓖ 50   Ⓙ 5

GO ON

Grade 2 **79**

Name _____

CHAPTER **5** **TEST**
FORM A
PAGE 2

7. There are 10 beans in the smaller jar.

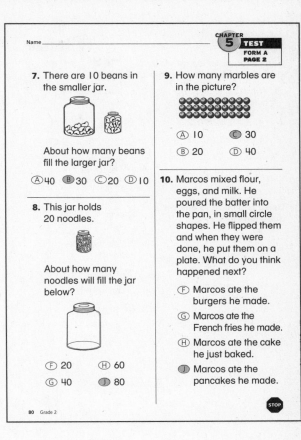

About how many beans fill the larger jar?

Ⓐ 40 Ⓑ 30 Ⓒ 20 Ⓓ 10

8. This jar holds 20 noodles.

About how many noodles will fill the jar below?

Ⓕ 20   Ⓗ 60

Ⓖ 40   Ⓙ 80

9. How many marbles are in the picture?

Ⓐ 10   Ⓒ 30

Ⓑ 20   Ⓓ 40

10. Marcos mixed flour, eggs, and milk. He poured the batter into the pan, in small circle shapes. He flipped them and when they were done, he put them on a plate. What do you think happened next?

   Ⓕ Marcos ate the burgers he made.

   Ⓖ Marcos ate the French fries he made.

   Ⓗ Marcos ate the cake he just baked.

   Ⓙ Marcos ate the pancakes he made.

STOP

80 Grade 2

Name _____

CHAPTER **5** **TEST**
FORM B
PAGE 1

Read each question carefully. Write your answer on the line.

1. Write another way to show 7 tens.

   70

2. What is another name for 40 ones?

   4 tens

3. How many tens and ones are these?

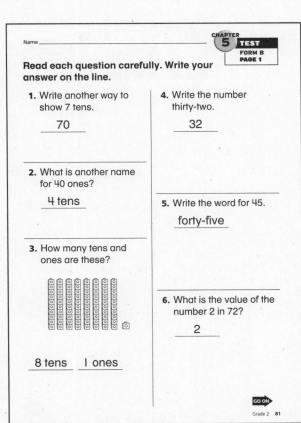

   8 tens   1 ones

4. Write the number thirty-two.

   32

5. Write the word for 45.

   forty-five

6. What is the value of the number 2 in 72?

   2

GO ON

Grade 2 **81**

Name _____

CHAPTER **5** **TEST**
FORM B
PAGE 2

7. There are 15 beans in the smaller jar.

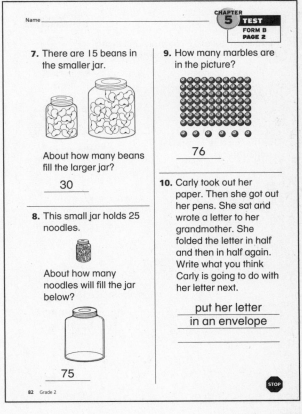

About how many beans fill the larger jar?

   30

8. This small jar holds 25 noodles.

About how many noodles will fill the jar below?

   75

9. How many marbles are in the picture?

   76

10. Carly took out her paper. Then she got out her pens. She sat and wrote a letter to her grandmother. She folded the letter in half and then in half again. Write what you think Carly is going to do with her letter next.

   put her letter
   in an envelope

STOP

82 Grade 2

Chapter 6

Form A, Page 1

Name _____

Read each question carefully.
Darken the circle for the correct answer.

1. Which set shows skip-counting by 5's?

Ⓐ 5, 10, 12, 20, 25

Ⓑ 5, 9, 15, 20, 23

Ⓒ 5, 10, 15, 20, 25

Ⓓ 5, 10, 15, 20, 24

Use this picture to answer questions 2–3.

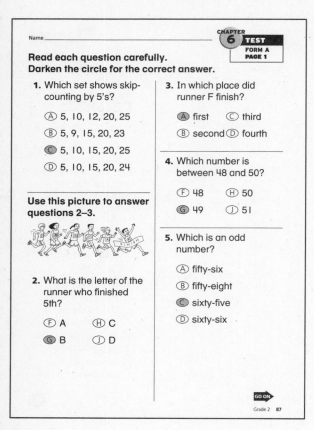

2. What is the letter of the runner who finished 5th?

Ⓕ A   Ⓗ C

Ⓖ B   Ⓙ D

3. In which place did runner F finish?

Ⓐ first   Ⓒ third

Ⓑ second   Ⓓ fourth

4. Which number is between 48 and 50?

Ⓕ 48   Ⓗ 50

Ⓖ 49   Ⓙ 51

5. Which is an odd number?

Ⓐ fifty-six

Ⓑ fifty-eight

Ⓒ sixty-five

Ⓓ sixty-six

GO ON

Grade 2   87

Name _____

6. David sits behind John. John sits behind Mark. Isaac sits in front of Mark. Who sits in the front?

Ⓕ David

Ⓖ Isaac

Ⓗ John

Ⓙ Mark

7. The square is in front of the triangle. The circle is in front of the square. The rectangle is behind the triangle. Which shape is last in the row?

Ⓐ circle

Ⓑ rectangle

Ⓒ square

Ⓓ triangle

8. Which shows a group of even numbers?

Ⓕ 22, 24, 68, 77

Ⓖ 33, 34, 38, 90

Ⓗ 54, 56, 80, 98

Ⓙ 72, 88, 94, 97

9. What number is missing?

74, ☐, 78, 80, 82, 84

Ⓐ 75   Ⓒ 77

Ⓑ 76   Ⓓ 79

10. What symbol makes this sentence true?

42 ◯ 42

Ⓕ >   Ⓗ =

Ⓖ <   Ⓙ +

STOP

88   Grade 2

Form B, Page 1

Name _____

Read each question carefully. Fill in the correct answer in the space provided.

1. Finish counting by 3's.

37, 40, 43, 47, 50, __53__

Use this picture to answer questions 2–3.

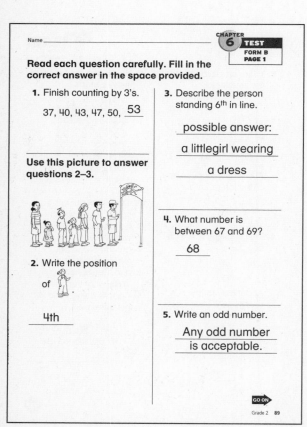

2. Write the position of 🧍

__4th__

3. Describe the person standing 6ᵗʰ in line.

possible answer:
a littlegirl wearing
a dress

4. What number is between 67 and 69?

68

5. Write an odd number.

Any odd number
is acceptable.

GO ON

Grade 2   89

Name _____

6. Max sits behind Zach. Zach sits behind Francis. Gene sits in front of Francis. Who sits in the front?

Gene

7. The frog is in front of the log. The butterfly is in front of the tulip. The tulip is behind the log. What item is in the front?

frog

8. Write 3 even numbers.

Any 3 even
numbers
are acceptable.

9. Write the missing number.

39, 42, 45, __48__, 51, 54

10. Write <, >, or = to make a true sentence.

37 < 89

STOP

90   Grade 2

Chapter 7

Read each question carefully.
Darken the circle for the correct answer.

1. What is the name of this coin?

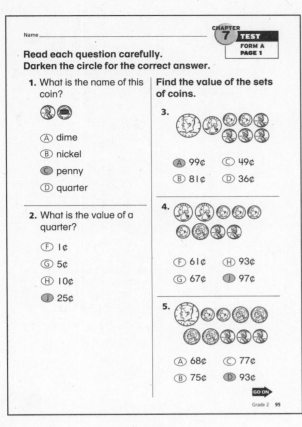

Ⓐ dime

Ⓑ nickel

Ⓒ penny

Ⓓ quarter

2. What is the value of a quarter?

Ⓕ 1¢

Ⓖ 5¢

Ⓗ 10¢

Ⓙ 25¢

Find the value of the sets of coins.

3.

Ⓐ 99¢   Ⓒ 49¢

Ⓑ 81¢   Ⓓ 36¢

4.

Ⓕ 61¢   Ⓗ 93¢

Ⓖ 67¢   Ⓙ 97¢

5.

Ⓐ 68¢   Ⓒ 77¢

Ⓑ 75¢   Ⓓ 93¢

GO ON

---

6. Which of these describes the value of a quarter?

Ⓕ 5 tens 2 ones

Ⓖ 2 tens 5 ones

Ⓗ 7 tens

Ⓙ 3 ones

7. Which is a way to show 74¢?

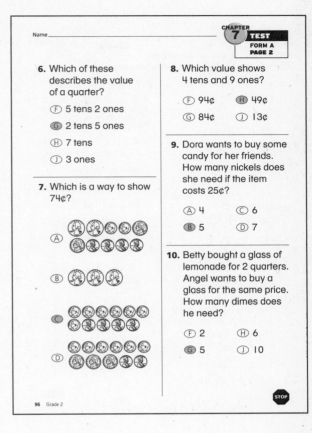

Ⓐ

Ⓑ

Ⓒ

Ⓓ

8. Which value shows 4 tens and 9 ones?

Ⓕ 94¢   Ⓗ 49¢

Ⓖ 84¢   Ⓙ 13¢

9. Dora wants to buy some candy for her friends. How many nickels does she need if the item costs 25¢?

Ⓐ 4   Ⓒ 6

Ⓑ 5   Ⓓ 7

10. Betty bought a glass of lemonade for 2 quarters. Angel wants to buy a glass for the same price. How many dimes does he need?

Ⓕ 2   Ⓗ 6

Ⓖ 5   Ⓙ 10

STOP

Read each question carefully. Fill in your answer in the space provided.

1. What is the name of this coin?

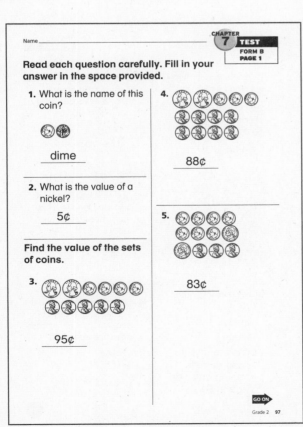

dime

2. What is the value of a nickel?

5¢

Find the value of the sets of coins.

3.

95¢

4.

88¢

5.

83¢

GO ON

---

6. Write the value of 5 tens and 8 ones?

58 ¢

7. Circle the coins to show 38¢.

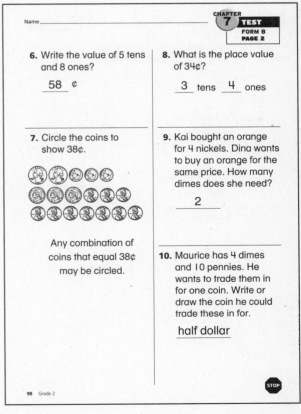

Any combination of coins that equal 38¢ may be circled.

8. What is the place value of 34¢?

3 tens 4 ones

9. Kai bought an orange for 4 nickels. Dina wants to buy an orange for the same price. How many dimes does she need?

2

10. Maurice has 4 dimes and 10 pennies. He wants to trade them in for one coin. Write or draw the coin he could trade these in for.

half dollar

STOP

© Macmillan/McGraw-Hill

Chapter 8

CHAPTER 8 TEST — FORM A, PAGE 1

Name _____

Read each question carefully.
Darken the circle for the correct answer.

1. Which of these is NOT equal to one dollar?

- Ⓐ 4 quarters
- Ⓑ 10 nickels
- Ⓒ 10 dimes
- Ⓓ 100 pennies

2. How much money does Emily have?

- Ⓕ $1.84
- Ⓗ $1.64
- Ⓖ $1.74
- Ⓙ $1.54

3. Miguel buys a flower for 59¢. He gives the clerk 75¢. How much change should he get back?

- Ⓐ 18¢
- Ⓒ 16¢
- Ⓑ 17¢
- Ⓓ 14¢

4. Anne has these coins.

Which coins does Anne need to make a dollar?

- Ⓕ 1 dime, 1 quarter
- Ⓖ 2 nickels, 2 quarters
- Ⓗ 2 quarters, 5 pennies
- Ⓙ 3 nickels, 1 quarter

5. How much money is shown?

- Ⓐ $2.92
- Ⓒ $2.72
- Ⓑ $2.82
- Ⓓ $2.52

GO ON

Grade 2 **103**

CHAPTER 8 TEST — FORM A, PAGE 2

Name _____

6. Which is greater than $1.76?

- Ⓕ
- Ⓖ
- Ⓗ
- Ⓙ

7. Which is NOT equal to $2.00?

- Ⓐ 20 dimes
- Ⓑ 4 half dollars
- Ⓒ 30 nickels
- Ⓓ 200 pennies

8. Jenna has 1 quarter and 2 dimes. She finds 30¢. How much does she have in all?

- Ⓕ 33¢
- Ⓗ 65¢
- Ⓖ 57¢
- Ⓙ 75¢

9. Paulo has 3 quarters. He buys a juice box for 60¢. How much change should he get?

- Ⓐ 15¢
- Ⓒ 57¢
- Ⓑ 30¢
- Ⓓ 75¢

10. Eli has 8 dimes. He buys a card for 47¢. How much change should he get?

- Ⓕ 33¢
- Ⓖ 39¢
- Ⓗ 43¢
- Ⓙ 80¢

STOP

104 Grade 2

CHAPTER 8 TEST — FORM B, PAGE 1

Name _____

Read each question carefully. Write or circle your answer in the space provided.

1. Draw or write the coins you can use to equal one dollar.

possible answer:
__4 quarters__

2. How much money does Benito have?

__$2.64__

3. Denise buys a flower for 89¢. She gives the clerk $1.00. How much change should she get back?

__11¢__

4. Philippa has these coins.

What coins does Philippa need to make a dollar?

possible answer:
__10 pennies__

5. How much money is shown?

__$1.72__

GO ON

Grade 2 **105**

CHAPTER 8 TEST — FORM B, PAGE 2

Name _____

6. Circle the group that is less than $1.52.

7. Draw coins that equal $1.00.

possible answer:
any drawing
of coins that add
up to $1.00

8. Carl had 5 nickels and 8 pennies. He earned 27¢. How much money does he have now?

__60¢__

9. Raylene has 6 dimes and 1 nickel. She buys a hotdog for 37¢. How much does she have left?

__28¢__

10. Leona has 2 dimes and 7 nickels. She buys a book for 19¢. How much does she have left?

__36¢__

STOP

106 Grade 2

© Macmillan/McGraw-Hill

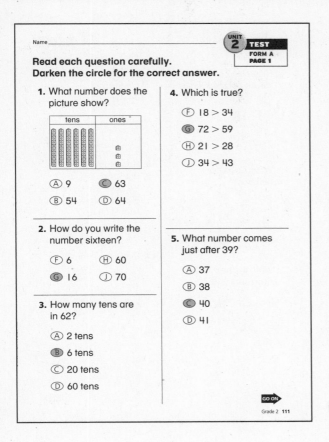

Name _____

UNIT **2 TEST**
FORM A
PAGE 1

**Read each question carefully.
Darken the circle for the correct answer.**

1. What number does the picture show?

tens	ones

- Ⓐ 9
- Ⓑ 54
- Ⓒ 63
- Ⓓ 64

2. How do you write the number sixteen?

- Ⓕ 6
- Ⓖ 16
- Ⓗ 60
- Ⓙ 70

3. How many tens are in 62?

- Ⓐ 2 tens
- Ⓑ 6 tens
- Ⓒ 20 tens
- Ⓓ 60 tens

4. Which is true?

- Ⓕ 18 > 34
- Ⓖ 72 > 59
- Ⓗ 21 > 28
- Ⓙ 34 > 43

5. What number comes just after 39?

- Ⓐ 37
- Ⓑ 38
- Ⓒ 40
- Ⓓ 41

GO ON

Grade 2 **111**

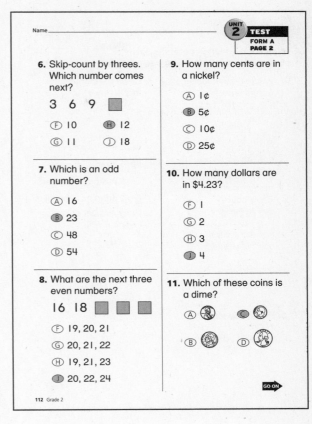

Name _____

UNIT **2 TEST**
FORM A
PAGE 2

6. Skip-count by threes. Which number comes next?

3   6   9   ■

- Ⓕ 10
- Ⓖ 11
- Ⓗ 12
- Ⓙ 18

7. Which is an odd number?

- Ⓐ 16
- Ⓑ 23
- Ⓒ 48
- Ⓓ 54

8. What are the next three even numbers?

16   18   ■   ■   ■

- Ⓕ 19, 20, 21
- Ⓖ 20, 21, 22
- Ⓗ 19, 21, 23
- Ⓙ 20, 22, 24

9. How many cents are in a nickel?

- Ⓐ 1¢
- Ⓑ 5¢
- Ⓒ 10¢
- Ⓓ 25¢

10. How many dollars are in $4.23?

- Ⓕ 1
- Ⓖ 2
- Ⓗ 3
- Ⓙ 4

11. Which of these coins is a dime?

- Ⓐ
- Ⓑ
- Ⓒ
- Ⓓ

GO ON

112 Grade 2

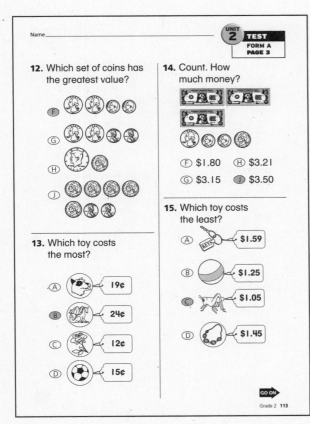

Name _____

UNIT **2 TEST**
FORM A
PAGE 3

12. Which set of coins has the greatest value?

- Ⓕ
- Ⓖ
- Ⓗ
- Ⓙ

13. Which toy costs the most?

- Ⓐ 19¢
- Ⓑ 24¢
- Ⓒ 12¢
- Ⓓ 15¢

14. Count. How much money?

- Ⓕ $1.80
- Ⓖ $3.15
- Ⓗ $3.21
- Ⓙ $3.50

15. Which toy costs the least?

- Ⓐ $1.59
- Ⓑ $1.25
- Ⓒ $1.05
- Ⓓ $1.45

GO ON

Grade 2 **113**

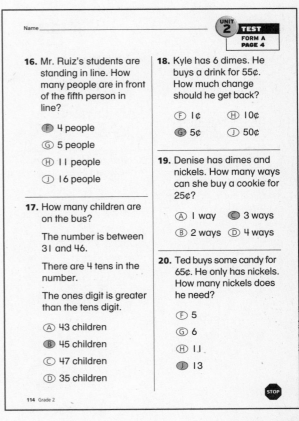

Name _____

UNIT **2 TEST**
FORM A
PAGE 4

16. Mr. Ruiz's students are standing in line. How many people are in front of the fifth person in line?

- Ⓕ 4 people
- Ⓖ 5 people
- Ⓗ 11 people
- Ⓙ 16 people

17. How many children are on the bus?

The number is between 31 and 46.

There are 4 tens in the number.

The ones digit is greater than the tens digit.

- Ⓐ 43 children
- Ⓑ 45 children
- Ⓒ 47 children
- Ⓓ 35 children

18. Kyle has 6 dimes. He buys a drink for 55¢. How much change should he get back?

- Ⓕ 1¢
- Ⓖ 5¢
- Ⓗ 10¢
- Ⓙ 50¢

19. Denise has dimes and nickels. How many ways can she buy a cookie for 25¢?

- Ⓐ 1 way
- Ⓑ 2 ways
- Ⓒ 3 ways
- Ⓓ 4 ways

20. Ted buys some candy for 65¢. He only has nickels. How many nickels does he need?

- Ⓕ 5
- Ⓖ 6
- Ⓗ 11
- Ⓙ 13

STOP

114 Grade 2

Unit 2

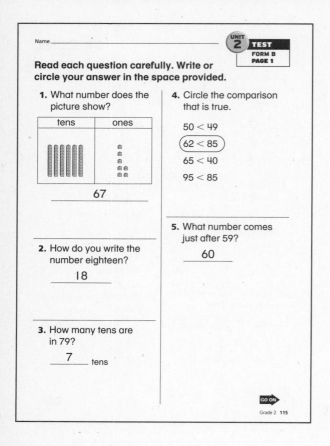

Name _____

Read each question carefully. Write or circle your answer in the space provided.

1. What number does the picture show?

tens	ones

67

2. How do you write the number eighteen?

18

3. How many tens are in 79?

7 tens

4. Circle the comparison that is true.

50 < 49

(62 < 85)

65 < 40

95 < 85

5. What number comes just after 59?

60

GO ON

Grade 2 115

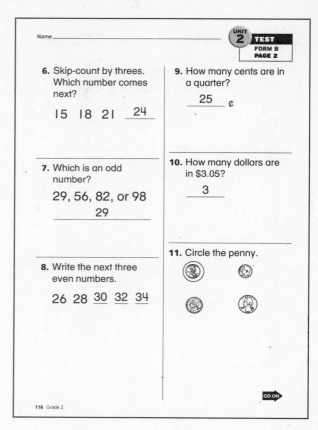

Name _____

6. Skip-count by threes. Which number comes next?

15 18 21 __24__

7. Which is an odd number?

29, 56, 82, or 98

29

8. Write the next three even numbers.

26 28 30 32 34

9. How many cents are in a quarter?

25 ¢

10. How many dollars are in $3.05?

3

11. Circle the penny.

GO ON

116 Grade 2

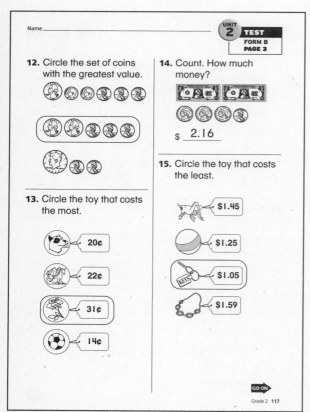

Name _____

12. Circle the set of coins with the greatest value.

13. Circle the toy that costs the most.

20¢

22¢

31¢

14¢

14. Count. How much money?

$ 2.16

15. Circle the toy that costs the least.

$1.45

$1.25

$1.05

$1.59

GO ON

Grade 2 117

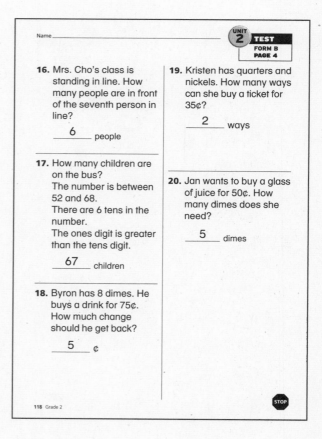

Name _____

16. Mrs. Cho's class is standing in line. How many people are in front of the seventh person in line?

6 people

17. How many children are on the bus?
The number is between 52 and 68.
There are 6 tens in the number.
The ones digit is greater than the tens digit.

67 children

18. Byron has 8 dimes. He buys a drink for 75¢. How much change should he get back?

5 ¢

19. Kristen has quarters and nickels. How many ways can she buy a ticket for 35¢?

2 ways

20. Jan wants to buy a glass of juice for 50¢. How many dimes does she need?

5 dimes

STOP

118 Grade 2

Chapter 9

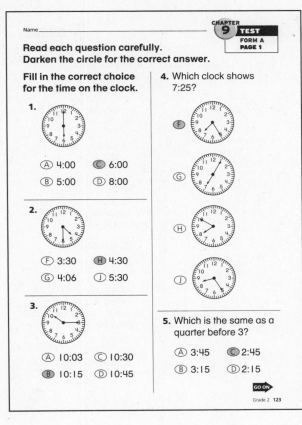

Name_____

Read each question carefully.
Darken the circle for the correct answer.

Fill in the correct choice for the time on the clock.

1.

- Ⓐ 4:00   Ⓒ 6:00
- Ⓑ 5:00   Ⓓ 8:00

2.

- Ⓕ 3:30   Ⓗ 4:30
- Ⓖ 4:06   Ⓙ 5:30

3.

- Ⓐ 10:03   Ⓒ 10:30
- Ⓑ 10:15   Ⓓ 10:45

4. Which clock shows 7:25?

- Ⓕ
- Ⓖ
- Ⓗ
- Ⓙ

5. Which is the same as a quarter before 3?

- Ⓐ 3:45   Ⓒ 2:45
- Ⓑ 3:15   Ⓓ 2:15

GO ON

Grade 2 **123**

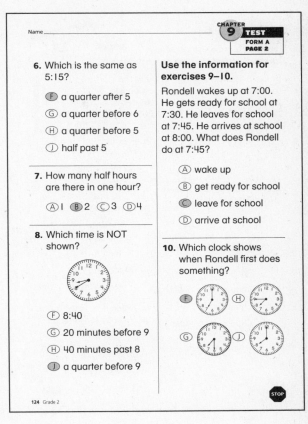

Name_____

6. Which is the same as 5:15?

- Ⓕ a quarter after 5
- Ⓖ a quarter before 6
- Ⓗ a quarter before 5
- Ⓙ half past 5

7. How many half hours are there in one hour?

- Ⓐ 1   Ⓑ 2   Ⓒ 3   Ⓓ 4

8. Which time is NOT shown?

- Ⓕ 8:40
- Ⓖ 20 minutes before 9
- Ⓗ 40 minutes past 8
- Ⓙ a quarter before 9

Use the information for exercises 9–10.

Rondell wakes up at 7:00. He gets ready for school at 7:30. He leaves for school at 7:45. He arrives at school at 8:00. What does Rondell do at 7:45?

- Ⓐ wake up
- Ⓑ get ready for school
- Ⓒ leave for school
- Ⓓ arrive at school

10. Which clock shows when Rondell first does something?

- Ⓕ
- Ⓖ
- Ⓗ
- Ⓙ

STOP

124 Grade 2

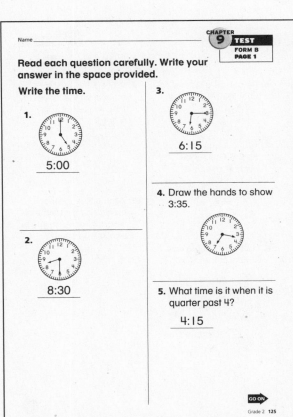

Name_____

Read each question carefully. Write your answer in the space provided.

Write the time.

1.

5:00

2.

8:30

3.

6:15

4. Draw the hands to show 3:35.

5. What time is it when it is quarter past 4?

4:15

GO ON

Grade 2 **125**

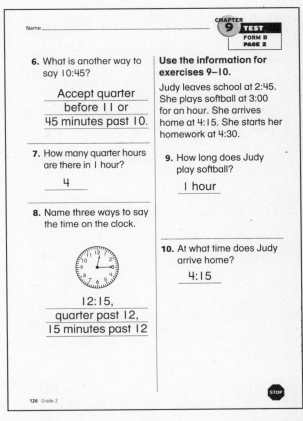

Name_____

6. What is another way to say 10:45?

Accept quarter
before 11 or
45 minutes past 10.

7. How many quarter hours are there in 1 hour?

4

8. Name three ways to say the time on the clock.

12:15,
quarter past 12,
15 minutes past 12

Use the information for exercises 9–10.

Judy leaves school at 2:45. She plays softball at 3:00 for an hour. She arrives home at 4:15. She starts her homework at 4:30.

9. How long does Judy play softball?

1 hour

10. At what time does Judy arrive home?

4:15

STOP

126 Grade 2

Chapter 10

FORM A, PAGE 1

Name_____

Read each question carefully.
Darken the circle for the correct answer.

1. What time do you wake up?

Ⓐ 7:00 A.M.
Ⓑ 11:00 A.M.
Ⓒ 7:00 P.M.
Ⓓ 11:00 P.M.

2. How much time is there until 12:00?

Ⓕ 3 hours
Ⓖ 3 hours, 30 minutes
Ⓗ 4 hours
Ⓙ 4 hours, 30 minutes

Use the calendar for items 3–5.

March 2004

3. How many days are in March?

Ⓐ 28   Ⓒ 30
Ⓑ 29   Ⓓ 31

4. What is the date one week after March 10?

Ⓕ March 11
Ⓖ March 15
Ⓗ March 17
Ⓙ March 20

5. Which date is the fourth Tuesday in March?

Ⓐ March 18
Ⓑ March 23
Ⓒ March 25
Ⓓ March 30

GO ON

FORM A, PAGE 2

Name_____

6. What time is it 2 hours after 5:30?

Ⓕ 5:32   Ⓗ 7:30
Ⓖ 5:50   Ⓙ 7:52

7. Which clock shows the time 30 minutes after 2:15?

Ⓐ

Ⓑ

Ⓒ

Ⓓ

8. How long was Maura at the movies?

Ⓕ 1 hour   Ⓗ 3 hours
Ⓖ 2 hours   Ⓙ 4 hours

9. Which unit is best for measuring the length of time it takes to wash your face?

Ⓐ minute   Ⓒ day
Ⓑ hour   Ⓓ week

10. Which unit is best for measuring the length of time it will take for you to enter fourth grade?

Ⓕ day   Ⓗ month
Ⓖ minute   Ⓙ year

STOP

FORM B, PAGE 1

Name_____

Read each question carefully. Write your answer in the space provided.

1. What time do you go to sleep?

Accept reasonable
P.M. answers.

2. How much time is there until 1:00?

2 hours and
45 minutes

Use the calendar for items 3–5.

October 2004

3. How many days are in October?

31

4. What is the date one week after October 7?

October 14

5. What date is the third Friday in October?

October 15

GO ON

FORM B, PAGE 2

Name_____

6. What time is it 2 hours after 2:30?

4:30

7. Show the time 30 minutes after 6:15.

8. How many hours was Manny at the movies?

2   hours

9. What unit is best for measuring the length of time it takes to walk a dog?

minute

10. What unit is best for measuring the length of time it will take for you to become an adult?

year

STOP

Chapter 11

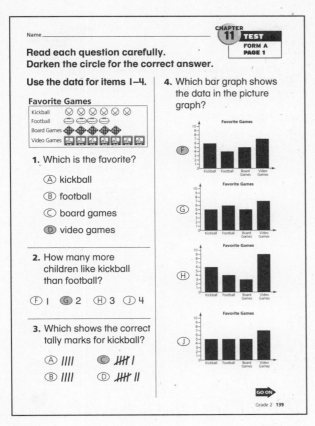

Name_____

Read each question carefully.
Darken the circle for the correct answer.

Use the data for items 1–4.

Favorite Games

Kickball	⊗ ⊗ ⊗ ⊗ ⊗
Football	⬭ ⬭ ⬭ ⬭
Board Games	◈ ◈ ◈ ◈
Video Games	▦ ▦ ▦ ▦ ▦

1. Which is the favorite?

Ⓐ kickball

Ⓑ football

Ⓒ board games

Ⓓ video games

2. How many more children like kickball than football?

Ⓕ 1   Ⓖ 2   Ⓗ 3   Ⓙ 4

3. Which shows the correct tally marks for kickball?

Ⓐ ////

Ⓑ ////

Ⓒ 卌 /

Ⓓ 卌 //

4. Which bar graph shows the data in the picture graph?

Ⓕ

Ⓖ

Ⓗ

Ⓙ

Favorite Games

GO ON

Grade 2 **139**

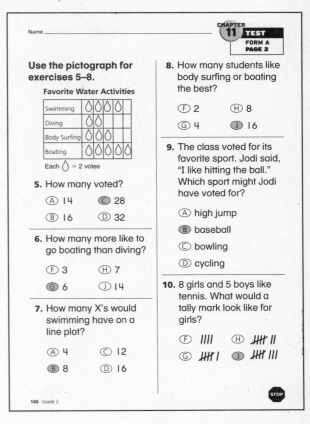

Name_____

Use the pictograph for exercises 5–8.

Favorite Water Activities

Swimming	〇〇〇〇
Diving	〇〇
Body Surfing	〇〇〇
Boating	〇〇〇〇

Each 〇 = 2 votes

5. How many voted?

Ⓐ 14   Ⓒ 28

Ⓑ 16   Ⓓ 32

6. How many more like to go boating than diving?

Ⓕ 3   Ⓗ 7

Ⓖ 6   Ⓙ 14

7. How many X's would swimming have on a line plot?

Ⓐ 4   Ⓒ 12

Ⓑ 8   Ⓓ 16

8. How many students like body surfing or boating the best?

Ⓕ 2   Ⓗ 8

Ⓖ 4   Ⓙ 16

9. The class voted for its favorite sport. Jodi said, "I like hitting the ball." Which sport might Jodi have voted for?

Ⓐ high jump

Ⓑ baseball

Ⓒ bowling

Ⓓ cycling

10. 8 girls and 5 boys like tennis. What would a tally mark look like for girls?

Ⓕ ////   Ⓗ 卌 //

Ⓖ 卌 /   Ⓙ 卌 ///

STOP

140 Grade 2

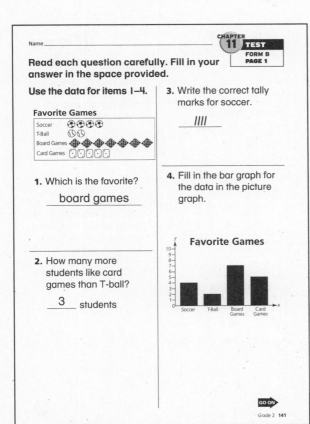

Name_____

Read each question carefully. Fill in your answer in the space provided.

Use the data for items 1–4.

Favorite Games

Soccer	⊕ ⊕ ⊕ ⊕
T-Ball	◐ ◐
Board Games	◈ ◈ ◈ ◈ ◈ ◈ ◈
Card Games	▢ ▢ ▢ ▢ ▢

1. Which is the favorite?

___board games___

2. How many more students like card games than T-ball?

___3___ students

3. Write the correct tally marks for soccer.

___////___

4. Fill in the bar graph for the data in the picture graph.

Favorite Games

| Soccer | T-Ball | Board Games | Card Games |

GO ON

Grade 2 **141**

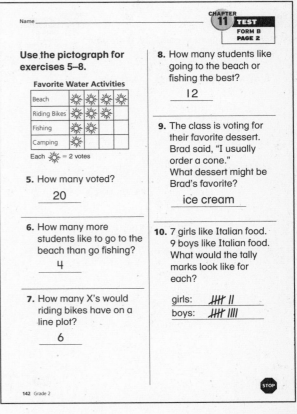

Name_____

Use the pictograph for exercises 5–8.

Favorite Water Activities

Beach	☀ ☀ ☀ ☀
Riding Bikes	☀ ☀ ☀
Fishing	☀ ☀
Camping	☀

Each ☀ = 2 votes

5. How many voted?

___20___

6. How many more students like to go to the beach than go fishing?

___4___

7. How many X's would riding bikes have on a line plot?

___6___

8. How many students like going to the beach or fishing the best?

___12___

9. The class is voting for their favorite dessert. Brad said, "I usually order a cone." What dessert might be Brad's favorite?

___ice cream___

10. 7 girls like Italian food. 9 boys like Italian food. What would the tally marks look like for each?

girls: ___卌 //___

boys: ___卌 ////___

STOP

142 Grade 2

Chapter 12

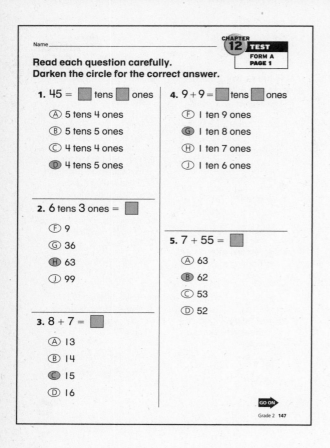

Name _____

CHAPTER **12** **TEST**
FORM A
PAGE 1

Read each question carefully.
Darken the circle for the correct answer.

1. 45 = ▨ tens ▨ ones

   Ⓐ 5 tens 4 ones

   Ⓑ 5 tens 5 ones

   Ⓒ 4 tens 4 ones

   Ⓓ 4 tens 5 ones

4. 9 + 9 = ▨ tens ▨ ones

   Ⓕ 1 ten 9 ones

   Ⓖ 1 ten 8 ones

   Ⓗ 1 ten 7 ones

   Ⓙ 1 ten 6 ones

2. 6 tens 3 ones = ▨

   Ⓕ 9

   Ⓖ 36

   Ⓗ 63

   Ⓙ 99

5. 7 + 55 = ▨

   Ⓐ 63

   Ⓑ 62

   Ⓒ 53

   Ⓓ 52

3. 8 + 7 = ▨

   Ⓐ 13

   Ⓑ 14

   Ⓒ 15

   Ⓓ 16

GO ON

Grade 2 **147**

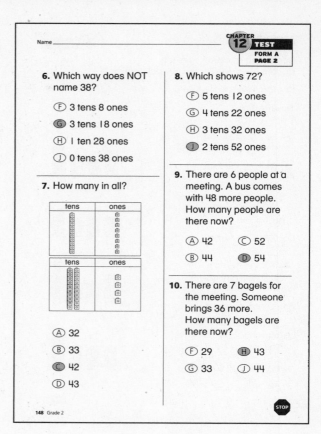

Name _____

CHAPTER **12** **TEST**
FORM A
PAGE 2

6. Which way does NOT name 38?

   Ⓕ 3 tens 8 ones

   Ⓖ 3 tens 18 ones

   Ⓗ 1 ten 28 ones

   Ⓙ 0 tens 38 ones

8. Which shows 72?

   Ⓕ 5 tens 12 ones

   Ⓖ 4 tens 22 ones

   Ⓗ 3 tens 32 ones

   Ⓙ 2 tens 52 ones

7. How many in all?

tens	ones

tens	ones

   Ⓐ 32

   Ⓑ 33

   Ⓒ 42

   Ⓓ 43

9. There are 6 people at a meeting. A bus comes with 48 more people. How many people are there now?

   Ⓐ 42   Ⓒ 52

   Ⓑ 44   Ⓓ 54

10. There are 7 bagels for the meeting. Someone brings 36 more. How many bagels are there now?

   Ⓕ 29   Ⓗ 43

   Ⓖ 33   Ⓙ 44

STOP

148 Grade 2

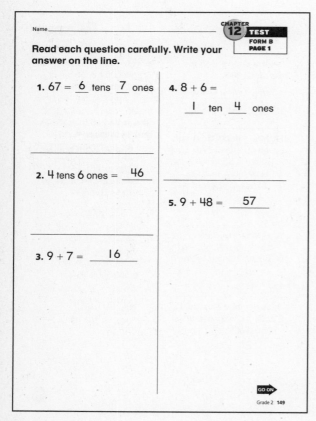

Name _____

CHAPTER **12** **TEST**
FORM B
PAGE 1

Read each question carefully. Write your answer on the line.

1. 67 = _6_ tens _7_ ones

4. 8 + 6 =
   _1_ ten _4_ ones

2. 4 tens 6 ones = _46_

5. 9 + 48 = _57_

3. 9 + 7 = _16_

GO ON

Grade 2 **149**

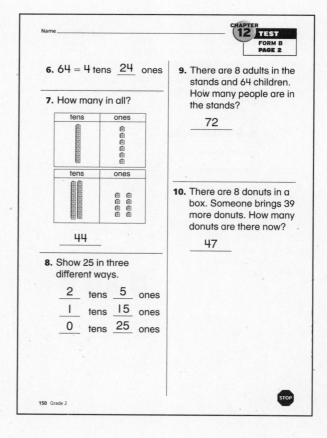

Name _____

CHAPTER **12** **TEST**
FORM B
PAGE 2

6. 64 = 4 tens _24_ ones

7. How many in all?

tens	ones

tens	ones

   _44_

8. Show 25 in three different ways.

   _2_ tens _5_ ones

   _1_ tens _15_ ones

   _0_ tens _25_ ones

9. There are 8 adults in the stands and 64 children. How many people are in the stands?

   _72_

10. There are 8 donuts in a box. Someone brings 39 more donuts. How many donuts are there now?

   _47_

STOP

150 Grade 2

© Macmillan/McGraw-Hill

366 Grade 2

Unit 3

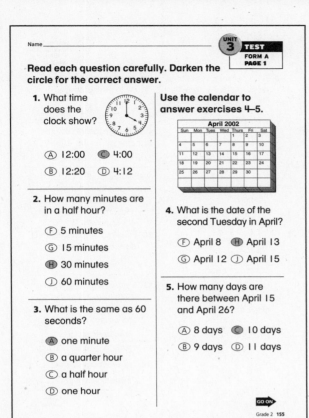

Name _____

UNIT 3 TEST
FORM A
PAGE 1

Read each question carefully. Darken the circle for the correct answer.

1. What time does the clock show?

① 12:00   ③ 4:00

② 12:20   ④ 4:12

Use the calendar to answer exercises 4–5.

April 2002

Sun	Mon	Tues	Wed	Thurs	Fri	Sat
	1	2	3	4	5	6
7	8	9	10	11	12	13
14	15	16	17	18	19	20
21	22	23	24	25	26	27
28	29	30				

2. How many minutes are in a half hour?

Ⓓ 5 minutes

Ⓔ 15 minutes

Ⓕ 30 minutes

Ⓛ 60 minutes

3. What is the same as 60 seconds?

① one minute

② a quarter hour

③ a half hour

④ one hour

4. What is the date of the second Tuesday in April?

Ⓓ April 8   Ⓗ April 13

Ⓔ April 12   Ⓛ April 15

5. How many days are there between April 15 and April 26?

① 8 days   ③ 10 days

② 9 days   ④ 11 days

GO ON

Grade 2 **155**

Name _____

UNIT 3 TEST
FORM A
PAGE 2

6. It is nighttime. What time does the clock show?

Ⓓ 3:55 A.M.

Ⓔ 10:15 P.M.

Ⓕ 11:15 P.M.

Ⓛ 12:15 A.M.

7. How many hours have passed?

① 2 hours   ③ 5 hours

② 3 hours   ④ 7 hours

8. What time does the clock show?

Ⓓ 1:35

Ⓔ 2:35

Ⓕ 7:05

Ⓛ 12:35

9. What is another way to write the number 4?

① IIII   ② ⅰⅰⅰ   ③ ⅰⅰI   ④ ⅰII

Use the graph below to answer items 10–12.

Saturday Morning Bike Rides

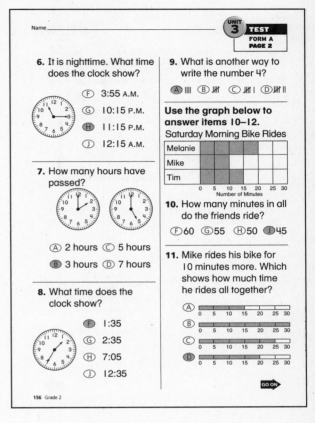

10. How many minutes in all do the friends ride?

Ⓓ 60   Ⓔ 55   Ⓕ 50   Ⓛ 45

11. Mike rides his bike for 10 minutes more. Which shows how much time he rides all together?

①
②
③
④

GO ON

156 Grade 2

Name _____

UNIT 3 TEST
FORM A
PAGE 3

12. Tim rides his bike for 15 minutes more. Which shows how much time he rides all together?

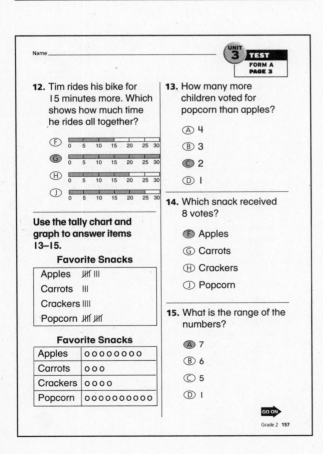

Ⓓ
Ⓔ
Ⓕ
Ⓛ

Use the tally chart and graph to answer items 13–15.

Favorite Snacks

Apples	裀 III
Carrots	III
Crackers	IIII
Popcorn	裀 裀

Favorite Snacks

Apples	o o o o o o o o
Carrots	o o o
Crackers	o o o o
Popcorn	o o o o o o o o o o

13. How many more children voted for popcorn than apples?

① 4

② 3

③ 2

④ 1

14. Which snack received 8 votes?

Ⓓ Apples

Ⓔ Carrots

Ⓕ Crackers

Ⓛ Popcorn

15. What is the range of the numbers?

① 7

② 6

③ 5

④ 1

GO ON

Grade 2 **157**

Name _____

UNIT 3 TEST
FORM A
PAGE 4

16. What is the mode of the numbers?

Ⓓ 7   Ⓗ 5

Ⓔ 6   Ⓛ 2

17. Mrs. Ahart's class puts on puppet shows. Each show is 30 minutes long. How many minutes does it take to put on 2 puppet shows?

① 30 minutes

② 40 minutes

③ 50 minutes

④ 60 minutes

18. The students eat lunch at 12:30. They finish 30 minutes later. At what time do they finish?

Ⓓ 12:00   Ⓗ 1:00

Ⓔ 12:30   Ⓛ 1:30

Fill in the table. Then answer items 19–20.

Sasha is saving money for a gift. She saved $3 in week 1 and $2 in week 2. She saved $5 in week 3 and $4 in week 4.

Sasha's Gift Money

Week	1	2	3	4
How Much	3	2	5	4

19. How much more money does Sasha save in week 3 than in week 1?

① $9   ③ $5

② $6   ④ $2

20. How much money did Sasha save in all?

Ⓓ $15   Ⓗ $11

Ⓔ $14   Ⓛ $8

STOP

158 Grade 2

© Macmillan/McGraw-Hill

Grade 2 **367**

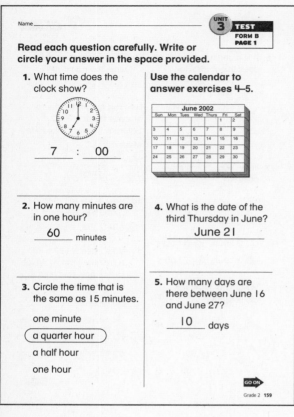

Name

UNIT 3 TEST
FORM B
PAGE 1

Read each question carefully. Write or circle your answer in the space provided.

1. What time does the clock show?

7 : 00

2. How many minutes are in one hour?

60 minutes

3. Circle the time that is the same as 15 minutes.

one minute

(a quarter hour)

a half hour

one hour

Use the calendar to answer exercises 4–5.

June 2002

Sun	Mon	Tues	Wed	Thurs	Fri	Sat
						1
2	3	4	5	6	7	8
9	10	11	12	13	14	15
16	17	18	19	20	21	22
23	24	25	26	27	28	29
30						

4. What is the date of the third Thursday in June?

June 21

5. How many days are there between June 16 and June 27?

10 days

GO ON

Grade 2 **159**

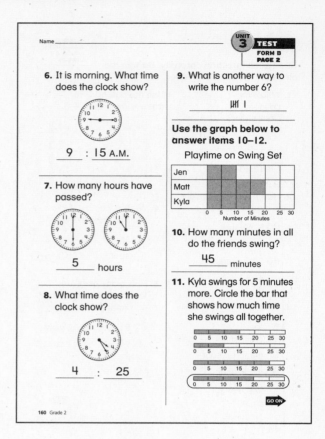

Name

UNIT 3 TEST
FORM B
PAGE 2

6. It is morning. What time does the clock show?

9 : 15 A.M.

7. How many hours have passed?

5 hours

8. What time does the clock show?

4 : 25

9. What is another way to write the number 6?

丗 I

Use the graph below to answer items 10–12.

Playtime on Swing Set

Jen / Matt / Kyla — Number of Minutes (0, 5, 10, 15, 20, 25, 30)

10. How many minutes in all do the friends swing?

45 minutes

11. Kyla swings for 5 minutes more. Circle the bar that shows how much time she swings all together.

0 5 10 15 20 25 30

0 5 10 15 20 25 30

0 5 10 15 20 25 30

(0 5 10 15 20 25 30)

GO ON

160 Grade 2

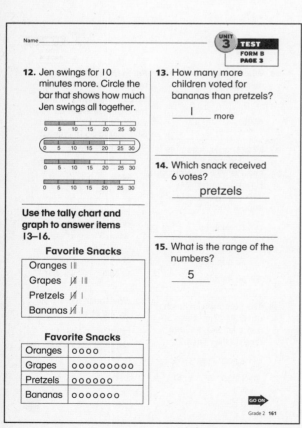

Name

UNIT 3 TEST
FORM B
PAGE 3

12. Jen swings for 10 minutes more. Circle the bar that shows how much Jen swings all together.

0 5 10 15 20 25 30

(0 5 10 15 20 25 30)

0 5 10 15 20 25 30

Use the tally chart and graph to answer items 13–16.

Favorite Snacks

Oranges	III
Grapes	丗 III
Pretzels	丗 I
Bananas	丗 I

Favorite Snacks

Oranges	o o o o
Grapes	o o o o o o o o
Pretzels	o o o o o o
Bananas	o o o o o o o

13. How many more children voted for bananas than pretzels?

1 more

14. Which snack received 6 votes?

pretzels

15. What is the range of the numbers?

5

GO ON

Grade 2 **161**

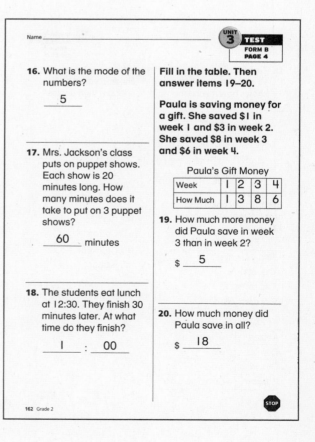

Name

UNIT 3 TEST
FORM B
PAGE 4

16. What is the mode of the numbers?

5

17. Mrs. Jackson's class puts on puppet shows. Each show is 20 minutes long. How many minutes does it take to put on 3 puppet shows?

60 minutes

18. The students eat lunch at 12:30. They finish 30 minutes later. At what time do they finish?

1 : 00

Fill in the table. Then answer items 19–20.

Paula is saving money for a gift. She saved $1 in week 1 and $3 in week 2. She saved $8 in week 3 and $6 in week 4.

Paula's Gift Money

Week	1	2	3	4
How Much	1	3	8	6

19. How much more money did Paula save in week 3 than in week 2?

$ 5

20. How much money did Paula save in all?

$ 18

STOP

162 Grade 2

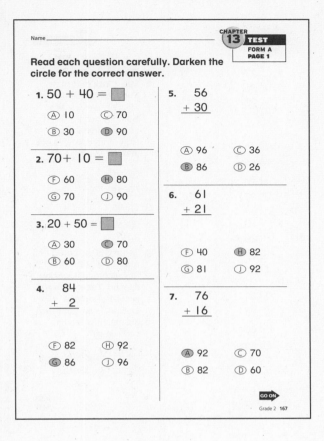

Name _____

Read each question carefully. Darken the circle for the correct answer.

1. $50 + 40 = $ ▢

- Ⓐ 10
- Ⓒ 70
- Ⓑ 30
- Ⓓ 90

2. $70 + 10 = $ ▢

- Ⓕ 60
- Ⓗ 80
- Ⓖ 70
- Ⓙ 90

3. $20 + 50 = $ ▢

- Ⓐ 30
- Ⓒ 70
- Ⓑ 60
- Ⓓ 80

4.
$$84 \atop +\ 2$$

- Ⓕ 82
- Ⓗ 92
- Ⓖ 86
- Ⓙ 96

5.
$$56 \atop +30$$

- Ⓐ 96
- Ⓒ 36
- Ⓑ 86
- Ⓓ 26

6.
$$61 \atop +21$$

- Ⓕ 40
- Ⓗ 82
- Ⓖ 81
- Ⓙ 92

7.
$$76 \atop +16$$

- Ⓐ 92
- Ⓒ 70
- Ⓑ 82
- Ⓓ 60

GO ON

Name _____

Use this story for questions 8–9.

The second grade class needs to make money for their spring party. The class voted on what they can do, and the winning vote went to a car wash.

8. What problem does the second grade class have?

- Ⓕ They are having a spring party.
- Ⓖ They don't have enough math books.
- Ⓗ They need money for their spring party.
- Ⓙ They don't have enough chalk.

9. What did the class decide was the best solution for their problem?

- Ⓐ Have a car wash.
- Ⓑ Have a bake sale.
- Ⓒ Sell sandwiches.
- Ⓓ Put on a magic show.

10.
$$29 \atop +\ 7$$

- Ⓕ 37
- Ⓖ 36
- Ⓗ 35
- Ⓙ 22

STOP

Name _____

Read each question carefully. Write your answer on the line.

1. $20 + 40 = $ _60_

2. $10 + 10 = $ _20_

3. $10 + 80 = $ _90_

4.
$$32 \atop {+\ 2} \atop \overline{34}$$

5.
$$60 \atop {+30} \atop \overline{90}$$

6.
$$23 \atop {+72} \atop \overline{95}$$

7.
$$48 \atop {+16} \atop \overline{64}$$

GO ON

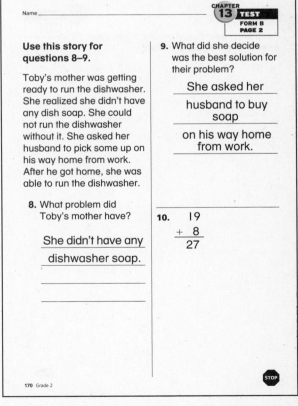

Name _____

Use this story for questions 8–9.

Toby's mother was getting ready to run the dishwasher. She realized she didn't have any dish soap. She could not run the dishwasher without it. She asked her husband to pick some up on his way home from work. After he got home, she was able to run the dishwasher.

8. What problem did Toby's mother have?

She didn't have any
dishwasher soap.
_____

9. What did she decide was the best solution for their problem?

She asked her
husband to buy
soap
on his way home
from work.

10.
$$19 \atop {+\ 8} \atop \overline{27}$$

STOP

Chapter 14

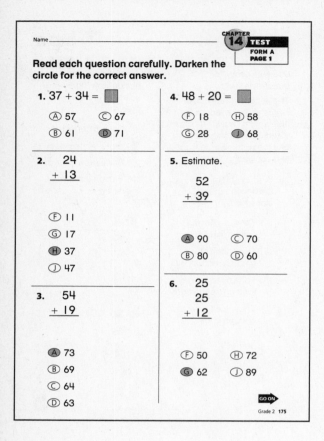

CHAPTER **14** **TEST**
FORM A
PAGE 1

Read each question carefully. Darken the circle for the correct answer.

1. $37 + 34 =$ ▨
- Ⓐ 57
- Ⓒ 67
- Ⓑ 61
- Ⓓ 71

4. $48 + 20 =$ ▨
- Ⓕ 18
- Ⓗ 58
- Ⓖ 28
- Ⓙ 68

2.
$$\begin{array}{r} 24 \\ + 13 \\ \hline \end{array}$$
- Ⓕ 11
- Ⓖ 17
- Ⓗ 37
- Ⓙ 47

5. Estimate.
$$\begin{array}{r} 52 \\ + 39 \\ \hline \end{array}$$
- Ⓐ 90
- Ⓒ 70
- Ⓑ 80
- Ⓓ 60

3.
$$\begin{array}{r} 54 \\ + 19 \\ \hline \end{array}$$
- Ⓐ 73
- Ⓑ 69
- Ⓒ 64
- Ⓓ 63

6.
$$\begin{array}{r} 25 \\ 25 \\ + 12 \\ \hline \end{array}$$
- Ⓕ 50
- Ⓗ 72
- Ⓖ 62
- Ⓙ 89

GO ON ▶

Grade 2 **175**

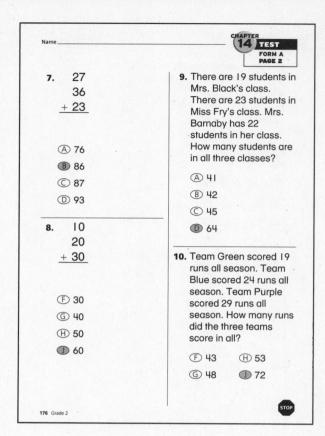

CHAPTER **14** **TEST**
FORM A
PAGE 2

7.
$$\begin{array}{r} 27 \\ 36 \\ + 23 \\ \hline \end{array}$$
- Ⓐ 76
- Ⓑ 86
- Ⓒ 87
- Ⓓ 93

8.
$$\begin{array}{r} 10 \\ 20 \\ + 30 \\ \hline \end{array}$$
- Ⓕ 30
- Ⓖ 40
- Ⓗ 50
- Ⓙ 60

9. There are 19 students in Mrs. Black's class. There are 23 students in Miss Fry's class. Mrs. Barnaby has 22 students in her class. How many students are in all three classes?
- Ⓐ 41
- Ⓑ 42
- Ⓒ 45
- Ⓓ 64

10. Team Green scored 19 runs all season. Team Blue scored 24 runs all season. Team Purple scored 29 runs all season. How many runs did the three teams score in all?
- Ⓕ 43
- Ⓗ 53
- Ⓖ 48
- Ⓙ 72

STOP

176 Grade 2

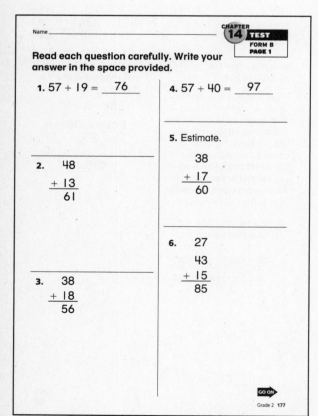

CHAPTER **14** **TEST**
FORM B
PAGE 1

Read each question carefully. Write your answer in the space provided.

1. $57 + 19 =$ ___76___

4. $57 + 40 =$ ___97___

2.
$$\begin{array}{r} 48 \\ + 13 \\ \hline 61 \end{array}$$

5. Estimate.
$$\begin{array}{r} 38 \\ + 17 \\ \hline 60 \end{array}$$

3.
$$\begin{array}{r} 38 \\ + 18 \\ \hline 56 \end{array}$$

6.
$$\begin{array}{r} 27 \\ 43 \\ + 15 \\ \hline 85 \end{array}$$

GO ON ▶

Grade 2 **177**

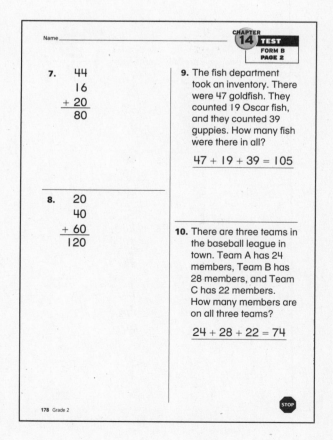

CHAPTER **14** **TEST**
FORM B
PAGE 2

7.
$$\begin{array}{r} 44 \\ 16 \\ + 20 \\ \hline 80 \end{array}$$

8.
$$\begin{array}{r} 20 \\ 40 \\ + 60 \\ \hline 120 \end{array}$$

9. The fish department took an inventory. There were 47 goldfish. They counted 19 Oscar fish, and they counted 39 guppies. How many fish were there in all?

$47 + 19 + 39 = 105$

10. There are three teams in the baseball league in town. Team A has 24 members, Team B has 28 members, and Team C has 22 members. How many members are on all three teams?

$24 + 28 + 22 = 74$

STOP

178 Grade 2

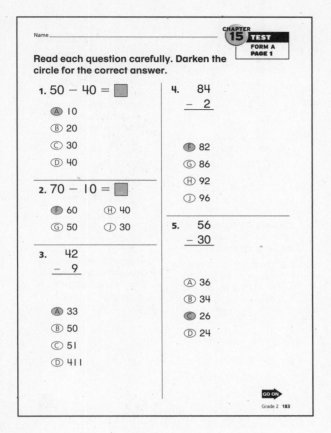

Name _____

CHAPTER 15 TEST
FORM A
PAGE 1

Read each question carefully. Darken the circle for the correct answer.

1. $50 - 40 =$ ⬜
   - Ⓐ 10
   - Ⓑ 20
   - Ⓒ 30
   - Ⓓ 40

2. $70 - 10 =$ ⬜
   - Ⓕ 60   Ⓗ 40
   - Ⓖ 50   Ⓙ 30

3. $\begin{array}{r} 42 \\ -\ 9 \\ \hline \end{array}$
   - Ⓐ 33
   - Ⓑ 50
   - Ⓒ 51
   - Ⓓ 411

4. $\begin{array}{r} 84 \\ -\ 2 \\ \hline \end{array}$
   - Ⓕ 82
   - Ⓖ 86
   - Ⓗ 92
   - Ⓙ 96

5. $\begin{array}{r} 56 \\ -\ 30 \\ \hline \end{array}$
   - Ⓐ 36
   - Ⓑ 34
   - Ⓒ 26
   - Ⓓ 24

GO ON

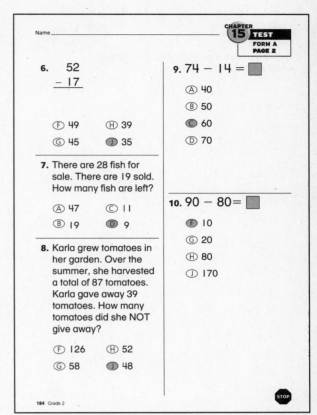

Name _____

CHAPTER 15 TEST
FORM A
PAGE 2

6. $\begin{array}{r} 52 \\ -\ 17 \\ \hline \end{array}$
   - Ⓕ 49   Ⓗ 39
   - Ⓖ 45   Ⓙ 35

7. There are 28 fish for sale. There are 19 sold. How many fish are left?
   - Ⓐ 47   Ⓒ 11
   - Ⓑ 19   Ⓓ 9

8. Karla grew tomatoes in her garden. Over the summer, she harvested a total of 87 tomatoes. Karla gave away 39 tomatoes. How many tomatoes did she NOT give away?
   - Ⓕ 126   Ⓗ 52
   - Ⓖ 58   Ⓙ 48

9. $74 - 14 =$ ⬜
   - Ⓐ 40
   - Ⓑ 50
   - Ⓒ 60
   - Ⓓ 70

10. $90 - 80 =$ ⬜
    - Ⓕ 10
    - Ⓖ 20
    - Ⓗ 80
    - Ⓙ 170

STOP

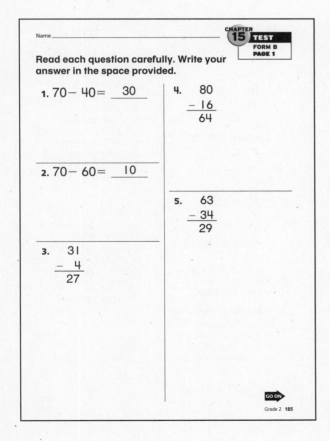

Name _____

CHAPTER 15 TEST
FORM B
PAGE 1

Read each question carefully. Write your answer in the space provided.

1. $70 - 40 =$ ___30___

2. $70 - 60 =$ ___10___

3. $\begin{array}{r} 31 \\ -\ 4 \\ \hline 27 \end{array}$

4. $\begin{array}{r} 80 \\ -\ 16 \\ \hline 64 \end{array}$

5. $\begin{array}{r} 63 \\ -\ 34 \\ \hline 29 \end{array}$

GO ON

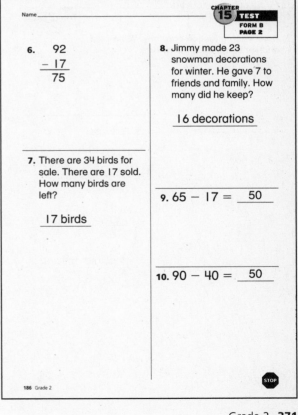

Name _____

CHAPTER 15 TEST
FORM B
PAGE 2

6. $\begin{array}{r} 92 \\ -\ 17 \\ \hline 75 \end{array}$

7. There are 34 birds for sale. There are 17 sold. How many birds are left?

   ___17 birds___

8. Jimmy made 23 snowman decorations for winter. He gave 7 to friends and family. How many did he keep?

   ___16 decorations___

9. $65 - 17 =$ ___50___

10. $90 - 40 =$ ___50___

STOP

Chapter 16

Read each question carefully. Darken the circle for the correct answer.

1. 78 − 20 =

- Ⓐ 58
- Ⓒ 48
- Ⓑ 52
- Ⓓ 42

2. 39 − 18 =

- Ⓕ 29
- Ⓗ 19
- Ⓖ 21
- Ⓙ 11

3.
$$72 - 47 =$$

- Ⓐ 35
- Ⓑ 34
- Ⓒ 25
- Ⓓ 24

4.
$$\begin{array}{r} 42 \\ -\ 5 \\ \hline \end{array}$$

- Ⓕ 27
- Ⓖ 33
- Ⓗ 36
- Ⓙ 37

5. How would you check this subtraction?

$$\begin{array}{r} 76 \\ -\ 22 \\ \hline 54 \end{array}$$

- Ⓐ 76 + 22 = 54
- Ⓑ 22 + 76 = 54
- Ⓒ 54 + 22 = 76
- Ⓓ 76 + 54 = 22

GO ON

Grade 2 **191**

---

6. Estimate.
$$\begin{array}{r} 52 \\ -\ 39 \\ \hline \end{array}$$

- Ⓕ 10
- Ⓖ 20
- Ⓗ 30
- Ⓙ 40

7. Estimate.
$$\begin{array}{r} 59 \\ -\ 38 \\ \hline \end{array}$$

- Ⓐ 10
- Ⓑ 20
- Ⓒ 30
- Ⓓ 40

Choose the answer that shows how you could solve each problem.

8. There are 48 children in the second grade. The music teacher calls all 27 boys out of class. How many girls are left in class?

- Ⓕ 48 − 27 = 19
- Ⓖ 48 − 27 = 21
- Ⓗ 48 + 27 = 65
- Ⓙ 48 + 27 = 75

9. The school play had 74 people try out for the show. The director can only choose 45 people. How many people will not be in the show?

- Ⓐ 74 + 45 = 119
- Ⓑ 74 + 45 = 129
- Ⓒ 74 − 45 = 31
- Ⓓ 74 − 45 = 29

10. Tommy went to 63 baseball games in the summer. He then got to go to 19 more games on the weekends in the fall. How many baseball games did he go to?

- Ⓕ 63 − 19 = 44
- Ⓖ 63 − 19 = 56
- Ⓗ 63 + 19 = 72
- Ⓙ 63 + 19 = 82

STOP

192 Grade 2

Read each question carefully. Write your answer in the space provided.

1. 56 − 10 = _46_

2. 47 − 28 = _19_

3.
$$\begin{array}{r} 62 \\ -\ 45 \\ \hline 17 \end{array}$$

4.
$$\begin{array}{r} 63 \\ -\ 8 \\ \hline 55 \end{array}$$

5. Check the subtraction by adding.

$$\begin{array}{r} 87 \\ -\ 32 \\ \hline 55 \end{array}$$

possible answer:
_55 + 32 = 87_

GO ON

Grade 2 **193**

---

6. Estimate.
$$\begin{array}{r} 49 \\ -\ 18 \\ \hline \end{array}$$

possible answer: 30

7. Estimate.
$$\begin{array}{r} 64 \\ -\ 49 \\ \hline \end{array}$$

possible answer: 20

Write how you would solve each problem.

8. There are 37 children in the second grade. The gym teacher calls all 19 girls out of class. How many boys are left in class?

_37 − 19 = 18_

9. The school had 53 people try out for the soccer team. The coach can only choose 25 people. How many people will not be on the team?

_53 − 25 = 28_

10. Tommy went to 26 basketball games in the winter. He went to 18 more games during the spring. How many basketball games did Tommy go to?

_26 + 18 = 44_

STOP

194 Grade 2

Unit 4

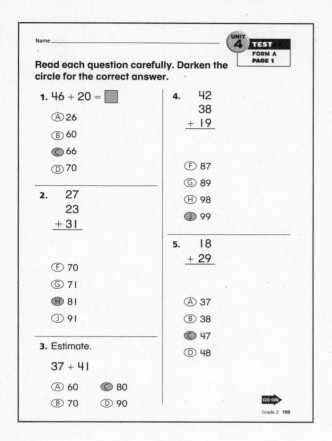

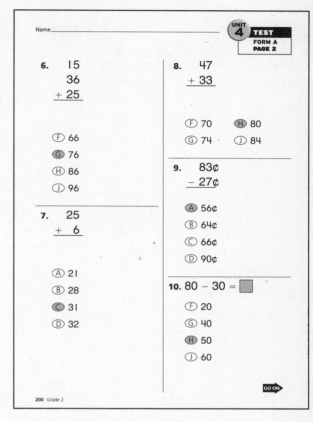

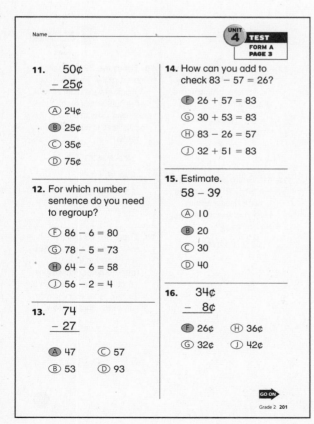

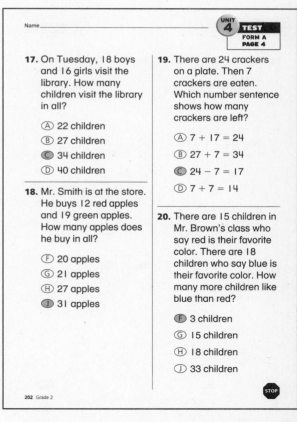

Grade 2 **373**

Name_____

Read each question carefully. Write or circle your answer in the space provided.

1. 52 + 20 = ___72___

2.
```
   46
   23
 + 17
 ─────
   86
```

3. Estimate.

43 + 51 = _____

possible answer: 90

4.
```
   35
   29
 + 15
 ─────
   79
```

5.
```
   17
 + 18
 ─────
   35
```

Name_____

6.
```
   16
   25
 + 35
 ─────
   76
```

7.
```
   22
 +  7
 ─────
   29
```

8.
```
   64
 + 19
 ─────
   83
```

9.
```
   63¢
 − 28¢
 ─────
   35¢
```

10. 90 − 20 = ___70___

Name_____

11.
```
   50¢
 − 15¢
 ─────
   35¢
```

12. For which number sentence do you need to regroup?

Circle the answer.

65 − 3 = 62

89 − 8 = 81

57 − 6 = 51

(74 − 7 = 67)

13.
```
   86
 − 39
 ─────
   47
```

14. Show how you can add to check 92 − 48 = 44.

 48 + 44 = 92

15. Estimate.

87 − 49

possible answer: 40

16.
```
   43¢
 −  7¢
 ─────
   36¢
```

Name_____

17. On Friday, 19 boys and 15 girls visit the library. How many children are at the library?

___34___ children

18. Mr. Smith is at the store. He buys 15 red apples and 28 green apples. How many apples does he buy in all?

___43___ apples

19. There are 32 crackers on a plate. Then 9 crackers are eaten. Circle the number sentence that shows how many crackers are on the plate now?

(32 − 9 = 23)

23 − 9 = 14

23 + 9 = 32

9 − 9 = 0

20. There are 20 children in Mr. Chester's class who say green is their favorite color. There are 15 children who picked yellow. How many more like green than yellow?

___5___ children

Chapter 17

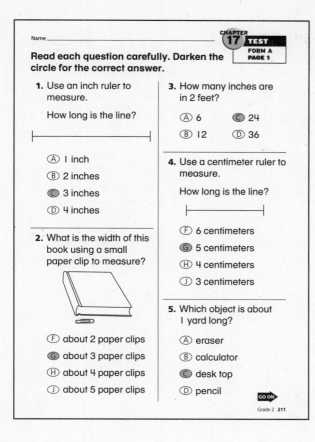

Read each question carefully. Darken the circle for the correct answer.

1. Use an inch ruler to measure.

How long is the line?

Ⓐ 1 inch
Ⓑ 2 inches
Ⓒ 3 inches
Ⓓ 4 inches

2. What is the width of this book using a small paper clip to measure?

Ⓕ about 2 paper clips
Ⓖ about 3 paper clips
Ⓗ about 4 paper clips
Ⓙ about 5 paper clips

3. How many inches are in 2 feet?

Ⓐ 6   Ⓒ 24
Ⓑ 12   Ⓓ 36

4. Use a centimeter ruler to measure.

How long is the line?

Ⓕ 6 centimeters
Ⓖ 5 centimeters
Ⓗ 4 centimeters
Ⓙ 3 centimeters

5. Which object is about 1 yard long?

Ⓐ eraser
Ⓑ calculator
Ⓒ desk top
Ⓓ pencil

GO ON

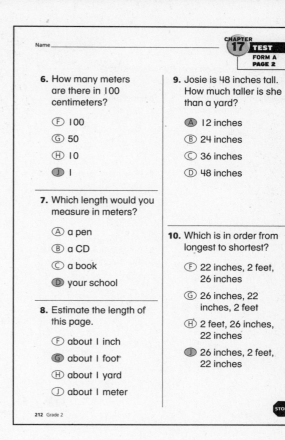

6. How many meters are there in 100 centimeters?

Ⓕ 100
Ⓖ 50
Ⓗ 10
Ⓙ 1

7. Which length would you measure in meters?

Ⓐ a pen
Ⓑ a CD
Ⓒ a book
Ⓓ your school

8. Estimate the length of this page.

Ⓕ about 1 inch
Ⓖ about 1 foot
Ⓗ about 1 yard
Ⓙ about 1 meter

9. Josie is 48 inches tall. How much taller is she than a yard?

Ⓐ 12 inches
Ⓑ 24 inches
Ⓒ 36 inches
Ⓓ 48 inches

10. Which is in order from longest to shortest?

Ⓕ 22 inches, 2 feet, 26 inches
Ⓖ 26 inches, 22 inches, 2 feet
Ⓗ 2 feet, 26 inches, 22 inches
Ⓙ 26 inches, 2 feet, 22 inches

STOP

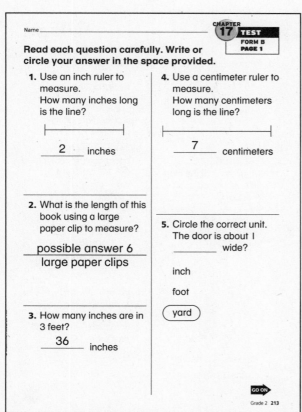

Read each question carefully. Write or circle your answer in the space provided.

1. Use an inch ruler to measure.
How many inches long is the line?

_2_ inches

2. What is the length of this book using a large paper clip to measure?

possible answer 6 large paper clips

3. How many inches are in 3 feet?

_36_ inches

4. Use a centimeter ruler to measure.
How many centimeters long is the line?

_7_ centimeters

5. Circle the correct unit. The door is about 1 _____ wide?

inch

foot

(yard)

GO ON

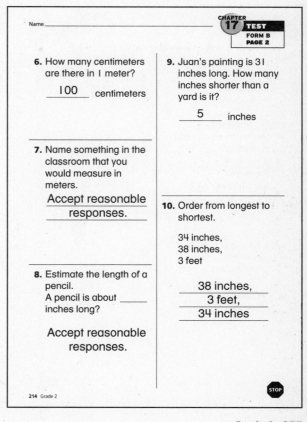

6. How many centimeters are there in 1 meter?

_100_ centimeters

7. Name something in the classroom that you would measure in meters.

Accept reasonable responses.

8. Estimate the length of a pencil.
A pencil is about _____ inches long?

Accept reasonable responses.

9. Juan's painting is 31 inches long. How many inches shorter than a yard is it?

_5_ inches

10. Order from longest to shortest.

34 inches,
38 inches,
3 feet

38 inches,
3 feet,
34 inches

STOP

Chapter 18

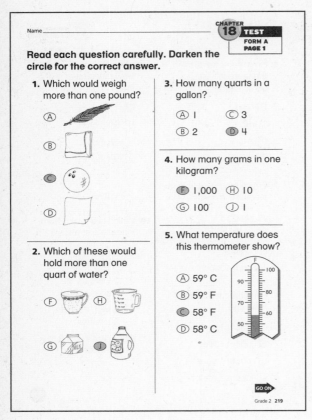

Name _____

Read each question carefully. Darken the circle for the correct answer.

1. Which would weigh more than one pound?

Ⓐ

Ⓑ

Ⓒ

Ⓓ

2. Which of these would hold more than one quart of water?

Ⓕ   Ⓗ

Ⓖ   Ⓙ

3. How many quarts in a gallon?

Ⓐ 1   Ⓒ 3

Ⓑ 2   Ⓓ 4

4. How many grams in one kilogram?

Ⓕ 1,000   Ⓗ 10

Ⓖ 100   Ⓙ 1

5. What temperature does this thermometer show?

Ⓐ 59° C

Ⓑ 59° F

Ⓒ 58° F

Ⓓ 58° C

GO ON

Grade 2 **219**

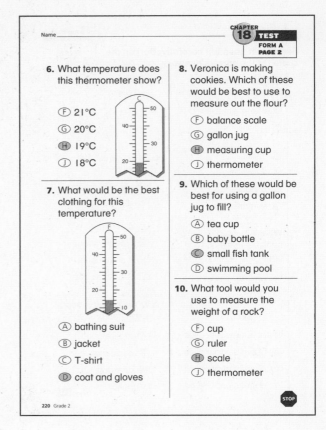

Name _____

6. What temperature does this thermometer show?

Ⓕ 21°C

Ⓖ 20°C

Ⓗ 19°C

Ⓙ 18°C

7. What would be the best clothing for this temperature?

Ⓐ bathing suit

Ⓑ jacket

Ⓒ T-shirt

Ⓓ coat and gloves

8. Veronica is making cookies. Which of these would be best to use to measure out the flour?

Ⓕ balance scale

Ⓖ gallon jug

Ⓗ measuring cup

Ⓙ thermometer

9. Which of these would be best for using a gallon jug to fill?

Ⓐ tea cup

Ⓑ baby bottle

Ⓒ small fish tank

Ⓓ swimming pool

10. What tool would you use to measure the weight of a rock?

Ⓕ cup

Ⓖ ruler

Ⓗ scale

Ⓙ thermometer

220 Grade 2

STOP

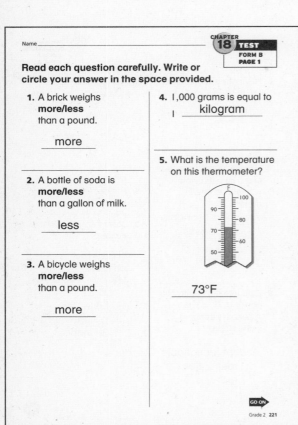

Name _____

Read each question carefully. Write or circle your answer in the space provided.

1. A brick weighs **more/less** than a pound.

more

2. A bottle of soda is **more/less** than a gallon of milk.

less

3. A bicycle weighs **more/less** than a pound.

more

4. 1,000 grams is equal to 1 ___kilogram___

5. What is the temperature on this thermometer?

73°F

GO ON

Grade 2 **221**

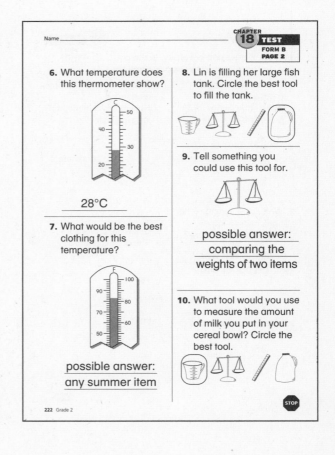

Name _____

6. What temperature does this thermometer show?

28°C

7. What would be the best clothing for this temperature?

possible answer: any summer item

8. Lin is filling her large fish tank. Circle the best tool to fill the tank.

9. Tell something you could use this tool for.

possible answer: comparing the weights of two items

10. What tool would you use to measure the amount of milk you put in your cereal bowl? Circle the best tool.

222 Grade 2

STOP

© Macmillan/McGraw-Hill

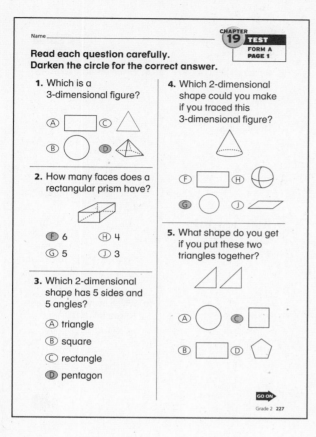

Name _____

CHAPTER **19** **TEST**
FORM A
PAGE 1

Read each question carefully.
Darken the circle for the correct answer.

1. Which is a 3-dimensional figure?
Ⓐ ▭   Ⓒ △
Ⓑ ◯   **Ⓓ** ◿

2. How many faces does a rectangular prism have?
Ⓕ 6   Ⓗ 4
Ⓖ 5   Ⓙ 3

3. Which 2-dimensional shape has 5 sides and 5 angles?
Ⓐ triangle
Ⓑ square
Ⓒ rectangle
Ⓓ pentagon

4. Which 2-dimensional shape could you make if you traced this 3-dimensional figure?
Ⓕ ▭   Ⓗ ◯
Ⓖ ◯   Ⓙ ▱

5. What shape do you get if you put these two triangles together?
Ⓐ ◯   **Ⓒ** ▢
Ⓑ ▭   Ⓓ ⬠

GO ON
Grade 2 **227**

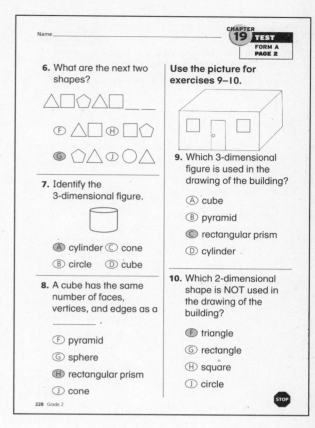

Name _____

CHAPTER **19** **TEST**
FORM A
PAGE 2

6. What are the next two shapes?
△ ▢ ⬠ △ ▢ __ __
Ⓕ △ ▢   Ⓗ ▢ ⬠
Ⓖ ⬠ △   Ⓙ ◯ △

7. Identify the 3-dimensional figure.
Ⓐ cylinder   Ⓒ cone
Ⓑ circle   Ⓓ cube

8. A cube has the same number of faces, vertices, and edges as a _____
Ⓕ pyramid
Ⓖ sphere
Ⓗ rectangular prism
Ⓙ cone

Use the picture for exercises 9–10.

9. Which 3-dimensional figure is used in the drawing of the building?
Ⓐ cube
Ⓑ pyramid
Ⓒ rectangular prism
Ⓓ cylinder

10. Which 2-dimensional shape is NOT used in the drawing of the building?
Ⓕ triangle
Ⓖ rectangle
Ⓗ square
Ⓙ circle

STOP
228 Grade 2

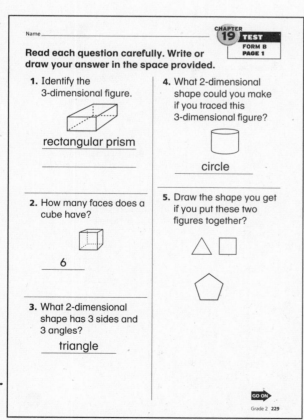

Name _____

CHAPTER **19** **TEST**
FORM B
PAGE 1

Read each question carefully. Write or draw your answer in the space provided.

1. Identify the 3-dimensional figure.
rectangular prism
_____

2. How many faces does a cube have?
6
_____

3. What 2-dimensional shape has 3 sides and 3 angles?
triangle
_____

4. What 2-dimensional shape could you make if you traced this 3-dimensional figure?
circle
_____

5. Draw the shape you get if you put these two figures together?

GO ON
Grade 2 **229**

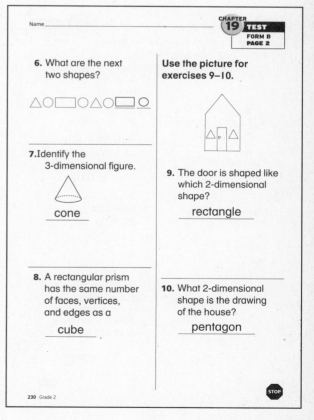

Name _____

CHAPTER **19** **TEST**
FORM B
PAGE 2

6. What are the next two shapes?
△ ◯ ▢ ▭ ◯ △ ◯ ▭ ◯

7. Identify the 3-dimensional figure.
cone
_____

8. A rectangular prism has the same number of faces, vertices, and edges as a
cube
_____

Use the picture for exercises 9–10.

9. The door is shaped like which 2-dimensional shape?
rectangle
_____

10. What 2-dimensional shape is the drawing of the house?
pentagon
_____

STOP
230 Grade 2

Chapter 20

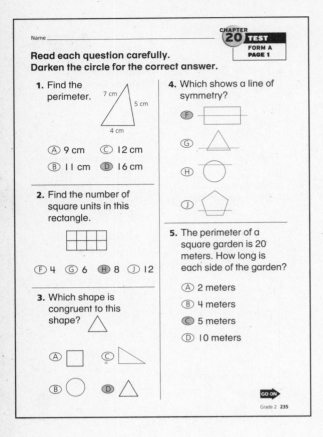

Name _____

CHAPTER 20 TEST
FORM A
PAGE 1

Read each question carefully.
Darken the circle for the correct answer.

1. Find the perimeter.

7 cm 5 cm
4 cm

Ⓐ 9 cm   Ⓒ 12 cm
Ⓑ 11 cm   Ⓓ 16 cm

2. Find the number of square units in this rectangle.

Ⓕ 4   Ⓖ 6   Ⓗ 8   Ⓙ 12

3. Which shape is congruent to this shape?

Ⓐ ☐   Ⓒ ◺
Ⓑ ◯   Ⓓ △

4. Which shows a line of symmetry?

Ⓕ ▭
Ⓖ △
Ⓗ ◯
Ⓙ ⬠

5. The perimeter of a square garden is 20 meters. How long is each side of the garden?

Ⓐ 2 meters
Ⓑ 4 meters
Ⓒ 5 meters
Ⓓ 10 meters

GO ON
Grade 2 **235**

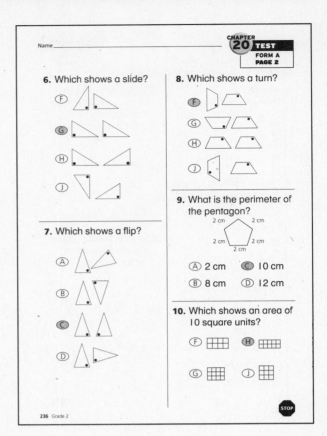

Name _____

CHAPTER 20 TEST
FORM A
PAGE 2

6. Which shows a slide?

Ⓕ   Ⓖ   Ⓗ   Ⓙ

7. Which shows a flip?

Ⓐ   Ⓑ   Ⓒ   Ⓓ

8. Which shows a turn?

Ⓕ   Ⓖ   Ⓗ   Ⓙ

9. What is the perimeter of the pentagon?

2 cm 2 cm
2 cm 2 cm
2 cm

Ⓐ 2 cm   Ⓒ 10 cm
Ⓑ 8 cm   Ⓓ 12 cm

10. Which shows an area of 10 square units?

Ⓕ   Ⓗ
Ⓖ   Ⓙ

STOP
236 Grade 2

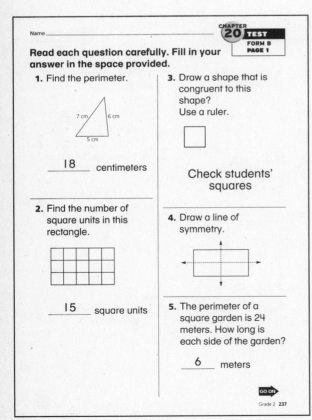

Name _____

CHAPTER 20 TEST
FORM B
PAGE 1

Read each question carefully. Fill in your answer in the space provided.

1. Find the perimeter.

7 cm 6 cm
5 cm

___18___ centimeters

2. Find the number of square units in this rectangle.

___15___ square units

3. Draw a shape that is congruent to this shape?
Use a ruler.

☐

Check students' squares

4. Draw a line of symmetry.

5. The perimeter of a square garden is 24 meters. How long is each side of the garden?

___6___ meters

GO ON
Grade 2 **237**

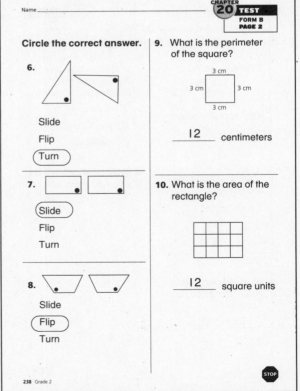

Name _____

CHAPTER 20 TEST
FORM B
PAGE 2

Circle the correct answer.

6.

Slide
Flip
(Turn)

7.

(Slide)
Flip
Turn

8.

Slide
(Flip)
Turn

9. What is the perimeter of the square?

3 cm
3 cm 3 cm
3 cm

___12___ centimeters

10. What is the area of the rectangle?

___12___ square units

STOP
238 Grade 2

© Macmillan/McGraw-Hill

Unit 5

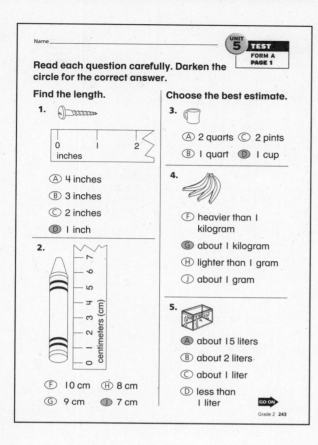

UNIT 5 TEST — FORM A PAGE 1

Name _____

Read each question carefully. Darken the circle for the correct answer.

Find the length.

1.
```
0     I     2
inches
```
- Ⓐ 4 inches
- Ⓑ 3 inches
- Ⓒ 2 inches
- Ⓓ I inch

2.
```
7 6 5 4 3 2 1 0
centimeters (cm)
```
- Ⓕ I0 cm
- Ⓖ 9 cm
- Ⓗ 8 cm
- Ⓙ 7 cm

Choose the best estimate.

3.
- Ⓐ 2 quarts
- Ⓒ 2 pints
- Ⓑ I quart
- Ⓓ I cup

4.
- Ⓕ heavier than I kilogram
- Ⓖ about I kilogram
- Ⓗ lighter than I gram
- Ⓙ about I gram

5.
- Ⓐ about I5 liters
- Ⓑ about 2 liters
- Ⓒ about I liter
- Ⓓ less than I liter

GO ON

Grade 2 243

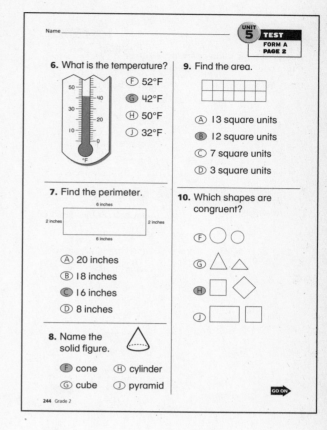

UNIT 5 TEST — FORM A PAGE 2

Name _____

6. What is the temperature?
- Ⓕ 52°F
- Ⓖ 42°F
- Ⓗ 50°F
- Ⓙ 32°F

7. Find the perimeter.
```
       6 inches
2 inches        2 inches
       6 inches
```
- Ⓐ 20 inches
- Ⓑ I8 inches
- Ⓒ I6 inches
- Ⓓ 8 inches

8. Name the solid figure.
- Ⓕ cone
- Ⓖ cube
- Ⓗ cylinder
- Ⓙ pyramid

9. Find the area.
- Ⓐ I3 square units
- Ⓑ I2 square units
- Ⓒ 7 square units
- Ⓓ 3 square units

10. Which shapes are congruent?
- Ⓕ
- Ⓖ
- Ⓗ
- Ⓙ

GO ON

244 Grade 2

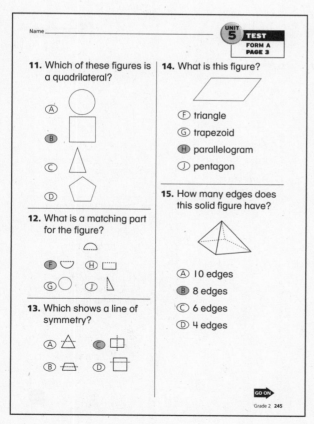

UNIT 5 TEST — FORM A PAGE 3

Name _____

11. Which of these figures is a quadrilateral?
- Ⓐ
- Ⓑ
- Ⓒ
- Ⓓ

12. What is a matching part for the figure?
- Ⓕ
- Ⓖ
- Ⓗ
- Ⓙ

13. Which shows a line of symmetry?
- Ⓐ
- Ⓑ
- Ⓒ
- Ⓓ

14. What is this figure?
- Ⓕ triangle
- Ⓖ trapezoid
- Ⓗ parallelogram
- Ⓙ pentagon

15. How many edges does this solid figure have?
- Ⓐ I0 edges
- Ⓑ 8 edges
- Ⓒ 6 edges
- Ⓓ 4 edges

GO ON

Grade 2 245

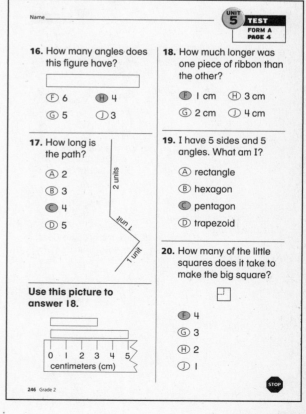

UNIT 5 TEST — FORM A PAGE 4

Name _____

16. How many angles does this figure have?
- Ⓕ 6
- Ⓖ 5
- Ⓗ 4
- Ⓙ 3

17. How long is the path?
- Ⓐ 2
- Ⓑ 3
- Ⓒ 4
- Ⓓ 5

Use this picture to answer 18.
```
0 I 2 3 4 5
centimeters (cm)
```

18. How much longer was one piece of ribbon than the other?
- Ⓕ I cm
- Ⓖ 2 cm
- Ⓗ 3 cm
- Ⓙ 4 cm

19. I have 5 sides and 5 angles. What am I?
- Ⓐ rectangle
- Ⓑ hexagon
- Ⓒ pentagon
- Ⓓ trapezoid

20. How many of the little squares does it take to make the big square?
- Ⓕ 4
- Ⓖ 3
- Ⓗ 2
- Ⓙ I

STOP

246 Grade 2

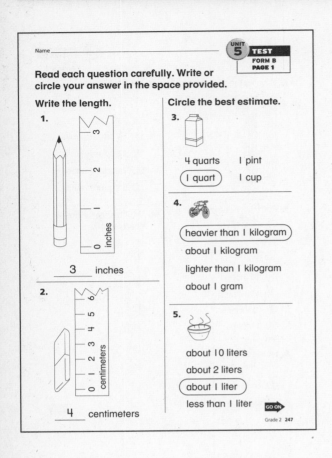

Name _____

Read each question carefully. Write or circle your answer in the space provided.

Write the length.

1.

_____3_____ inches

2.

_____4_____ centimeters

Circle the best estimate.

3.

4 quarts   I pint

(I quart)   I cup

4.

(heavier than I kilogram)

about I kilogram

lighter than I kilogram

about I gram

5.

about 10 liters

about 2 liters

(about I liter)

less than I liter

GO ON

Grade 2 **247**

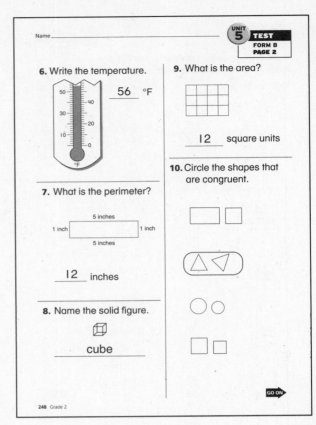

Name _____

6. Write the temperature.

_____56_____ °F

7. What is the perimeter?

5 inches

1 inch   1 inch

5 inches

_____12_____ inches

8. Name the solid figure.

_____cube_____

9. What is the area?

_____12_____ square units

10. Circle the shapes that are congruent.

248 Grade 2

GO ON

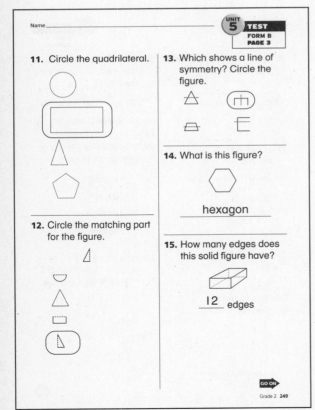

Name _____

11. Circle the quadrilateral.

12. Circle the matching part for the figure.

13. Which shows a line of symmetry? Circle the figure.

14. What is this figure?

_____hexagon_____

15. How many edges does this solid figure have?

_____12_____ edges

GO ON

Grade 2 **249**

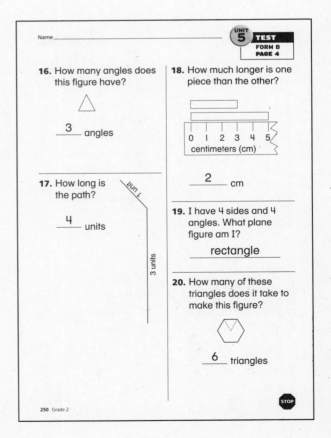

Name _____

16. How many angles does this figure have?

_____3_____ angles

17. How long is the path?

_____4_____ units

18. How much longer is one piece than the other?

centimeters (cm)

_____2_____ cm

19. I have 4 sides and 4 angles. What plane figure am I?

_____rectangle_____

20. How many of these triangles does it take to make this figure?

_____6_____ triangles

250 Grade 2

STOP

Chapter 21

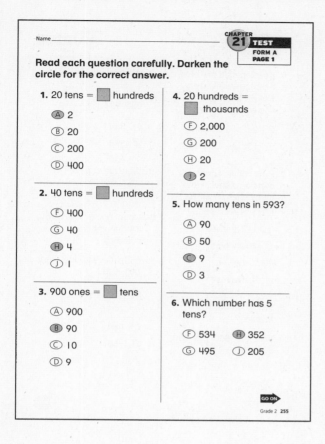

Name_____

Read each question carefully. Darken the circle for the correct answer.

1. 20 tens = ☐ hundreds

Ⓐ 2
Ⓑ 20
Ⓒ 200
Ⓓ 400

2. 40 tens = ☐ hundreds

Ⓕ 400
Ⓖ 40
Ⓗ 4
Ⓙ 1

3. 900 ones = ☐ tens

Ⓐ 900
Ⓑ 90
Ⓒ 10
Ⓓ 9

4. 20 hundreds = ☐ thousands

Ⓕ 2,000
Ⓖ 200
Ⓗ 20
Ⓙ 2

5. How many tens in 593?

Ⓐ 90
Ⓑ 50
Ⓒ 9
Ⓓ 3

6. Which number has 5 tens?

Ⓕ 534   Ⓗ 352
Ⓖ 495   Ⓙ 205

GO ON

Grade 2 **255**

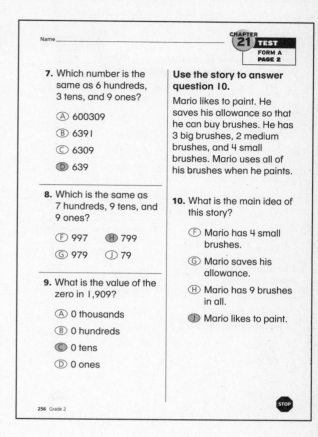

Name_____

7. Which number is the same as 6 hundreds, 3 tens, and 9 ones?

Ⓐ 600309
Ⓑ 6391
Ⓒ 6309
Ⓓ 639

8. Which is the same as 7 hundreds, 9 tens, and 9 ones?

Ⓕ 997   Ⓗ 799
Ⓖ 979   Ⓙ 79

9. What is the value of the zero in 1,909?

Ⓐ 0 thousands
Ⓑ 0 hundreds
Ⓒ 0 tens
Ⓓ 0 ones

Use the story to answer question 10.

Mario likes to paint. He saves his allowance so that he can buy brushes. He has 3 big brushes, 2 medium brushes, and 4 small brushes. Mario uses all of his brushes when he paints.

10. What is the main idea of this story?

Ⓕ Mario has 4 small brushes.
Ⓖ Mario saves his allowance.
Ⓗ Mario has 9 brushes in all.
Ⓙ Mario likes to paint.

STOP

256 Grade 2

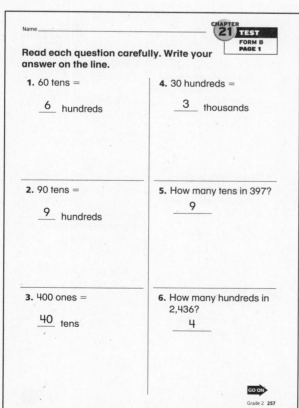

Name_____

Read each question carefully. Write your answer on the line.

1. 60 tens =

_6_ hundreds

2. 90 tens =

_9_ hundreds

3. 400 ones =

_40_ tens

4. 30 hundreds =

_3_ thousands

5. How many tens in 397?

_9_

6. How many hundreds in 2,436?

_4_

GO ON

Grade 2 **257**

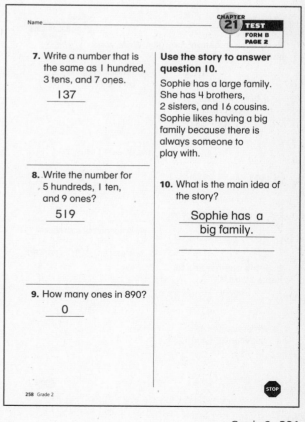

Name_____

7. Write a number that is the same as 1 hundred, 3 tens, and 7 ones.

_137_

8. Write the number for 5 hundreds, 1 ten, and 9 ones.

_519_

9. How many ones in 890?

_0_

Use the story to answer question 10.

Sophie has a large family. She has 4 brothers, 2 sisters, and 16 cousins. Sophie likes having a big family because there is always someone to play with.

10. What is the main idea of the story?

Sophie has a
big family.

STOP

258 Grade 2

Chapter 22

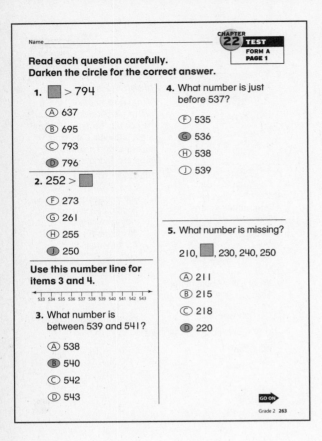

Name _____

CHAPTER **22** TEST
FORM A
PAGE 1

Read each question carefully.
Darken the circle for the correct answer.

1. ▨ > 794

Ⓐ 637
Ⓑ 695
Ⓒ 793
Ⓓ 796

2. 252 > ▨

Ⓕ 273
Ⓖ 261
Ⓗ 255
Ⓙ 250

Use this number line for items 3 and 4.

533 534 535 536 537 538 539 540 541 542 543

3. What number is between 539 and 541?

Ⓐ 538
Ⓑ 540
Ⓒ 542
Ⓓ 543

4. What number is just before 537?

Ⓕ 535
Ⓖ 536
Ⓗ 538
Ⓙ 539

5. What number is missing?

210, ▨, 230, 240, 250

Ⓐ 211
Ⓑ 215
Ⓒ 218
Ⓓ 220

GO ON

Grade 2 **263**

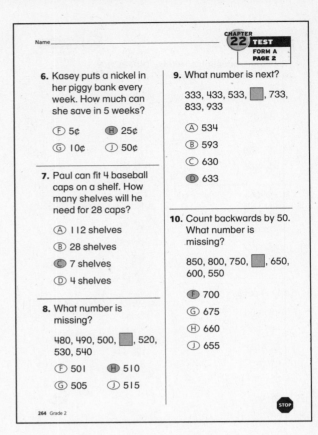

Name _____

CHAPTER **22** TEST
FORM A
PAGE 2

6. Kasey puts a nickel in her piggy bank every week. How much can she save in 5 weeks?

Ⓕ 5¢   Ⓗ 25¢
Ⓖ 10¢   Ⓙ 50¢

7. Paul can fit 4 baseball caps on a shelf. How many shelves will he need for 28 caps?

Ⓐ 112 shelves
Ⓑ 28 shelves
Ⓒ 7 shelves
Ⓓ 4 shelves

8. What number is missing?

480, 490, 500, ▨, 520, 530, 540

Ⓕ 501   Ⓗ 510
Ⓖ 505   Ⓙ 515

9. What number is next?

333, 433, 533, ▨, 733, 833, 933

Ⓐ 534
Ⓑ 593
Ⓒ 630
Ⓓ 633

10. Count backwards by 50. What number is missing?

850, 800, 750, ▨, 650, 600, 550

Ⓕ 700
Ⓖ 675
Ⓗ 660
Ⓙ 655

STOP

264 Grade 2

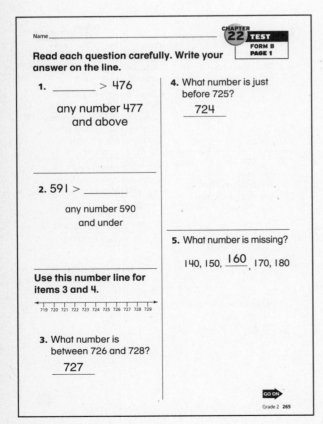

Name _____

CHAPTER **22** TEST
FORM B
PAGE 1

Read each question carefully. Write your answer on the line.

1. _____ > 476

any number 477 and above

2. 591 > _____

any number 590 and under

Use this number line for items 3 and 4.

719 720 721 722 723 724 725 726 727 728 729

3. What number is between 726 and 728?

727

4. What number is just before 725?

724

5. What number is missing?

140, 150, 160, 170, 180

GO ON

Grade 2 **265**

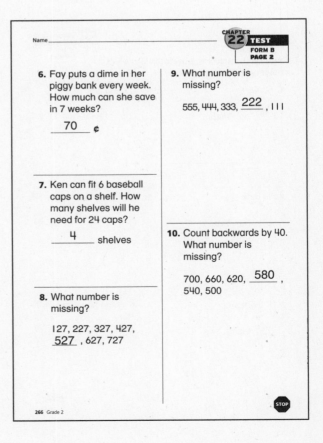

Name _____

CHAPTER **22** TEST
FORM B
PAGE 2

6. Fay puts a dime in her piggy bank every week. How much can she save in 7 weeks?

70 ¢

7. Ken can fit 6 baseball caps on a shelf. How many shelves will he need for 24 caps?

4 shelves

8. What number is missing?

127, 227, 327, 427, 527, 627, 727

9. What number is missing?

555, 444, 333, 222, 111

10. Count backwards by 40. What number is missing?

700, 660, 620, 580, 540, 500

STOP

266 Grade 2

© Macmillan/McGraw-Hill

Chapter 23

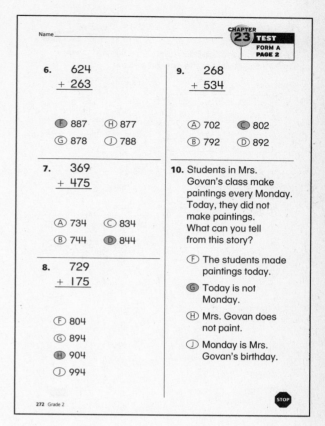

Read each question carefully. Darken the circle for the correct answer.

CHAPTER 23 TEST FORM A PAGE 1

1. 200 + 400 = ☐
   - Ⓐ 200
   - Ⓑ 300
   - Ⓒ 500
   - Ⓓ 600

2. 271
   + 164
   - Ⓕ 435
   - Ⓖ 335
   - Ⓗ 235
   - Ⓙ 135

3. 157
   + 136
   - Ⓐ 293
   - Ⓑ 283
   - Ⓒ 193
   - Ⓓ 183

4. 659 + 300 = ☐
   - Ⓕ 359
   - Ⓖ 689
   - Ⓗ 900
   - Ⓙ 959

5. 195 + 404 = ☐
   - Ⓐ 594
   - Ⓑ 599
   - Ⓒ 604
   - Ⓓ 609

GO ON
Grade 2 271

CHAPTER 23 TEST FORM A PAGE 2

6. 624
   + 263
   - Ⓕ 887
   - Ⓖ 878
   - Ⓗ 877
   - Ⓙ 788

7. 369
   + 475
   - Ⓐ 734
   - Ⓑ 744
   - Ⓒ 834
   - Ⓓ 844

8. 729
   + 175
   - Ⓕ 804
   - Ⓖ 894
   - Ⓗ 904
   - Ⓙ 994

9. 268
   + 534
   - Ⓐ 702
   - Ⓑ 792
   - Ⓒ 802
   - Ⓓ 892

10. Students in Mrs. Govan's class make paintings every Monday. Today, they did not make paintings. What can you tell from this story?
   - Ⓕ The students made paintings today.
   - Ⓖ Today is not Monday.
   - Ⓗ Mrs. Govan does not paint.
   - Ⓙ Monday is Mrs. Govan's birthday.

STOP
272 Grade 2

CHAPTER 23 TEST FORM B PAGE 1

Read each question carefully. Write your answer in the space provided.

1. 500 + 400 = __900__

2. 371
   + 567
   ─────
   938

3. 198
   + 248
   ─────
   446

4. 799 + 200 = __999__

5. 392 + 403 = __795__

GO ON
Grade 2 273

CHAPTER 23 TEST FORM B PAGE 2

6. 437
   + 312
   ─────
   749

7. 157
   + 368
   ─────
   525

8. 819
   + 119
   ─────
   938

9. 647
   + 216
   ─────
   863

10. Students in Mrs. Levine's class have a milk box with each snack. The class has two snacks a day. What can you tell about students in the class?

   possible answer:
   They have two milk boxes.

STOP
274 Grade 2

Chapter 24

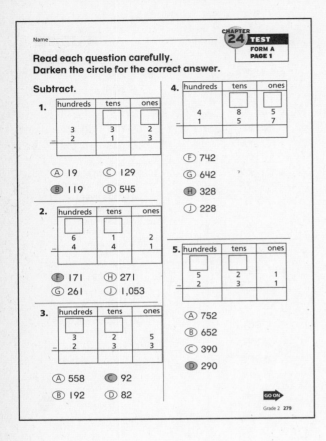

Name_____

TEST
FORM A
PAGE 1

**Read each question carefully.
Darken the circle for the correct answer.**

Subtract.

1.

hundreds	tens	ones
	☐	☐
3	3	2
− 2	1	3

Ⓐ 19   Ⓒ 129
Ⓑ 119   Ⓓ 545

2.

hundreds	tens	ones
☐	☐	
6	1	2
− 4	4	1

Ⓕ 171   Ⓗ 271
Ⓖ 261   Ⓙ 1,053

3.

hundreds	tens	ones
☐	☐	
3	2	5
− 2	3	3

Ⓐ 558   Ⓒ 92
Ⓑ 192   Ⓓ 82

4.

hundreds	tens	ones
	☐	☐
4	8	5
− 1	5	7

Ⓕ 742
Ⓖ 642
Ⓗ 328
Ⓙ 228

5.

hundreds	tens	ones
☐		
5	2	1
− 2	3	1

Ⓐ 752
Ⓑ 652
Ⓒ 390
Ⓓ 290

GO ON

Grade 2 **279**

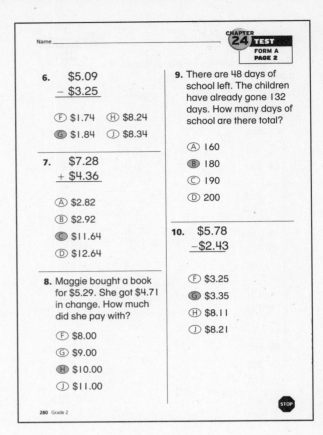

Name_____

TEST
FORM A
PAGE 2

6.
$5.09
− $3.25

Ⓕ $1.74   Ⓗ $8.24
Ⓖ $1.84   Ⓙ $8.34

7.
$7.28
+ $4.36

Ⓐ $2.82
Ⓑ $2.92
Ⓒ $11.64
Ⓓ $12.64

8. Maggie bought a book
for $5.29. She got $4.71
in change. How much
did she pay with?

Ⓕ $8.00
Ⓖ $9.00
Ⓗ $10.00
Ⓙ $11.00

9. There are 48 days of
school left. The children
have already gone 132
days. How many days of
school are there total?

Ⓐ 160
Ⓑ 180
Ⓒ 190
Ⓓ 200

10.
$5.78
− $2.43

Ⓕ $3.25
Ⓖ $3.35
Ⓗ $8.11
Ⓙ $8.21

STOP

280 Grade 2

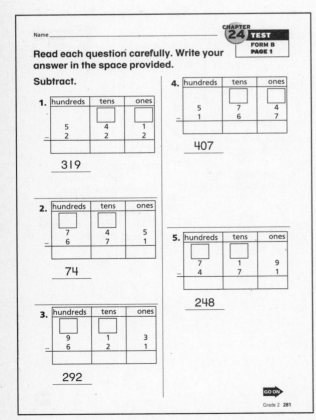

Name_____

TEST
FORM B
PAGE 1

**Read each question carefully. Write your
answer in the space provided.**

Subtract.

1.

hundreds	tens	ones
	☐	☐
5	4	1
− 2	2	2

319

2.

hundreds	tens	ones
☐	☐	
7	4	5
− 6	7	1

74

3.

hundreds	tens	ones
☐		
9	1	3
− 6	2	1

292

4.

hundreds	tens	ones
	☐	☐
5	7	4
− 1	6	7

407

5.

hundreds	tens	ones
☐		
7	1	9
− 4	7	1

248

GO ON

Grade 2 **281**

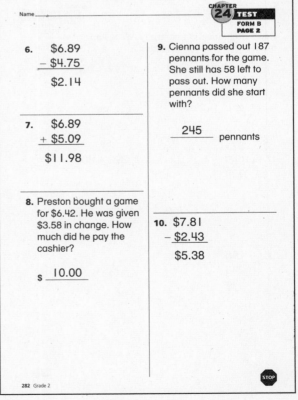

Name_____

TEST
FORM B
PAGE 2

6.
$6.89
− $4.75
$2.14

7.
$6.89
+ $5.09
$11.98

8. Preston bought a game
for $6.42. He was given
$3.58 in change. How
much did he pay the
cashier?

$ 10.00

9. Cienna passed out 187
pennants for the game.
She still has 58 left to
pass out. How many
pennants did she start
with?

245 pennants

10. $7.81
− $2.43
$5.38

STOP

282 Grade 2

© Macmillan/McGraw-Hill

384 Grade 2

Unit 6

Read each question carefully. Darken the circle for the correct answer.

1. What number is shown?

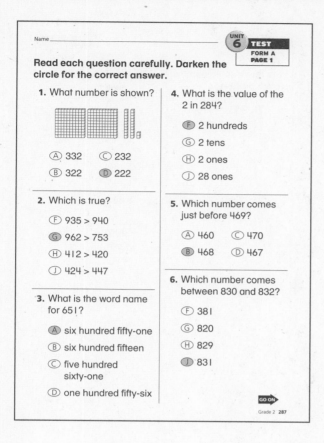

- Ⓐ 332   Ⓒ 232
- Ⓑ 322   Ⓓ 222

2. Which is true?

- Ⓕ 935 > 940
- Ⓖ 962 > 753
- Ⓗ 412 > 420
- Ⓙ 424 > 447

3. What is the word name for 651?

- Ⓐ six hundred fifty-one
- Ⓑ six hundred fifteen
- Ⓒ five hundred sixty-one
- Ⓓ one hundred fifty-six

4. What is the value of the 2 in 284?

- Ⓕ 2 hundreds
- Ⓖ 2 tens
- Ⓗ 2 ones
- Ⓙ 28 ones

5. Which number comes just before 469?

- Ⓐ 460   Ⓒ 470
- Ⓑ 468   Ⓓ 467

6. Which number comes between 830 and 832?

- Ⓕ 381
- Ⓖ 820
- Ⓗ 829
- Ⓙ 831

GO ON

Find the missing number in each pattern.

7. 145, 245, 345, ▢

- Ⓐ 346
- Ⓑ 355
- Ⓒ 440
- Ⓓ 445

8. 432, ▢, 434, 435

- Ⓕ 431
- Ⓖ 433
- Ⓗ 436
- Ⓙ 439

9.
```
  326
+ 243
```
- Ⓐ 669
- Ⓑ 579
- Ⓒ 569
- Ⓓ 529

10.
```
  648
+ 137
```
- Ⓕ 785
- Ⓖ 775
- Ⓗ 771
- Ⓙ 512

GO ON

11.
```
  535
+ 386
```
- Ⓐ 931   Ⓒ 831
- Ⓑ 921   Ⓓ 821

12.
```
  600
- 300
```
- Ⓕ 500   Ⓗ 300
- Ⓖ 400   Ⓙ 200

13.
```
  642
- 137
```
- Ⓐ 579   Ⓒ 506
- Ⓑ 519   Ⓓ 505

14.
```
  324
- 256
```
- Ⓕ 580
- Ⓖ 132
- Ⓗ 68
- Ⓙ 58

15.
```
  $9.37
- 6.54
```
- Ⓐ $15.91
- Ⓑ $3.23
- Ⓒ $2.84
- Ⓓ $2.83

GO ON

16.
```
  $7.81
+ 1.59
```
- Ⓕ $9.50   Ⓗ $8.40
- Ⓖ $9.40   Ⓙ $6.40

17. There are 257 people in line to buy tickets to the football game. Sam is the last person in line. How many people are in front of Sam?

- Ⓐ 256   Ⓒ 258
- Ⓑ 257   Ⓓ 260

18. How many pennies does Alex have?

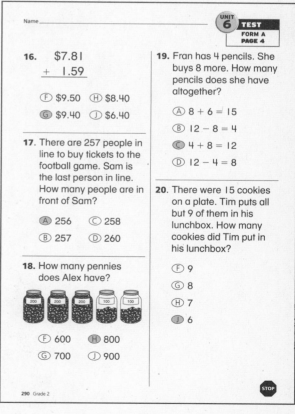

- Ⓕ 600   Ⓗ 800
- Ⓖ 700   Ⓙ 900

19. Fran has 4 pencils. She buys 8 more. How many pencils does she have altogether?

- Ⓐ 8 + 6 = 15
- Ⓑ 12 − 8 = 4
- Ⓒ 4 + 8 = 12
- Ⓓ 12 − 4 = 8

20. There were 15 cookies on a plate. Tim puts all but 9 of them in his lunchbox. How many cookies did Tim put in his lunchbox?

- Ⓕ 9
- Ⓖ 8
- Ⓗ 7
- Ⓙ 6

STOP

Unit 6

Name _____

Read each question carefully. Write your answer in the space provided.

1. What number is shown?

_____232_____

2. Use >, <, or 5 to compare.

542 $(>)$ 513

3. What is the word name for 745?

_____seven hundred_____
_____forty-five_____

4. What is the value of the 7 in 371?

_____7 tens_____

5. Which number comes just after 333?

_____334_____

6. Which number comes between 634 and 636?

_____635_____

GO ON

Grade 2 **291**

Name _____

Write the missing number in each pattern.

7. 235, 335, 435, _535_

8. 234, _235_, 236, 237

9.
$$\begin{array}{r} 627 \\ + 149 \\ \hline 776 \end{array}$$

10.
$$\begin{array}{r} 385 \\ + 61 \\ \hline 446 \end{array}$$

GO ON

292 Grade 2

Name _____

11.
$$\begin{array}{r} 577 \\ + 259 \\ \hline 836 \end{array}$$

12.
$$\begin{array}{r} 700 \\ - 300 \\ \hline 400 \end{array}$$

13.
$$\begin{array}{r} 451 \\ - 246 \\ \hline 205 \end{array}$$

14.
$$\begin{array}{r} 437 \\ - 288 \\ \hline 149 \end{array}$$

15.
$$\begin{array}{r} \$8.29 \\ - 6.47 \\ \hline \$1.82 \end{array}$$

GO ON

Grade 2 **293**

Name _____

16.
$$\begin{array}{r} \$4.72 \\ + 3.68 \\ \hline \$ 8.40 \end{array}$$

17. There are 324 people in line to buy tickets to the football game. How many people are in front of the last person in line?

_____323_____ people

18. How many pennies does Amanda have?

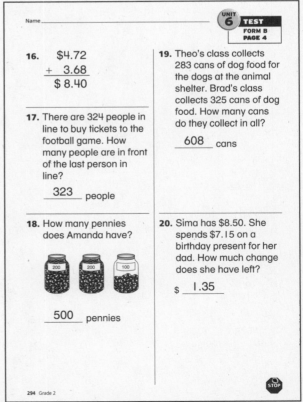

_____500_____ pennies

19. Theo's class collects 283 cans of dog food for the dogs at the animal shelter. Brad's class collects 325 cans of dog food. How many cans do they collect in all?

_____608_____ cans

20. Sima has $8.50. She spends $7.15 on a birthday present for her dad. How much change does she have left?

$ _____1.35_____

STOP

294 Grade 2

© Macmillan/McGraw-Hill

Chapter 25

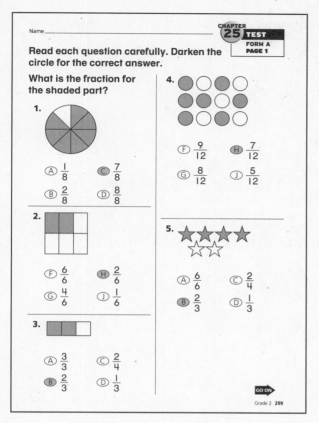

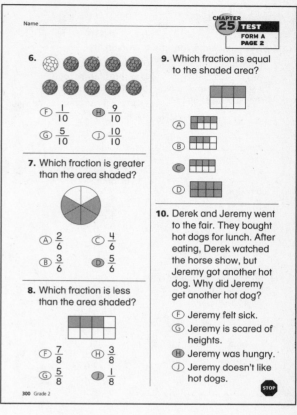

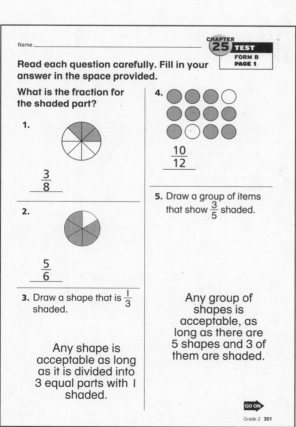

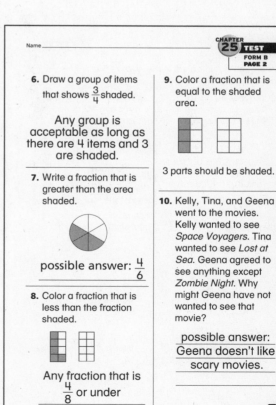

FORM A PAGE 1

Read each question carefully. Darken the circle for the correct answer.

What is the fraction for the shaded part?

1.
(A) $\frac{1}{8}$ (C) $\frac{7}{8}$
(B) $\frac{2}{8}$ (D) $\frac{8}{8}$

2.
(F) $\frac{6}{6}$ (H) $\frac{2}{6}$
(G) $\frac{4}{6}$ (J) $\frac{1}{6}$

3.
(A) $\frac{3}{3}$ (C) $\frac{2}{4}$
(B) $\frac{2}{3}$ (D) $\frac{1}{3}$

4.
(F) $\frac{9}{12}$ (H) $\frac{7}{12}$
(G) $\frac{8}{12}$ (J) $\frac{5}{12}$

5.
(A) $\frac{6}{6}$ (C) $\frac{2}{4}$
(B) $\frac{2}{3}$ (D) $\frac{1}{3}$

GO ON
Grade 2 299

FORM A PAGE 2

6.
(F) $\frac{1}{10}$ (H) $\frac{9}{10}$
(G) $\frac{5}{10}$ (J) $\frac{10}{10}$

7. Which fraction is greater than the area shaded?
(A) $\frac{2}{6}$ (C) $\frac{4}{6}$
(B) $\frac{3}{6}$ (D) $\frac{5}{6}$

8. Which fraction is less than the area shaded?
(F) $\frac{7}{8}$ (H) $\frac{3}{8}$
(G) $\frac{5}{8}$ (J) $\frac{1}{8}$

9. Which fraction is equal to the shaded area?
(A)
(B)
(C)
(D)

10. Derek and Jeremy went to the fair. They bought hot dogs for lunch. After eating, Derek watched the horse show, but Jeremy got another hot dog. Why did Jeremy get another hot dog?
(F) Jeremy felt sick.
(G) Jeremy is scared of heights.
(H) Jeremy was hungry.
(J) Jeremy doesn't like hot dogs.

STOP
300 Grade 2

FORM B PAGE 1

Read each question carefully. Fill in your answer in the space provided.

What is the fraction for the shaded part?

1.
$\frac{3}{8}$

2.
$\frac{5}{6}$

3. Draw a shape that is $\frac{1}{3}$ shaded.

Any shape is acceptable as long as it is divided into 3 equal parts with 1 shaded.

4.
$\frac{10}{12}$

5. Draw a group of items that show $\frac{3}{5}$ shaded.

Any group of shapes is acceptable, as long as there are 5 shapes and 3 of them are shaded.

GO ON
Grade 2 301

FORM B PAGE 2

6. Draw a group of items that shows $\frac{3}{4}$ shaded.

Any group is acceptable as long as there are 4 items and 3 are shaded.

7. Write a fraction that is greater than the area shaded.

possible answer: $\frac{4}{6}$

8. Color a fraction that is less than the fraction shaded.

Any fraction that is $\frac{4}{8}$ or under

9. Color a fraction that is equal to the shaded area.

3 parts should be shaded.

10. Kelly, Tina, and Geena went to the movies. Kelly wanted to see *Space Voyagers*. Tina wanted to see *Lost at Sea*. Geena agreed to see anything except *Zombie Night*. Why might Geena have not wanted to see that movie?

possible answer: Geena doesn't like scary movies.

STOP
302 Grade 2

© Macmillan/McGraw-Hill

Chapter 26

Name _____

Read each question carefully. Darken the circle for the correct answer.

1. You toss a coin 10 times. How many times should you get heads?

Ⓐ 0   Ⓑ 1   **Ⓒ 5**   Ⓓ 10

2. Which color is it impossible for the spinner to stop on?

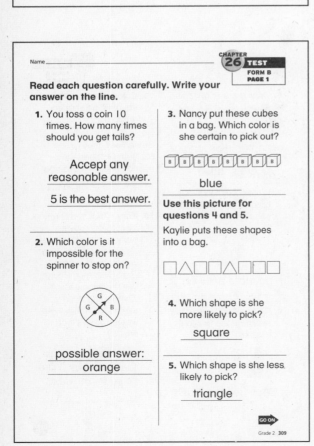

Ⓕ blue   Ⓗ red

Ⓖ green   Ⓙ yellow

3. Anthony put these cubes in a bag. Which color is he certain to pick out?

Ⓐ blue   **Ⓒ red**

Ⓑ green   Ⓓ yellow

Use this picture for questions 4 and 5.

Olga put these shapes into a bag.

4. Which shape is she more likely to pick?

Ⓕ circle

Ⓖ hexagon

Ⓗ square

Ⓙ triangle

5. Of the shapes in the bag, which is she less likely to pick?

Ⓐ circle

Ⓑ hexagon

Ⓒ square

Ⓓ triangle

GO ON

Grade 2 **307**

Name _____

6. Derrick used the numbers 3, 8, and 9 to make different 2-digit numbers. Which number would NOT be on his list of 2-digit numbers?

Ⓕ 38   Ⓗ 89

Ⓖ 39   **Ⓙ 90**

7. Marie was making color combinations with her fabric pieces. She used red, blue, and orange fabric. Which of these could be one of her color combinations?

Ⓐ blue and green

Ⓑ red and yellow

Ⓒ orange and blue

Ⓓ blue and pink

8. Which spinner is most likely to land on blue?

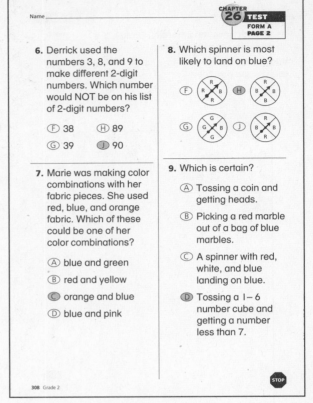

9. Which is certain?

Ⓐ Tossing a coin and getting heads.

Ⓑ Picking a red marble out of a bag of blue marbles.

Ⓒ A spinner with red, white, and blue landing on blue.

Ⓓ Tossing a 1–6 number cube and getting a number less than 7.

STOP

308 Grade 2

Name _____

Read each question carefully. Write your answer on the line.

1. You toss a coin 10 times. How many times should you get tails?

Accept any reasonable answer.

5 is the best answer.

2. Which color is it impossible for the spinner to stop on?

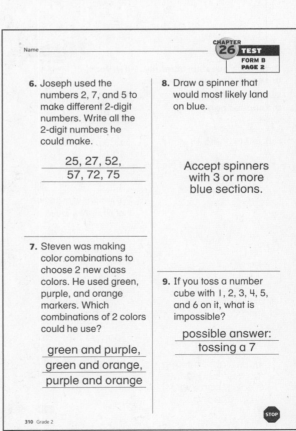

possible answer:
orange

3. Nancy put these cubes in a bag. Which color is she certain to pick out?

blue

Use this picture for questions 4 and 5.

Kaylie puts these shapes into a bag.

4. Which shape is she more likely to pick?

square

5. Which shape is she less likely to pick?

triangle

GO ON

Grade 2 **309**

Name _____

6. Joseph used the numbers 2, 7, and 5 to make different 2-digit numbers. Write all the 2-digit numbers he could make.

25, 27, 52,
57, 72, 75

7. Steven was making color combinations to choose 2 new class colors. He used green, purple, and orange markers. Which combinations of 2 colors could he use?

green and purple,
green and orange,
purple and orange

8. Draw a spinner that would most likely land on blue.

Accept spinners with 3 or more blue sections.

9. If you toss a number cube with 1, 2, 3, 4, 5, and 6 on it, what is impossible?

possible answer:
tossing a 7

STOP

310 Grade 2

© Macmillan/McGraw-Hill

Chapter 27

Form A, Page 1

CHAPTER 27 TEST
FORM A
PAGE 1

Read each question carefully.
Darken the circle for the correct answer.

Use the following sequence of numbers for exercises 1–3.

3, 3, 3, 5, 7, 8, 8

1. What is the range of the data?

Ⓐ 3   Ⓒ 5
Ⓑ 4   Ⓓ 6

2. What is the median of the data?

Ⓕ 3   Ⓗ 7
Ⓖ 5   Ⓙ 8

3. What is the mode of the data?

Ⓐ 3   Ⓒ 7
Ⓑ 5   Ⓓ 8

Use the coordinate graph for exercises 4 and 5.

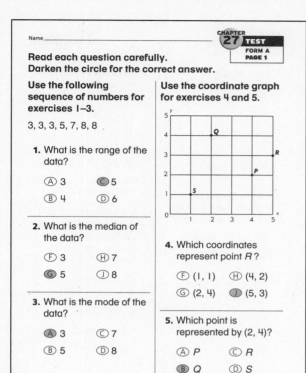

4. Which coordinates represent point *R*?

Ⓕ (1, 1)   Ⓗ (4, 2)
Ⓖ (2, 4)   Ⓙ (5, 3)

5. Which point is represented by (2, 4)?

Ⓐ *P*   Ⓒ *R*
Ⓑ *Q*   Ⓓ *S*

GO ON

Grade 2 315

Form A, Page 2

Name

CHAPTER 27 TEST
FORM A
PAGE 2

Use the following sequence of numbers for exercises 6–8.

1, 2, 4, 5, 6, 6, 7

6. What is the range of the data?

Ⓕ 7   Ⓖ 6   Ⓗ 5   Ⓙ 4

7. What is the median of the data?

Ⓐ 4   Ⓑ 5   Ⓒ 6   Ⓓ 7

8. What is the mode of the data?

Ⓕ 1   Ⓗ 2   Ⓖ 6   Ⓙ 7

Use the information below for exercises 9–10.

The school is selling concert tickets for $7 each. 23 students are in the concert, and 30 students are selling tickets. The concert is on March 25.

9. What is important in determining the amount the school makes?

Ⓐ the day of the concert
Ⓑ the number of students in all
Ⓒ the number of tickets sold

10. What is NOT important in determining the average amount of money each student collected?

Ⓕ the total number of tickets sold
Ⓖ the number of students in the concert
Ⓗ the amount charged for each ticket

STOP

316 Grade 2

Form B, Page 1

Name

CHAPTER 27 TEST
FORM B
PAGE 1

Read each question carefully. Write your answer on the line.

Use the following sequence of numbers for exercises 1–3.

5, 8, 8, 11, 14, 14, 14

1. What is the range of the data?

__9__

2. What is the median of the data?

__11__

3. What is the mode of the data?

__14__

Use the coordinate graph for exercises 4 and 5.

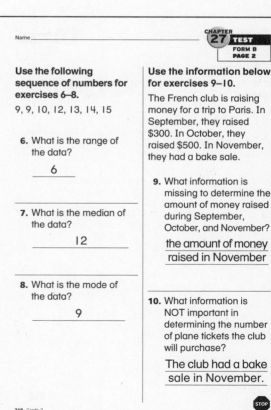

4. What coordinates represent point *A*?

__(1, 4)__

5. What point represents the coordinates (4, 5)?

__D__

GO ON

Grade 2 317

Form B, Page 2

Name

CHAPTER 27 TEST
FORM B
PAGE 2

Use the following sequence of numbers for exercises 6–8.

9, 9, 10, 12, 13, 14, 15

6. What is the range of the data?

__6__

7. What is the median of the data?

__12__

8. What is the mode of the data?

__9__

Use the information below for exercises 9–10.

The French club is raising money for a trip to Paris. In September, they raised $300. In October, they raised $500. In November, they had a bake sale.

9. What information is missing to determine the amount of money raised during September, October, and November?

the amount of money raised in November

10. What information is NOT important in determining the number of plane tickets the club will purchase?

The club had a bake sale in November.

STOP

318 Grade 2

© Macmillan/McGraw-Hill

Chapter 28

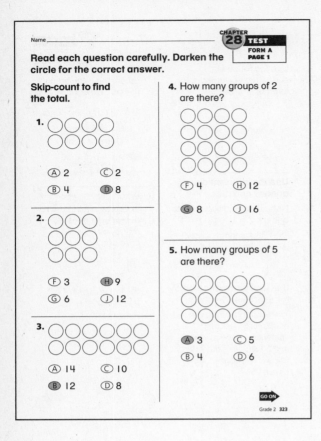

Read each question carefully. Darken the circle for the correct answer.

Skip-count to find the total.

1.
Ⓐ 2   Ⓒ 2
Ⓑ 4   **Ⓓ 8**

2.
Ⓕ 3   **Ⓗ 9**
Ⓖ 6   Ⓙ 12

3.
Ⓐ 14   Ⓒ 10
Ⓑ 12   Ⓓ 8

4. How many groups of 2 are there?
Ⓕ 4   Ⓗ 12
Ⓖ 8   Ⓙ 16

5. How many groups of 5 are there?
Ⓐ 3   Ⓒ 5
Ⓑ 4   Ⓓ 6

GO ON
Grade 2 **323**

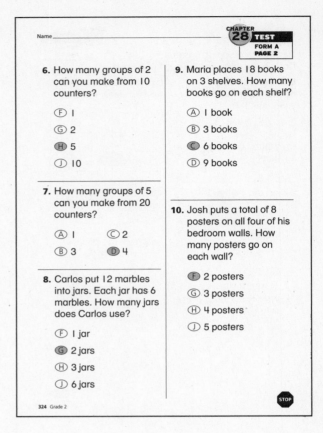

6. How many groups of 2 can you make from 10 counters?
Ⓕ 1
Ⓖ 2
Ⓗ 5
Ⓙ 10

7. How many groups of 5 can you make from 20 counters?
Ⓐ 1   Ⓒ 2
Ⓑ 3   **Ⓓ 4**

8. Carlos put 12 marbles into jars. Each jar has 6 marbles. How many jars does Carlos use?
Ⓕ 1 jar
Ⓖ 2 jars
Ⓗ 3 jars
Ⓙ 6 jars

9. Maria places 18 books on 3 shelves. How many books go on each shelf?
Ⓐ 1 book
Ⓑ 3 books
Ⓒ 6 books
Ⓓ 9 books

10. Josh puts a total of 8 posters on all four of his bedroom walls. How many posters go on each wall?
Ⓕ 2 posters
Ⓖ 3 posters
Ⓗ 4 posters
Ⓙ 5 posters

STOP
324 Grade 2

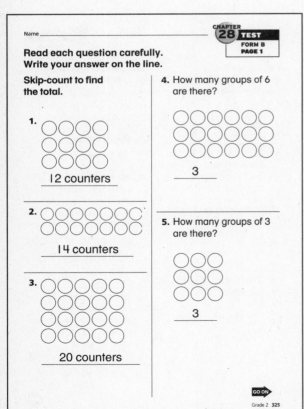

Read each question carefully. Write your answer on the line.

Skip-count to find the total.

1.
12 counters

2.
14 counters

3.
20 counters

4. How many groups of 6 are there?
3

5. How many groups of 3 are there?
3

GO ON
Grade 2 **325**

---

6. How many groups of 4 can you make from 24 counters?
6

7. How many groups of 3 can you make from 15 counters?
5

8. James puts 8 shirts in drawers. There are four shirts in each drawer. How many drawers is James using?
2 drawers

9. Marcus puts 30 stamps in 3 stamp albums. How many stamps are in each album?
10 stamps

10. Teresa places 14 stuffed animals on shelves. There are 7 stuffed animals per shelf. How many shelves is Teresa using?
2 shelves

STOP
326 Grade 2

Unit 7

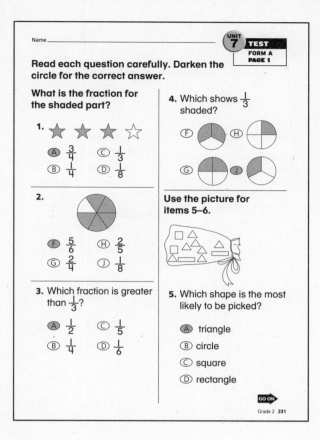

Name _____

Read each question carefully. Darken the circle for the correct answer.

What is the fraction for the shaded part?

1.
- Ⓐ $\frac{3}{4}$
- Ⓒ $\frac{1}{3}$
- Ⓑ $\frac{1}{4}$
- Ⓓ $\frac{1}{8}$

2.
- Ⓕ $\frac{5}{6}$
- Ⓗ $\frac{2}{5}$
- Ⓖ $\frac{2}{4}$
- Ⓙ $\frac{1}{8}$

3. Which fraction is greater than $\frac{1}{3}$?
- Ⓐ $\frac{1}{2}$
- Ⓒ $\frac{1}{5}$
- Ⓑ $\frac{1}{4}$
- Ⓓ $\frac{1}{6}$

4. Which shows $\frac{1}{3}$ shaded?
- Ⓕ
- Ⓗ
- Ⓖ
- Ⓙ

Use the picture for items 5–6.

5. Which shape is the most likely to be picked?
- Ⓐ triangle
- Ⓑ circle
- Ⓒ square
- Ⓓ rectangle

Grade 2 **331**

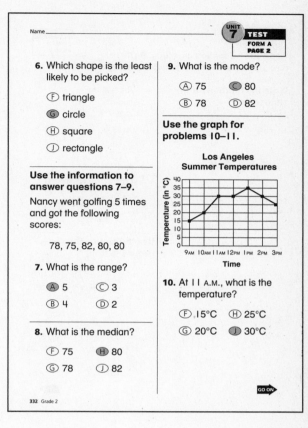

Name _____

6. Which shape is the least likely to be picked?
- Ⓕ triangle
- Ⓖ circle
- Ⓗ square
- Ⓙ rectangle

Use the information to answer questions 7–9.

Nancy went golfing 5 times and got the following scores:

78, 75, 82, 80, 80

7. What is the range?
- Ⓐ 5
- Ⓒ 3
- Ⓑ 4
- Ⓓ 2

8. What is the median?
- Ⓕ 75
- Ⓗ 80
- Ⓖ 78
- Ⓙ 82

9. What is the mode?
- Ⓐ 75
- Ⓒ 80
- Ⓑ 78
- Ⓓ 82

Use the graph for problems 10–11.

Los Angeles Summer Temperatures

10. At 11 A.M., what is the temperature?
- Ⓕ 15°C
- Ⓗ 25°C
- Ⓖ 20°C
- Ⓙ 30°C

332 Grade 2

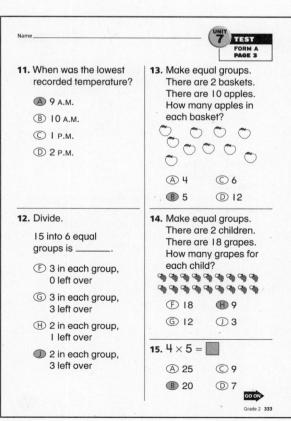

Name _____

11. When was the lowest recorded temperature?
- Ⓐ 9 A.M.
- Ⓑ 10 A.M.
- Ⓒ 1 P.M.
- Ⓓ 2 P.M.

12. Divide.

15 into 6 equal groups is _____.
- Ⓕ 3 in each group, 0 left over
- Ⓖ 3 in each group, 3 left over
- Ⓗ 2 in each group, 1 left over
- Ⓙ 2 in each group, 3 left over

13. Make equal groups. There are 2 baskets. There are 10 apples. How many apples in each basket?
- Ⓐ 4
- Ⓒ 6
- Ⓑ 5
- Ⓓ 12

14. Make equal groups. There are 2 children. There are 18 grapes. How many grapes for each child?
- Ⓕ 18
- Ⓗ 9
- Ⓖ 12
- Ⓙ 3

15. $4 \times 5 = \blacksquare$
- Ⓐ 25
- Ⓒ 9
- Ⓑ 20
- Ⓓ 7

Grade 2 **333**

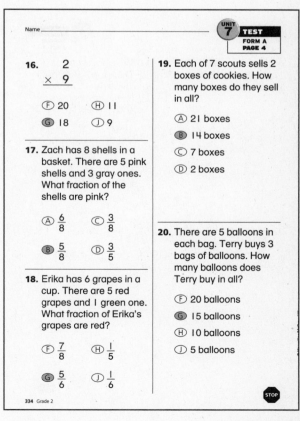

Name _____

16.
$$\begin{array}{r} 2 \\ \times\ 9 \\ \hline \end{array}$$
- Ⓕ 20
- Ⓗ 11
- Ⓖ 18
- Ⓙ 9

17. Zach has 8 shells in a basket. There are 5 pink shells and 3 gray ones. What fraction of the shells are pink?
- Ⓐ $\frac{6}{8}$
- Ⓒ $\frac{3}{8}$
- Ⓑ $\frac{5}{8}$
- Ⓓ $\frac{3}{5}$

18. Erika has 6 grapes in a cup. There are 5 red grapes and 1 green one. What fraction of Erika's grapes are red?
- Ⓕ $\frac{7}{8}$
- Ⓗ $\frac{1}{5}$
- Ⓖ $\frac{5}{6}$
- Ⓙ $\frac{1}{6}$

19. Each of 7 scouts sells 2 boxes of cookies. How many boxes do they sell in all?
- Ⓐ 21 boxes
- Ⓑ 14 boxes
- Ⓒ 7 boxes
- Ⓓ 2 boxes

20. There are 5 balloons in each bag. Terry buys 3 bags of balloons. How many balloons does Terry buy in all?
- Ⓕ 20 balloons
- Ⓖ 15 balloons
- Ⓗ 10 balloons
- Ⓙ 5 balloons

STOP

334 Grade 2

Unit 7

UNIT 7 TEST
FORM B
PAGE 1

Read each question carefully. Write or circle your answer in the space provided.

Write the fraction for the shaded part?

1. ★ ★ ☆ ☆

$$\frac{2}{4}$$

4. Which shows $\frac{1}{4}$ shaded? Circle the figure.

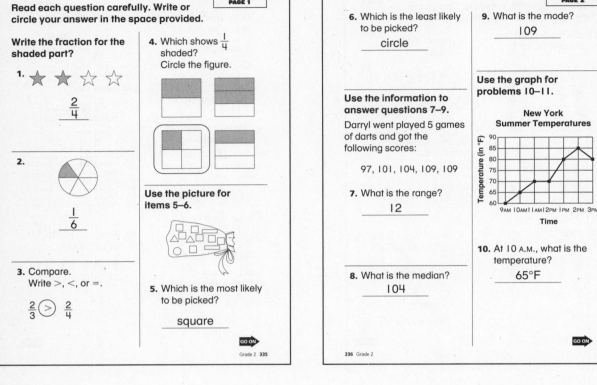

2.

$$\frac{1}{6}$$

Use the picture for items 5–6.

3. Compare. Write >, <, or =.

$$\frac{2}{3} \;\boxed{>}\; \frac{2}{4}$$

5. Which is the most likely to be picked?

square

GO ON

Grade 2 **335**

UNIT 7 TEST
FORM B
PAGE 2

6. Which is the least likely to be picked?

circle

9. What is the mode?

109

Use the information to answer questions 7–9.

Darryl went played 5 games of darts and got the following scores:

97, 101, 104, 109, 109

7. What is the range?

12

8. What is the median?

104

Use the graph for problems 10–11.

New York Summer Temperatures

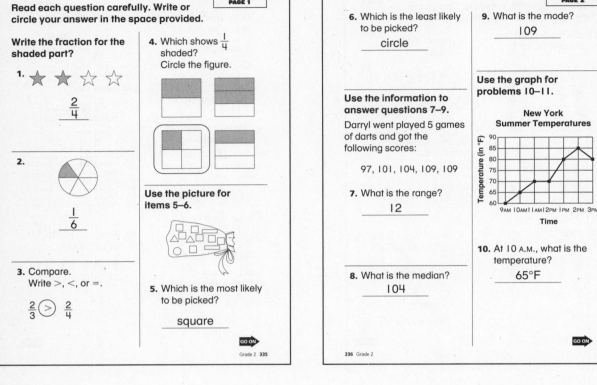

10. At 10 A.M., what is the temperature?

65°F

GO ON

336 Grade 2

UNIT 7 TEST
FORM B
PAGE 3

11. When was the highest recorded temperature?

2 P.M.

12. Divide.
18 into 4 equal groups is

4 in each group,

2 left over.

13. Make equal groups. There are 14 crayons. There are 2 boxes. How many crayons in each box?

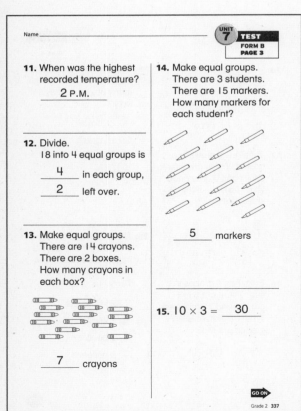

7 crayons

14. Make equal groups. There are 3 students. There are 15 markers. How many markers for each student?

5 markers

15. $10 \times 3 =$ 30

GO ON

Grade 2 **337**

UNIT 7 TEST
FORM B
PAGE 4

16.
$$\begin{array}{r} 3 \\ \times\, 5 \\ \hline 15 \end{array}$$

17. Shane has 6 shells in a basket. There are 5 pink shells and 1 gray one. What fraction of Shane's shells are pink?

$$\frac{5}{6}$$

18. Shanelle has 8 grapes in a cup. There are 3 red grapes and 5 green ones. What fraction of Shanelle's grapes are red?

$$\frac{3}{8}$$

19. Each of 10 scouts sells 4 boxes of cookies. How many boxes do they sell in all?

40 boxes

20. There are 7 balloons in each bag. Derrick buys 5 bags of balloons. How many balloons does Derrick buy in all?

35 balloons

STOP

338 Grade 2

Final

Page 1

Name _____

Read each question carefully. Darken the circle for the correct answer.

1. There are 12 people in line. Nanette is sixth. How many people are behind Nanette?

- Ⓐ 7
- Ⓒ 5
- Ⓑ 6
- Ⓓ 4

2. Estimate 48 + 33.

- Ⓕ 60
- Ⓖ 80
- Ⓗ 90
- Ⓙ 100

3. Which does not belong to the fact family?

- Ⓐ 9 + 8 = 17
- Ⓑ 17 − 10 = 7
- Ⓒ 17 − 9 = 8
- Ⓓ 8 + 9 = 17

4. Compare.

65 ◯ 57

- Ⓕ < Ⓖ > Ⓗ =

5. How much money is shown?

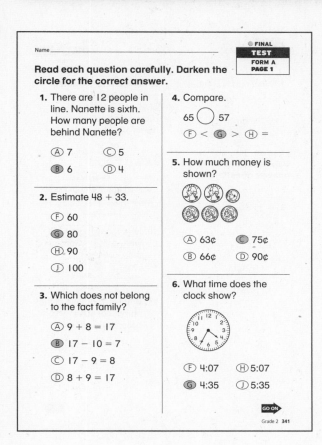

- Ⓐ 63¢
- Ⓒ 75¢
- Ⓑ 66¢
- Ⓓ 90¢

6. What time does the clock show?

- Ⓕ 4:07
- Ⓗ 5:07
- Ⓖ 4:35
- Ⓙ 5:35

GO ON

Grade 2 **341**

Page 2

Name _____

7. What part is shaded?

- Ⓐ $\frac{5}{6}$
- Ⓒ $\frac{3}{6}$
- Ⓑ $\frac{5}{8}$
- Ⓓ $\frac{3}{8}$

8.   253
    + 325

- Ⓕ 478
- Ⓗ 578
- Ⓖ 568
- Ⓙ 678

9.   788
    − 617

- Ⓐ 161
- Ⓒ 181
- Ⓑ 171
- Ⓓ 271

Anna's class collected pet food for the animal shelter. Use the pictograph to answer items 10–11.

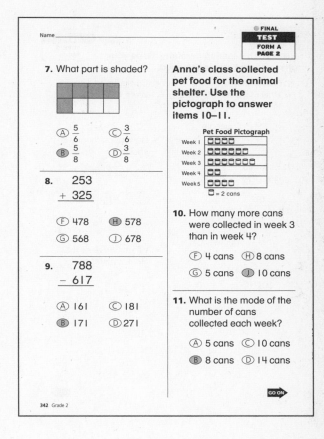

Pet Food Pictograph

◻ = 2 cans

10. How many more cans were collected in week 3 than in week 4?

- Ⓕ 4 cans
- Ⓗ 8 cans
- Ⓖ 5 cans
- Ⓙ 10 cans

11. What is the mode of the number of cans collected each week?

- Ⓐ 5 cans
- Ⓒ 10 cans
- Ⓑ 8 cans
- Ⓓ 14 cans

GO ON

342 Grade 2

Page 3

Name _____

12. Name the 3-dimensional figure.

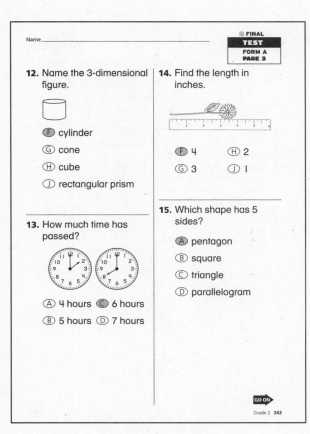

- Ⓕ cylinder
- Ⓖ cone
- Ⓗ cube
- Ⓙ rectangular prism

13. How much time has passed?

- Ⓐ 4 hours
- Ⓒ 6 hours
- Ⓑ 5 hours
- Ⓓ 7 hours

14. Find the length in inches.

- Ⓕ 4
- Ⓗ 2
- Ⓖ 3
- Ⓙ 1

15. Which shape has 5 sides?

- Ⓐ pentagon
- Ⓑ square
- Ⓒ triangle
- Ⓓ parallelogram

GO ON

Grade 2 **343**

Page 4

Name _____

16.   37
    24
  + 32

- Ⓕ 103
- Ⓗ 83
- Ⓖ 93
- Ⓙ 73

17. Compare.

$\frac{1}{3}$ ◯ $\frac{1}{4}$

- Ⓐ <
- Ⓑ >
- Ⓒ =

18. There are 3 cookies in each pack. Sasha has 5 packs. How many cookies does Sasha have?

- Ⓕ 16 cookies
- Ⓖ 15 cookies
- Ⓗ 8 cookies
- Ⓙ 2 cookies

19. Make equal groups. You have 20 boxes. You can put 4 boxes in each wagon. How many wagons do you need?

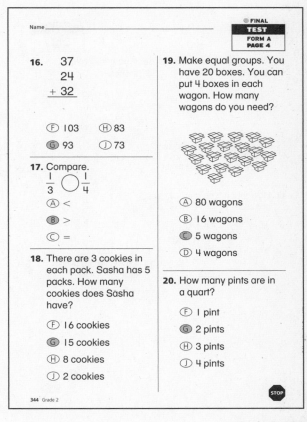

- Ⓐ 80 wagons
- Ⓑ 16 wagons
- Ⓒ 5 wagons
- Ⓓ 4 wagons

20. How many pints are in a quart?

- Ⓕ 1 pint
- Ⓖ 2 pints
- Ⓗ 3 pints
- Ⓙ 4 pints

STOP

344 Grade 2

Final

Name _____

Read each question carefully. Write your answer in the space provided.

1. Neil is seventh in line. How many people are in front of him?

___6___ people

2. Estimate

37 + 22

___60___

3. What subtraction fact is related to 7 + 6 = 13?

Accept 13 − 6 = 7 or 13 − 7 = 6.

4. Compare. Write <, >, or = .

42 (<) 53

5. How much money is shown?

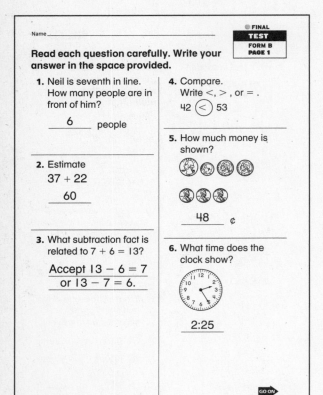

___48___ ¢

6. What time does the clock show?

2:25

GO ON

Name _____

7. What part is shaded?

$\dfrac{3}{8}$

8. 128
    + 311
    439

9. 824
    − 303
    521

Anna's class collected pet food for the animal shelter. Use the pictograph to answer items 10–11.

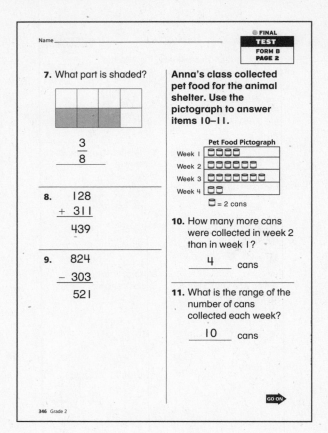

Pet Food Pictograph

Week 1
Week 2
Week 3
Week 4

= 2 cans

10. How many more cans were collected in week 2 than in week 1?

___4___ cans

11. What is the range of the number of cans collected each week?

___10___ cans

GO ON

Name _____

12. Name the 3-dimensional figure?

sphere

13. How much time has passed?

___5___ hours

14. Find the length in inches.

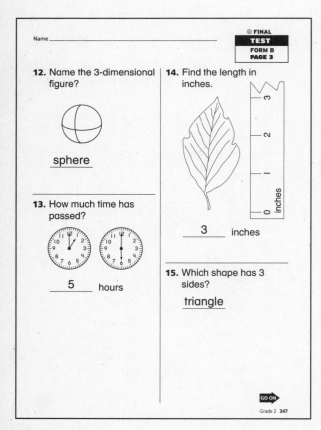

___3___ inches

15. Which shape has 3 sides?

triangle

GO ON

Name _____

16. 42
    36
   + 17
    95

17. Compare. Write <, >, or = .

$\dfrac{1}{5}$ (<) $\dfrac{1}{4}$

18. There are 4 brownies in each pack. Steve has 5 packs. How many brownies does Steve have?

___20___

19. Make equal groups. You have 15 boxes. You can put 5 boxes in each wagon.

How many wagons do you need?

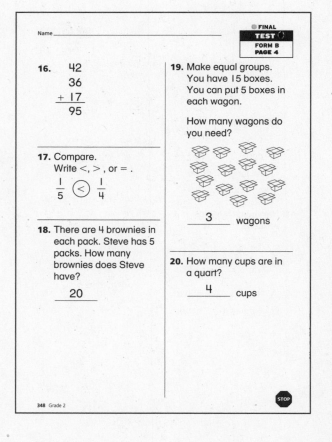

___3___ wagons

20. How many cups are in a quart?

___4___ cups

STOP

© Macmillan/McGraw-Hill